Praise for Satire In The Biden Years

"Dash MacIntyre is a bathroom stall graffiti news Herodotus of America's descent into fascist delusions and the MAGA movement's hysterical lunacies."

"Not quite as vulgar as the collection of abominations in MacIntyre's previous *Satire In The Trump Years*, but this disgraceful book is still a potential test case for how lenient courts have to be in weighing the Constitution's First Amendment free speech right to so relentlessly disrespect the President of the United States of America."

"Stupid, grotesquely sophomoric, an exhaustive compilation of Rabelaisian nonsense. This book is going on the very top of my next book burning pyre."

"How dare you, Dash MacIntyre?! Complete blasphemy! I suspect your alleged interviews with God and Jesus are whole cloth inventions!"

"…farfetched headlines."
—*Newsweek*

"If satire is best written sharp as if with a scalpel, MacIntyre goes into comedic surgery with a chainsaw tied up to a cinder block and shotgun."

"This book isn't how the Biden years were literally, but it kind of is how they were spiritually. Comedy just allows a cosmos of more truth and critical thinking than our contemporary news industry is capable of printing and broadcasting. Do drugs and read this, and start fighting back against the fascists yourself."

"Florida Republicans are going to love banning this book."

"Senator Chuck Grassley does not have an underground sex dungeon in the basement of his D.C. mansion, and he hasn't eaten ass in decades."
—an anonymity-requesting spokesman for Senator Grassley

"*Satire In The Trump Years* currently has a 5-star rating in the database of the Coyote Town, MO Public Library, our highest rating possible, and I'd bet its two reviewers eagerly anticipate Mr. MacIntyre's sequel, *Satire In The Biden Years*."
—Edna Wappleman, Director of the *Coyote Town Public Library*

"The graffiti news parodies throughout these pages are variously preposterous, absurd, stupid, and, most often, indistinguishable from reality."

"On May 8, 2023, a tweet went viral claiming that a Florida judge had banned the Bible in the state, largely due to mentions of murder, rape, genocide, and incest featured in the Old Testament […] But the tweet, which was posted by *The Halfway Post*, is a work of satire, and is not reflective of actual events."
—*Snopes.com*

"The fact that MacIntyre hasn't yet been declared an enemy of the state is either proof of free speech's survival in Trumpist America, or a sign that Trump really is illiterate."

"If the Founding Fathers had known juvenile satire like this would exist, they might have scrapped the whole freedom of speech thing."

"This book has much fewer references to white supremacist perverts obsessively preserving doomsday supplies of their own semen than MacIntyre's first book."

"*The Halfway Post* publishes chaos comedy, and I'm so here for it. Really appreciate your dark sense of humor."
—A satisfied *Substack* fan

"I believe Trump adviser Stephen Miller may someday arrest and eat Dash MacIntyre's corpse for all the stuff he's written about Emperor Trump."

"'Expired roast beef stench' has got to be the most original description of Donald Trump this year."
—A satisfied *Twitter* fan

SATIRE IN THE BIDEN YEARS

The Worst Of The Halfway Post

2021 - 2025

DASH MACINTYRE

Copyright © 2025 by Dash MacIntyre

All rights reserved. No part of this publication may be reproduced, distributed, or transmitted in any form or by any means without written permission of the publisher, except in the case of noncommercial uses permitted by copyright law.

For permission requests outside of fair use, contact Dash MacIntyre. Please don't be a dick and pretend my work is yours, or use it in commercial ways without at least giving me a cut of the profits and buying me coffee or beers while teaching me how you managed to do it.

Published by The Halfway Post
www.HalfwayPost.com

Printed in the United States of America
First edition

ISBN: 978-1-7365819-8-8 (Paperback)
ISBN: 978-1-7365819-7-1 (Ebook)

Book design, cover, and illustration by Dash MacIntyre

For more information, address:
TheHalfwayPost@gmail.com

This is a work of satirical fiction. All characterizations, quotes, and the situations in which public figures, companies, and organizations are described as participating in this book are entirely made up.

Any mention, description, or resemblance of public persons, living or dead, or corporate entities is intended solely as parody, spoof, and caricature of such persons and entities, and is not intended to communicate any true or factual information about them, no matter how unintentionally accurate or believable these comedic caricatures might be. Any other use of real names or events is accidental and coincidental.

Mention of specific companies, organizations, or authorities in this book neither implies endorsement by the author or publisher, nor implies that they endorse any aspect of this book or approve of its occasionally sophomoric sense of humor.

About The Halfway Post

The Halfway Post has been the newspaper of record for Dadaist graffiti news since 2017 providing comedic catharsis for Americans affected by the vulgarities of Donald Trump and his MAGA movement.

Written by Dash MacIntyre, a comedian and poet from St. Louis, *THP*'s comedy is award-winning, and has earned the most esteemed rating in the satire industry of "Pants On Fire!" by *PolitiFact*. *THP* has also been corrected by *The Associated Press*, *USA Today*, *Newsweek*, and *Snopes*.

Social Links

Linktr.ee/DashMacIntyre
TheHalfwayCafe.Substack.com
DashMacIntyre.Medium.com
X.com/HalfwayPost
HalfwayPost.Bsky.Social
Threads.net/@TheHalfwayPost
Instagram.com/TheHalfwayPost
HalfwayPost.com

Dash MacIntyre's Other Books

POLITICAL SATIRE
Satire In The Trump Years: The Best Of The Halfway Post (2021)
Satire In The Biden Years: The Worst Of The Halfway Post (2025)

COMEDY
Apéritifs (2025)

POETRY
Cabaret No Stare (2022)
Moon Goon (2023)
Hotel Golden Hours (2024)

Notice

This satirical collection is protected by numerous judicial interpretations and legal precedents established by the Supreme Court in validation of broad, inalienable rights to free speech via the First Amendment for satire and parody, no matter how triggered Donald Trump, or other unfunny public officials and figures, might be by its untiring criticism of their cultural, ideological, and personal flaws. Any attempt to sue the author or publisher of this book's obvious comedic fictions would charmingly prove further how deserving they are of its mockery.

In the iconic words of Donald Trump, "I don't take responsibility at all" that the behavior of the public persons lampooned here may make my parodying exaggerations seem indistinguishable from reality.

The book's only non-exaggeration is this picture of what Donald Trump looks like in the morning before beginning his daily, two-hour regimen of cosmetic styling:

For further reading, consult the Supreme Court decision in *Hustler Magazine, Inc. v. Falwell*, 485 U.S. 46, an 8-0 decision ruling that the First Amendment protects satirical allegations that famous televangelists have banged their moms in outhouses.

The Worst Of The Halfway Post

The Halfway Post's Dada News Manifesto

- Dada News doesn't report the facts, it improves them.
- Dada News is a harlequinade for eliciting social media doomscrollers' involuntary reactions, specifically fury from conservatives who love to dish fake news, but can't take it.
- Dada News is comedic catharsis for liberals who briefly fall for the Dadaist headlines before recognizing that the brazen fictional absurdity is actually nearly imperceptible from the absurdity of reality in contemporary politics.
- Dada News is absurd for absurdity's sake.
- Dada News is an antidote to fascism. When fascists lie to obstruct and confuse the masses' recognition of reality, Dadaists' lies are like a double-negative. A lie about a fascist lie is mathematically a truth.
- Dada News is the political equivalent of Hugo Ball reciting "Verse ohne Worte" at the Cabaret Voltaire in a cubist costume with lobster claws.
- Any expectations of Dada News to be objective will be happily unmet.
- Dada News doesn't tell how it is, Dada News tells how it *really* is.
- Dada journalists are easily repulsed by American conservatism's tyrannical demand for illiberalism to be taken seriously, so Dada News advocates for the total abolition of demagoguery, personality cults, ethno-nationalism, Christofascism, and dictatorial sympathies.
- Dada News is objectively subjective, and subjectively objective.
- Dada News is precisely calculated to inject enough nonsense into the national conversation to keep the universe from imploding or exploding (difficult to tell which until you've done the requisite daily doomscrolling).
- Dada News is not entirely stupid, though it is formidably stupid.
- Dada News headlines are most successful when received disapprovingly by liberal moral absolutists, and infuriatingly by conservative neo-monarchists.
- Dada News is most politically effective when it compels conservative critics to waste their free time crafting long, laborious responses attacking the integrity, intelligence, and sense of humor of Dada journalists that those same Dada journalists do not read and ignore completely.
- Dada News is an equal and opposite reaction to MAGA Trumpism, and a muscular flex of freedom of speech against authoritarianism in the defense of liberal democracy and American idealism.
- Dada News is a charming little reminder that if Donald Trump manages to strangle America's democracy and global hegemony in both soft and hard power, at least we Dadaists can giggle to ourselves while toiling and starving to death in a new generation of concentration camps remembering how utterly, spectacularly, and hilariously stupid Trump is, and how we never gave him any of the respect his malignant narcissism demanded.

Cheers to all fellow Dadaists!

Donald Trump's Cringiest Interview Of All Time

January 25, 2021
New York City, NY—

President Donald Trump today complimented the physical appearance of his daughter Ivanka again in a post-presidency interview with Sean Hannity, and it got a little weird. The following is a transcript of their conversation:

HANNITY: Let's start off with your kids. You have a great family, and they're following in your footsteps. Must make you proud. So how would you rate your kids' work ethics in your political career and the family company?

TRUMP: Oh, tremendous. Truly some of the best kids ever. Don Jr. is doing great work, and balancing the business with a lot of campaigning and television appearances defending me, and Eric is helping too. Since Eric's children's cancer charity got shut down by the State of New York so unfairly for just a little bit of alleged fraud, he has been helping out more around Trump Tower doing some janitorial jobs. And Jared is great, too. Everyone is being so unfair to him by assigning corrupt motives to his $2 billion investment from the Saudis. Nothing suspicious about that at all, I guarantee it. If you knew how innocent it was, it would blow your mind. People are saying it had absolutely nothing to do with the inter-palace coup Mohammed bin Salman did while we were negotiating deals with him. And we definitely didn't sell the Saudis nuclear secrets in exchange for them letting me host some of their LIV golf tournaments at my golf courses. What a ridiculous rumor! It's so absurd there's no reason to investigate further, or confiscate one of my accounting books, or hook me up to a lie detector test and ask me if I have another secret accounting book. The idea is preposterous.

HANNITY: And what about Ivanka? How would you rate her?

TRUMP: Total ten. Ten for her chest, ten for her legs, and her hips are unbelievable!

HANNITY: Oh—I meant more like her business endeavors.

TRUMP: Oh, ten for that as well. No one's done more for women in probably all of history. She's up there with all the other greats, like… What an incredible brain she has. Trump brain. Trumps have some of the biggest brains of all time. And she's got big other things, too. But her brain is just tremendous, especially for a woman. A tremendous woman. I'm sure she menstruates here and there, but she never lets you know when it's happening. That's very classy in a woman. And very rare. They usually never shut up about it! They get so nasty. But Ivanka's a real doll. And don't forget a genius thanks to her Trump brain. Our family just got really lucky with big brains. You know, a lot of people don't know this, but I went to Wharton, graduated top of my class, made billions and billions.

HANNITY: Really, the top of your class?

TRUMP: I was tremendous. I was the best of the best. They wanted to give me a business degree after my first year because I was practically teaching all the professors. All my professors couldn't believe the papers I turned in. They said, "Sir, your essays are the best we've ever read. You have deserved the Nobel Prize for Economics every year you've studied here!" But you know that stuff is all rigged. I should have gotten the Nobel Peace Prize several times as president, and the one for medicine for my amazing work stopping COVID like magic, and obviously literature for *The Art of the Deal*. But I barely paid attention in school. I spent my time drawing city skylines with my name on every single building, and planning out my business strategies to get rich fast by never paying my contractors or taxes. That's the Trump secret. Which is why I was smarter than the professors. If they're so smart, why are they paying taxes or their contractors? Only a genius like me could figure out how to never pay people or honor their contracts. Top of my class. Trust me, if you see my transcript, you'll see nothing but A's.

HANNITY: Wow! Will you release your transcript to show the liberals and finally, once and for all, shut them up about their fake news insults that you're an idiot's idea of a smart person and a povvo's idea of a rich person?

TRUMP: I'd love to, except the grades are being audited. You know how it goes...

HANNITY: Can't you request the university release your transcript?

TRUMP: If they do I will sue them for $5 billion... Because of the audit. No one takes audit integrity more seriously than Trump. They say I never shut up about personal integrity.

HANNITY: Of course, of course. And how are your other kids doing?

TRUMP: Stefanie is doing amazing, tremendous things.

HANNITY: Do you mean Tiffany?

TRUMP: That's what I said, Tiffany. Actually, Stefanie is her middle name, which I sometimes call her.

HANNITY: Her name is Tiffany Stefanie Trump?

TRUMP: And she's doing great. Somewhere between the ages of 25 and 35, and really doing so many amazing things, such as… And Barron is great, too. Melania really loves her son. They're very close. They speak in Slovenian all the time, and they have a lot of fun together. Every time I walk in the room they start saying jokes in Slovenian, and they burst out laughing. Actually, I'm not sure he even speaks English.

HANNITY: What do you think the impact of Melania's "Be Best" was?

TRUMP: She actually has more of a D-chest. Donald J. Trump does not marry women with B cups. But, honestly, Melania is starting to sag. She's getting up there in years. Usually when my wives pass forty it's time for an upgrade, but this time was a little different because the Christians, they really don't like divorce, and I need their votes. You know how it goes.

HANNITY: I meant her "Be Best" campaign… The anti-bullying project.

TRUMP: Ohhh! "Be Best!" It went so, so great. I know I've learned so much about bullying. It has made me see things in a whole new light. Like how much the fake news bullies me. I'm the nicest president of all time—everyone in America loves me—and they're so mean to me. No president has ever been treated like this. It's criminal.

HANNITY: The fake news media will never understand or acknowledge your greatness. Just like they'll never understand real America. The fake news at this point is practically addicted to lying about you. It's like, so what, you had some illegal immigrants concentrated indefinitely in camps with substandard living conditions, but that's the furthest thing from a concentration camp! It's not even close! And you went around allegedly dividing the country by calling Democrats "sub-human vermin," and Mexicans "rapists," and Blacks "thugs," and liberals "traitors who should be shot," but you're the furthest thing from divisive. If anything, you're uniting the country with hatred for the slight majority of the country that voted against you twice. Liberals are just losers who can't accept the fact that their three decades of popular vote victories aren't enough to win them majority representative power in Congress or a Supreme Court majority. Babies, right?

TRUMP: And they're even mean to Ivanka. How could you be mean to her? Look at her. Such a hot piece of meat you just want to get sizzling. You just want to take her off the grill and drizzle ketchup all over her. Get her nice and glistening. Her body is like a mouth-watering, well-done steak I'd do anything for—if she wasn't my daughter, of course.

HANNITY: Woah, haha, no filter, everybody! Blue collar again! We've got a man of the people over here who says exactly what he's thinking!

TRUMP: Sometimes I think about what I'd look like as a girl. Occasionally after a shower I'll tuck it in and take a look, but it's not the same. And Ivanka is tremendous, but she only has half of my genes. I've got 100% of them. Can you imagine how hot I'd be if I were a chick for real? I'd love to see myself at 13. Yowza! I'd be a piece of ass I could do locker room talk about all day! I'd have to keep myself away from Epstein, if you know what I mean! Or, from what they say, you know? I barely even knew him. If he was here in this room with you and me, I wouldn't be able to pick him out. Maybe he got coffee for me one time. Everyone is talking about how they never saw me at his parties, or his private islands, or the birthday parties he apparently used to throw for me every year. But yeah, I'd have one of the great bodies of all time if I were a broad. And tremendous tits. Way bigger than I have now. I'll tell you what, though, I wouldn't have any kids. I'd keep my body untainted by all that. As soon as all my wives had kids, their bodies went straight down the toilet. You just can't respect or admire a woman after she has carried a baby around for nine months and become a mother. People call it a beautiful miracle, but it's like Vietnam. And a total boner killer. Pregnant women just give up on having a thin waist around month five. Nothing ruins a woman like motherhood.

HANNITY: Telling it like it is! No lame, Woke political-correctness from you, Mr. President. The libs who respect their wives and women in general are so owned right now. Get me my cup of liberal tears! Time to fill up!

TRUMP: The only good thing about a pregnant wife is that she stops having a period for nine months, and stops bleeding all over the place from her wherever. What a relief those nine months are! But the birth thing is just a total mess. I can't watch it. I always let my wives do that stuff on their own. And I let the mothers raise the kids. I call the kids on their birthdays and stuff, but it's like, "See me when you're 18." And it works. My kids turned out so great. Who knew parenting was so easy? My ex-wives always said it was hard doing everything themselves while I was making money or taking other women out furniture shopping, but they didn't have a Trump brain so I can understand why it was difficult for them.

HANNITY: Incredible. Thank you so much for granting me this interview. Would you like to spit in my mouth? Mr. President, it would be the honor of my life if you spit right into my mouth, right now.

Donald Trump Explains His Favorite Bible Stories

February 14, 2021
Palm Springs, FL—

Donald Trump has a shaky grasp of the *Bible*, and it's always obvious he has no clue what he's talking about when he tries to answer questions about his favorite *Bible* stories.

The following are things Trump said today during a Q&A portion of a prayer breakfast event regarding his thoughts about Jesus:

The Ark
"A lot of people don't know this, but Jesus was a great boatbuilder. Maybe the best boatbuilder of all time. His Ark was just incredible, especially at that time. A lot of people had no idea arks could be so great. The way he sailed the Jewish people out of Egypt to the Promised Land of Sodomy and Gonorrhea during the Great Flood showed such intelligence and courage. He must have had a big brain. Sometimes I wonder how the brains of the Trump family compare to the big brains of the Christ family. The doctor told my mother when I was born, 'Ma'am, your baby has the biggest brain I've ever seen!' He couldn't believe it. He told me, with tears in his eyes, 'Sir, you are the biggest brained baby maybe of all time.' I wonder if baby Jesus's doctor said the same thing to Mrs. Christ. In a way, building arks is kind of like building big, beautiful casinos. I could build a big, beautiful ark. No one knows more about arks than me. Except maybe Jesus."

The Trojan War
"The Trojan War was one of the greats, wasn't it? It's right up there with the other great American wars, like World War II, the Civil War, the War of... and all the other big, beautiful wars. Back when America won its wars. The generals used to tell me, 'Sir, if only you had been president back then, we'd have won the Trojan War so much faster!' Jesus was a good general, too. His idea to build the wooden horse was so smart. And then he snuck out and opened the gate so America could walk right in. A lot of people don't know this, but after the war Jesus had a lot of trouble getting back home to Bethlehem. Jesus got lost at sea, fought a cyclops, and sirens turned his Twelve Disciples into pigs!"

The Battle Against the Minotaur
"Jesus defeated so many evil, nasty monsters for mankind. You wouldn't believe how dangerous the world was before Jesus came around. And it wasn't easy. No one could do what Jesus did. Only the true savior of mankind could get through the labyrinth without getting eaten by the Minotaur. People say

my victory over Crooked Hillary's cheated popular vote majority reminds them of Jesus navigating King Midas's maze. Winning Wisconsin when everyone said I couldn't was like Jesus finding the Golden Fleece when everyone said it was impossible!"

Defeating Medusa
"Having to deal with Nancy Pelosi, Hillary Clinton, and Megyn Kelly makes me know exactly how Jesus felt dealing with Medusa. Those are the four nastiest women of all time. Fortunately for Jesus, he only had to fight one of them! I had to fight the other three! After seeing how much blood was coming out of Megyn Kelly's wherever on that *Fox News* debate stage when she was so mean to me, and so vicious like no one has ever been vicious before, I'd rather take my chances with Medusa and all her snakes than have to answer another nasty question from bloody Megyn Kelly!"

The Eagle
"Jesus had a lot of mean people do bad things to him, which I totally relate to. People tell me all the time, 'Sir, we can't believe how unfair you've been treated your entire life! It's like Jesus the way the fake news media crucifies you every day with lies!' I bet Jesus on the Cross was relieved he'd never have to face what I face. I don't like to compare myself to Jesus, but I'm not sure Jesus could have handled how the fake news attacks me every day. The radical leftists who attack me might be worse than Jesus being hung up on the cross, and the eagle with razor-sharp talons coming every day to tear open his chest and eat his organs for eternity for our sins. And as a punishment from God for giving us the gift of fire. And for curing all the leopards of the diseases I guess cats back in the *Bible* days used to get because you're always hearing about Jesus curing the leopards."

The Ides of March
"I think the greatest tragedy, maybe of all time, was when Jesus was stabbed by the Senators after all he did for the Roman people. I tear up every time I think of Jesus on the floor of the Roman Senate whispering with his last breaths to his trusted Disciple, 'Et tu, Judas?' It reminds me of how Georgia Secretary of State Brad Raffensperger betrayed me by not finding the 11,780 votes I needed to beat Joe Biden in Georgia. I maybe even had it worse than Jesus, because Jesus didn't have any evil socialist Democrats to steal the election for Messiah from him! His election was fair and square, and Mark Antony didn't rig the vote. Jesus never had an election stolen like mine was. I wish I could trade places with Jesus. His political enemies didn't do two totally unfair impeachments, or make up a Carthaginian collusion scandal!"

The Daughter Seduction of Lot
"Hey, Ivanka, if you're listening, look up Genesis 19:34. Wink, wink!"

Life Hacks From The Republican Party On Thriving In Every Aspect Of Your Life

March 17, 2021
Palm Beach, FL—

Are you trying to cut out the stress in your life? Free yourself from the shackles of civic responsibility and societal obligations? The Republican Party of Coyote Town, Missouri, has published a how-to guide on how to **"Live Like A Republican"** with the following tried-and-true life hacks:

Are you hopelessly in debt and supporting yourself on deficit-spending? Ask your boss for a pay cut! His company will save so much money he's surely going to trickle down an unbelievable amount of wealth to you. And who knows how many extra jobs he'll create for you? Maybe you can start working two full-time jobs! Or three! When your entire daily schedule gets to full employment for all 24 hours, you'll be living the high life!

Is your neighborhood filled with litter and trash? Forget about picking it up yourself! Why start doing anything to clean up before all your neighbors do something first? You don't want to harm your personal financial situation by spending your time gathering up all the garbage and driving it to a dumpster down the street. And, besides, there's no reason to believe the little bits of litter you throw out the window every few hours are directly contributing to that mountain of trash in your backyard. The Earth has always had trash, and always will! Anyone who tells you otherwise is secretly getting paid in an international green conspiracy funded by Big Garbage.

Is your property crumbling apart after decades of neglect? Spend only the bare minimum on maintenance! Is a leaky roof or a rickety staircase worth going into debt to replace when doing so will set back your potential stock gains? Don't worry about preventative maintenance! Only when your problems become catastrophic emergencies and disasters should you think about interfering in your free personal market with interventionist regulations because you'll never become a billionaire while spending frivolously on things like a new water heater, air conditioner, or fixing your ungrounded electrical outlets! If your family members don't want to be shocked when they plug in their devices, maybe they ought to take on a little personal responsibility and bring their own portable external batteries. And don't worry if your pipes are getting bad and poisoning your guests with lead. Your brain is doing just fine!

Are you privatizing enough? Instead of spending your own money to fix things around your house, why not let a private company come in and fix your broken electrical outlets, dishwasher, etc., and then charge fees for your family members to pay the next time they come over? Nickel-and-diming all your house guests could really add up to some nice profits throughout the year! So start charging your guests for the coffee, snacks, or meals they consume at your house. Bill them every time they flush your toilet, or drink water from your sink. It'll be a great lesson on self-sufficiency for all your entitled, communist nephews and nieces who expect free stuff.

Does your brown-skinned neighbor look "sketchy?" Report him to the Department of Homeland Security! If he's a real, red-blooded American, he has nothing to worry about with a friendly checkup, and if he's an illegal terrorist, you've done your civic duty. Also, make sure to stockpile guns and ammo in your house, and make sure you're always spending more on weapons than all your neighbors combined. And don't stop at conventional guns, buy some grenades and rocket launchers too. This is the one expenditure you should definitely put on a credit card.

You should probably make budget cuts everywhere in your life to make up for how much you'll be spending on guns. Only buy used cars from now on, trade your healthcare plan for a cheaper one, and start rationing your food and medical supplies. No less than half of your discretionary spending should go toward maintaining overwhelming fire superiority over the rest of the neighborhood. Have you considered invading your neighbors' houses preemptively? Who knows what weapons of mass destruction they could be hoarding in their homes, or what schemes they're thinking up to threaten you. Maybe force some regime change at those addresses, and hear their wives and kids thank you for liberating them!

Is your HOA trying to raise dues—ahem—taxes? Go to your next homeowners' association meeting dressed like a Tea Party patriot and raise Hell! Don't let them steal your hard-earned money to fix the neighborhood pool, or add workout machines in the apartment complex gym, or do yard work in all the communal spaces! Demand the HOA cut your dues at least by half, and then insist that everyone buys their own pools, workout equipment, and lawnmowers from now on. Accuse your HOA of being "Marxist fascists" who are trying to bribe your minority neighbors for their votes with socialist gym equipment, then organize a mob to invade the HOA office and threaten to hang the HOA's vice president if your demands are not met in full! When the police investigate later, just assure them that you're a patriot who loves the community, and it's better to just move on rather than obsess over the past.

Remember that no communal problem or issue ever has to be your personal problem! Just worry about yourself, and everything will work itself out. And if it doesn't, it's definitely your sketchy neighbors' fault.

Mike Lindell Claims Democrats Paid "Mole People" To Bury Thousands Of Trump Ballots

April 2, 2021
Washington D.C.—

MyPillow CEO Mike Lindell says Democrats signed a nefarious, secret alliance in 2020 with an underground race of Mole People, and paid the Mole People to dig underneath the ballot drop boxes in the election and steal all the Trump ballots to hide them "deep underground through the Earth halfway to China."

The following are quotes Lindell made during a recent interview he did with the conservative news outlet *The Armed Freedom Eagle News Network*, an ultra MAGA media company whose motto is "*Newsmax* is RINO, *Fox* is Socialist":

- "The Democrats stole this election from Donald Trump, and I'm going to prove it. I've spent hundreds of thousands of dollars of my pillow profits traveling to Wisconsin, Michigan, Georgia, Arizona and Pennsylvania and setting all kinds of elaborately designed traps and nets to catch a Mole Person so I can get a confession out of him. I haven't caught a Mole Man yet, but, as soon as I do, Sean Hannity told me I can bring the Mole Man onto his show for a live, public interrogation—or waterboarding, depending on how talkative the Mole Man will be."

- "I have it on good authority the Mole People have dug several holes through the center of the earth that connect America to China on the other side of the globe. That's why the Democrats thought it would be the perfect crime to steal sacks of Trump ballots and toss them into the holes so some Chinese people could catch it on the other end and dispose of them. But Democrats were clumsy, and left clues everywhere. I've found micro bamboo fibers on some of the swing state Biden ballots. The bamboo fibers likely fell off the Mole People's clothes while they were rifling through all the ballots to find the Trump votes."

- "Folks, it's just how gravity works. You throw a burlap sack of Trump ballots into the big hole, and it picks up velocity as it descends through the mantle, outer core, and inner core of the Earth, and it gets going so fast it slingshots through to the other side all the way to Xi Jinping! I'd estimate it takes only five minutes for the sacks to get to the Chinese."

- "If the core of the Earth is filled with hot, liquid magma, how do the Mole People go back and forth between America and China? The

Marxist, leftist scientists and geologists have no explanation for that! Maybe it's a cable car or bullet train. My point is we just don't know."

- "I myself have seen some grainy photos of Mole People that coal miners have taken. Some say it's a hoax, but that's what the liberals want us to believe. I reuse to refuse to believe!"

- "We don't know for a fact the inner core of the Earth is over 9,000 degrees, so, if I were you, I wouldn't be so sure that the burlap sacks full of Trump votes would melt or catch fire on their way to China. Ask yourself, who will profit the most if everyone freaks out about the climate change hoax, and moves underground? The Mole People are building thousands of hotels and condominiums underground right now so they can profit when the liberals force everyone at gunpoint to move underground because of global warming. That's the big payoff these lying, socialist scientists have been waiting for all these years with their fake news climate science and charts and graphs. Your 'gotcha questions' can't trick me! The Democrats and the Mole People are doing whatever it takes to stop Donald Trump from keeping America above ground where all the freedom is!"

- "All I'm saying is we shouldn't believe the scientists and all their peer-reviewed evidence of so-called seismic waves, the planet's magnetic fields, and underground magma until we catch one of these Mole People. For all we know, the Earth's core is entirely hollow. Have you ever been there? Of course not. No one has. But I've been working with several mining company CEOs to get to the bottom of this, pun intended. I have a big announcement coming in two weeks, so stay tuned! And, while you wait, why not check out the *MyPillow* website and get yourself one of our many fine pillow products? You spend a third of your life in bed, why not make it comfy? Please buy a pillow. Even just one. I'm four months behind on *Fox* advertising bills, and they're going to stop airing my ads. This is kind of the end of the line for *MyPillow*. Also, I maybe don't have any more money to find the voter fraud I've kind of been making big promises about."

- "I think President Obama may have been personally involved in the conspiracy. In fact, I don't think he was really Black. I think his skin was just dirty from crawling through all the holes back and forth to China!"

- "And, in case anyone is wondering, if the Mole People have a hereditary monarchy type of government, I've already called dibs on marrying the Mole King's hottest daughter, unless Donald Trump wants her, in which case I have dibs on the Mole King's second hottest daughter!"

Melania Trump's New Book "Becoming Melania" Kind Of Trashes Her Husband Donald

New York City, NY
June 3, 2021—

Melania Trump has a new book coming out titled *Beyond First Lady*, and early reviewers are expressing shock at how negatively she writes about her husband, Donald Trump.

The following are exclusive excerpts from the book:

- Donald's morning hair and makeup routine takes twice as long as hers.

- Donald's hair is implanted and 3-feet long, and is only attached in the back. The hair is wrapped around his head like a turban and then saturated with a full can of hairspray.

- Donald asked her to call him "John Barron" on their early dates.

- Donald has a TV in every room of his penthouse suites so he can watch and listen to what *Fox News* is saying about him wherever he goes.

- Whenever he hears his name said on TV, he yells at everyone to shut up so he can hear what they say about him.

- Donald keeps the TV on while sleeping, and snaps awake every time his name is mentioned as he mumble-yells, "What are they saying about me?"

- When Donald farts he bends his head down to his knees, takes a big whiff, and yells, "Take that, climate change!"

- Donald has "saucer nipples."

- Melania has lunch with Stormy Daniels once a month where they laugh at Donald.

- Donald has a tattoo of his own signature on his mons pubis.

- The first time Melania met Donald's son Eric, Donald whispered in her ear, "I'm not really the father of that one."

- Throughout Donald's presidency, Melania threatened to humiliate him with a divorce several times to win all kinds of concessions from him. She procured Barron more money in Donald's will than either Eric or Don Jr. will get, and she will receive Trump Tower in New York.

- She won't vote for Donald in 2024 because if he gets reelected she'll have to decorate the White House for Christmas four more times.

- Every time Melania and Barron are in the room with Donald, they pantomime little improvisational scenes when his back is turned where they act out stabbing him, choking him to death, or shooting him and burst out laughing.

- Donald kept a dog kennel in the Oval Office, and when he was angry he'd force Ted Cruz, Lindsey Graham, Kevin McCarthy, Mark Meadows, or someone else nearby to get inside so he could scream at them, hit the sides of the kennel with a baseball bat, spit on them, and pour *Diet Coke* cans all over them.

- When Donald sees a spider he screams and yells for Melania or Barron to come kill it.

- Candles cannot be lit in any of his bathrooms because of how many years' worth of hairspray is coated on every surface.

- Donald didn't think he'd actually win the 2016 election, and he smelled particularly bad that night because a few times on election night, when he remembered he'd actually have to do the job for four years, some pee dribbled out.

- While Donald was president, Melania would occasionally buy cockroaches and let them loose in Ivanka's White House office, and mail boxes of them to Ivanka's house.

- Ivanka has turned down several requests from Donald that she tattoo his signature somewhere on her body.

- Donald has several locked, fire-proof safes in all of his properties filled with spare copies of the blackmail he has accumulated on his friends, enemies, members of Congress, and a long list of state and federal prosecutors.

- Eric, to this day, continues to call her "Malaria."

Donald Trump Is Now Selling Timeshares At Mar-A-Lago

July 10, 2021
Palm Beach, FL—

Former President Donald Trump just launched a new business venture called *Trump Vacations* to sell timeshares at his various hotels and golf courses.

Mr. Trump has reportedly already begun pitching timeshare contracts to his Mar-a-Lago guests, and even subjected a recent Republican National Committee meeting of top GOP party officials to a three-hour presentation led by him and his adult children, Don Jr., Ivanka, and Eric.

According to sources who attended the meeting, Donald Trump led off the presentation with a slideshow of pictures of sexy women in bikinis, and he claimed to the gathered RNC officials that "hot young women, and men, couldn't resist" the allure of a *Trump Vacations* member, and that paying for the *Trump Vacations* "Platinum Level" membership was "guaranteed to quadruple your sex life, and halve the age of your sexual partners." At the end of the slideshow was a picture of Ivanka in a bikini, and Trump paused on it, and stared at it without saying a word for an amount of time several attendees said afterwards was "uncomfortably long, considering it was his daughter."

Ivanka hosted the second segment of the presentation, and showed off the various Ivanka-branded amenities available at every *Trump Vacations* property, including *Ivanka Saunas*™, *Ivanka Massage Chairs*™, *Ivanka Robes*™, and complimentary *Ivanka Husband Protein Powder*™. All of the *Ivanka*-branded luxuries cost extra, though Ivanka requested that none of the gathered prospective members look up the online reviews to her products.

Presenting third was Donald Jr., who assured the RNC officials that, at every *Trump Vacations* property, he "knew a guy" who could get them whatever they wanted. Then he emphasized a second time the word "whatever." Then he winked. Then, just to be extra clear, he made a circle with his thumb and index finger of one hand, and then poked his index finger of his other hand into the circle several times. Then he imitated someone snorting a line of cocaine. Then he gave two thumbs up, winked again, and made a shushing gesture with his pointer finger over his mouth.

Presenting fourth was Eric, who told the audience that all the *Trump Vacations* properties had fun, little cheese dispensers "everywhere on the ground" like a scavenger hunt that were IQ-testing puzzles as well because you had to figure out how to get the cheese without letting a spring-loaded metal bar snap on your fingers. Eric repeated that these fun little puzzles were everywhere at all their properties, especially the restaurants.

A concerned looking Donald Trump then came back up front and gave Eric a "wrap it up" signal. Then a lawyer read aloud the following terms and conditions for becoming a *Trump Vacations* member:

- You have to sign a non-disclosure agreement, and can never publicly or privately talk about your stay at any *Trump Vacations* property, especially to the Better Business Bureau or prospective future members. If you do, Mr. Trump reserves the right to sue you for $5 billion for damages to his brand.
- Mr. Trump personally has first dibs on any property, and can supersede any reservation.
- You agree to never tamper with the little glass circles found above rooms' shower, or the glass circles embedded in the dressers facing the bed because they're "definitely not hidden cameras."
- If you're on the beach while Eric is playing in the ocean, you agree to watch him to make sure he doesn't drown. (Then Trump added, "Although, if he gets taken way out in the ocean by a sudden riptide, what are you gonna do, you know?")
- Any cans of *Diet Coke* in common or public areas are off-limits, and reserved exclusively for Mr. Trump.
- Mr. Trump reserves the right to walk into women's bathrooms and changing rooms at any time for "random service quality checks."
- No refunds.
- All tips for servers, bartenders, and hotel maids go to the Trump Org.
- You can never say the following words and phrases at any *Trump Vacations* property, or your membership will be revoked with no refunds: "Election 2020," "Biden," "Ron DeSantis," "Nancy Pelosi," "Barack Obama," "orangutan," "Why are there so many cockroaches," "What is that stench surrounding Trump?" "Donald Trump ate all the fried chicken out of the buffet again," "What is psychologically messed up about Trump that compels him to put his name on everything in his life from his buildings to his golf course napkins to his hotel bars of soap?"

After the presentation Trump asked who wanted to sign up, and none of the RNC officials raised their hands. Trump then threatened that, if they didn't all buy memberships today, he'd start a new MAGA political party and vow vengeance against every person who doesn't sign up for the rest of his life. Following that threat, all the RNC members registered and paid the exorbitant signup fees with Don Jr. and Eric while Trump put the slideshow back on and scrolled his way back to the picture of Ivanka in a bikini, and stared at it some more.

BIG IF TRUE I

- Following Florida Governor Ron DeSantis's political attacks against *Disney* for being "Woke," the animated film company is reportedly producing a new animated film about a flamboyantly homosexual drag queen named "Rhonda Santis."

- Conservative news mogul Rupert Murdoch has reportedly stopped filing and hiding the devil horns growing from his forehead.

- Bad news for Ron DeSantis: a new poll found that 86% of Republicans do not want to follow a "Donald" presidential nominee with a "Ronald" presidential nominee.

- Several GOP members of the Senate Subcommittee on Family Values say their Chairman Josh Hawley makes them watch "almost certainly way more gay porn than is necessary" during committee meetings for his stated goal of "studying the insidious network of gay pornographers throughout the US."

- Ivanka Trump spoke to the Female Empowerment Convention today, and said her family has been creating thousands of jobs for women for generations going back to when her great grandfather Friedrich Trump ran a brothel during the Canadian Gold Rush.

- Trump reportedly gave his remaining stolen classified files and national secrets to his doctor at Walter Reed Hospital so he can claim in court they're protected by HIPAA and "physician-patient privilege."

- The Trump Library is now postponing an exhibit it produced of all the famous women Trump has claimed asked him out on dates after virtually all the prospectively featured women claimed Trump was lying and threatened to sue the library.

- A self-proclaimed "MAGA hospital" in southern Idaho is using leeches on people to suck the COVID vaccines out from their blood because a nearby pastor has alleged that the "Kung Flu Fauci antibodies" were designed in cooperation with China to turn Americans' DNA Chinese.

- Florida Republicans say schools should censor images of the Founding Fathers in their textbooks so that Washington, Jefferson, Franklin and others aren't shown wearing high heels, stockings, long-haired wigs, makeup, or any other transgender-adjacent details.

- Amid rumors that Ivanka Trump ratted out the rest of the family for immunity in their family's criminal investigations, Eric Trump claims she was disowned by their father which means that now he's "the hot one."

- Trump just admitted in an unusually honest Father's Day reflection that he maybe wasn't the best father to any of his kids.

- The Proud Boys just announced their refusal to riot again for Trump because they suspect *Fox News* will just give all the credit to ANTIFA like they did after January 6th.

- The DOJ just subpoenaed Mar-a-Lago's *Diet Coke* delivery guy in his investigation over hoarding classified documents.

- Florida Republicans are lobbying for a bill to ban public schools from teaching the Gettysburg Address because it "makes the children feel uncomfortable knowing their state and ancestors fought for slavery."

- Democrats are offering an abortion compromise where doctors will be able to shoot fetuses with an AR-15 in elementary schools because Republicans are apparently unconcerned with that form of child murder.

- New documents from the *Dominion-Fox News* lawsuit shows that Tucker Carlson wrote "my audience" on the inside of his office's urinal and inside the toilet bowl.

- Republicans just started a support group for members of Congress whose Millennial and Gen Z children are calling them bigots, hypocrites, cultural dinosaurs, and Karens, and telling them, "OK, Boomer."

- Trump can't name any of the presidents between Abraham Lincoln and FDR.

- A GOP state party chair says his claim that "Satanist feminists are boycotting sex until Republicans die out so they can convert the US at vaginal gunpoint into a fascist, matriarchal triumvirate led by Beyoncé, Michelle Obama, and Oprah" was taken out of context to make him look crazy.

- Legal scholars say West Virginia's state constitution now officially gives more explicit rights to coal mines than it gives to women.

- Trump vowed today he'll run for president from Moscow, Riyadh, or Pyongyang if the Department of Justice continues to indict him. He reportedly likes Moscow because Putin is there and "has the best prostitutes," Riyadh because the women there legally can't sue him for sexual harassment or assault, and Pyongyang because the women are extra skinny and the lawyers will work for food.

- A confused Eric Trump just asked his dad if his dad's sexual assault accuser E. Jean Carroll is his real mom.

- *Fox News* hosts are mad today that President Biden reminded Americans to check the batteries in their fire alarms, with host Don Brockert saying, "Don't let the government tell you to fire-proof your home."

- Texas Republicans just legalized driving on state highways with a mounted AR-15 in the passenger side window for self-defense.

- Six months after its launch, the dating site for conservative gun owners called *"Red Flags"* still has no women signed up other than Lauren Boebert.

- Ron DeSantis just brought out a massive piñata in the shape of the word "WOKE" at his campaign fundraiser, and then beat on it with a baseball bat working up quite a sweat for twenty-five minutes as donors awkwardly watched thinking to themselves that he's kind of weird and unlikeable.

- The Florida state senator currently trying to ban pictures of nude statues like Michelangelo's David from school art textbooks has a pair of "truck nuts" hanging from his truck's tow hitch.

- Embattled Speaker of the House Kevin McCarthy just told the GOP House Caucus threatening to oust him, "I did way too many degrading things at Mar-a-Lago to lose my speakership after only four months."

- GOP Senator Herbert Rankford says he regrets saying "Women's uteruses will treat the conservative Supreme Court justices as liberators."

- Trump was asked which of God's 10 Commandments was his favorite, and he answered, "The one that allows me to not testify against myself."

- Wives of Republican members of Congress are increasingly interested to know why their husbands talk and think about trans people so much.

- Josh Hawley says he believes that if Republicans could just stop doing so many coke orgies they could capture control of the entire government.

- Trump says the Biden Administration "ruined the legal industry" because no lawyers want to work for him anymore without getting a year's worth of retainer fees in cash up front.

- Ted Cruz says that if GOP primary voters split evenly between Trump and DeSantis, he'll be nominated as the obvious compromise candidate.

- A new study found that 6% of all Manhattanites have personally experienced Trump announcing he'll pay their tabs at a restaurant, gala, or other event, but then leaving without paying.

- The Texas Supreme Court just ruled that the 2nd Amendment protects your right to buy a gun no matter how many times you mention, "I'm going to kill my ex-wife," during the transaction.

- A whistleblower at the Defense Department says Trump, during his last week as president, tried several times to order the generals to bring a nuclear missile to Mar-a-Lago for him to show off to members and charge them to look at it.

- Universities across the nation are now finding it financially imperative to charge students an extra $2,000 on their tuition to help cover the cost of insuring against mass shootings, which Republicans are affectionately calling a "Freedom Tax."

- Ivanka Trump says the fact that she's never invited to socialite parties anymore is violating her First Amendment right to participate in "Hot Girl Summer."

- A Florida GOP state senator accidentally said on a hot mic, "My plan is for school vouchers to allow public schools to go bankrupt while all the wealthy neighborhoods' tax money gets funneled to elitist suburban charter schools that can conveniently fill up availability before poor, ethnic kids can apply."

- Following the several shootings across the nation today, a *Fox News* host just claimed "mass shootings never used to happen until Biden took over."

- Trump accidentally dropped a candle at a Christian prayer dinner event tonight, and caught a *Bible* on fire.

Red States' Top 10 Craziest New Abortion Laws

August 16, 2021
Washington D.C.—

Now that the Roe V. Wade legal precedent on abortion has just been overturned, Republicans across the country are eagerly proposing and debating on some of the most sexist laws in modern US history.

Here are the top ten worst bills Republican officials are considering:

1. **Alabama**: The police shall arrest all unmarried women who are pregnant, and keep them in prison until their boyfriends, sperm donors, or rapists sign them out when they begin contractions to make sure they can't abort.

2. **Georgia**: "The Immaculate Conception bill." Within 10 business days of women finding out they're pregnant, all women must fill out and mail in a "Deed of Conception" with the state to track who is pregnant and who the father is so the government can track any possible miracle births, and find out fast if Jesus returns to Earth in Georgia.

3. **South Carolina**: The state shall allow only one exception for abortions: if the father of the fetus is a government official with a promising career (only applies for Republicans because conservatives understand the seriousness of their actions, unlike the Satanist Democrats who will just raise the baby to be a godless communist anyway).

4. **Mississippi**: Women can only have jobs until they get pregnant for the first time. After their first pregnancy, they must commit fully to being stay-at-home moms. Childless women can only work until the age of 35, at which point they must be shunned by society for being witchy spinsters incapable of love. Also, single women can only own one cat a time to avoid becoming "crazy cat ladies."

5. **Louisiana**: The police can take photos of women's vulva and keep them on file in case they're needed to solve any abortion-related crimes. This was immediately criticized by critics as "disgustingly perverted," "illegally voyeuristic," and "blatantly creepy," but the Republican state senator who wrote the bill said that any woman is welcome to come take a look at his penis as often as they want. Two days after submitting the bill, the state senator was arrested for flashing people in a public park. When released from jail he claimed the arrest was politically motivated by Cancel

Culture because, "The demonic, baby-eating Democrats hate me for being a proud Christian."

6. **Arkansas**: The state shall invest $15 million from unused COVID PPP loans to establish a Donald Trump Breeding Center that will be built big enough to take in 112 women at a time, and breed them with sperm deposits from Donald Trump. The mission statement of the proposed institution is to "Make America Great Again by filling the gene pool with Trump genetics," although one proposed amendment allows any fetuses that look like Eric in ultrasound imaging to be aborted.

7. **Kentucky**: A Constitutionally dubious bill wants to outlaw female masturbation by asking all smart watch products to track women's heart rates so when they have a high number of heartbeats per minute without moving spatially an alert is sent to the nearest police department to come knock on the door and arrest the woman if no man is present. The proposed legislation does not inhibit male masturbation in any way.

8. **Florida**: Representative Matt Gaetz has authored a piece of legislation he's calling the "Republicans Foster Young Teen Girls Act," but not much information is available about his proposal because in lieu of an explanation on how it would work or be implemented is just an emoji of an eggplant. His bill has earned no co-sponsors yet, with other GOP representatives citing his likely coming sex crime ethics investigation for having sex with a minor as the reason they're uninterested.

9. **Texas**: Louie Gohmert has proposed a bill that would ban all publicly funded schools from acknowledging the anatomical existence of the clitoris. "I'm sick of hearing people talk about the clitoris," Gohmert said last week, "talk about the greatest hoax ever perpetrated by biology! I'd love for some coastal elitist scientist to point on my body where my clitoris is. I sure as hell can't find it! I'll pull my pants down right now. There is absolutely no little erogenous fold of skin either above the stem of my penis, or below my sack. So where is it? The libs say it helps with climaxing, but, with God as my witness, I have never once even come close to climaxing by rubbing around my taint! Sometimes, when a finger slips in my bunghole, I feel a little something-something, but never just the taint. Why are women such conspiratorial liars about the clitoris? I don't have one, and no man I've ever met has said he has one either! And I've asked a lot of them!"

10. **Nebraska**: The state shall mandate every woman wear an ankle bracelet that loudly blares a police siren sound effect if she walks within 500 feet of a Planned Parenthood or Democratic Party field office.

Republicans Kill The "Puppy Mill Bill"

September 9, 2021
Washington D.C.—

Congressional Republicans just killed a bipartisan bill that would save puppies from puppy mills, and help them be adopted into forever homes.

The following are quotes from Republicans who voted or lobbied against it:

Mitch McConnell: "The Democrats want to tell you we Republicans are monsters for voting against this, but that's just socialism masquerading as compassion, and I will not fall for their tricks to use puppies as pawns in their political games. I'm a conservative, and will never condone the government interfering in the free market of puppy retail. Democrats are making irrational arguments based on their emotions to intervene in the economy. But I will not be intimidated by the alleged cuteness of puppies' domesticated features, like their cartoonishly big eyes and heads, or their disproportionately sized ears and paws. Puppies have never warmed my heart. I'm a reptile man, Goddammit!"

Ted Cruz: "The faster this dumb puppy bill dies, the faster I can get to Cancún! There's a heat wave coming to Texas this weekend threatening to kill the power grid, so I gotta get to a Cancún beach resort fast before my constituents notice I'm gone and start bitching about me leaving the state during an emergency! Dogs can't vote for me in presidential elections, so what do I care about what puppies think about me? I don't care about dogs at all, even if Donald Trump does call my wife one!"

Susan Collins: "I have been assured by my Republican colleagues that, if we regain the majority in Congress after the midterms, they will not pass any further anti-puppy legislation. So I trust that this bill from the Democrats is just not needed. Besides, I'm sure they'll be too busy reneging on all the promises they made to me about not ending abortion rights or access to birth control and contraception to think about taking away any rights from puppies! I think puppies will be just fine. It's human women who have to be concerned!"

Josh Hawley: "I gotta be honest, I'm too terrified of the January 6th protesters coming back and hanging all of us to pay any attention to what we vote on anymore. What was that sound? Are the protesters here? Ah, they're back!" *[Hawley then sprinted out of the Senate at top speed.]* "My book on manliness is now available for pre-orders!" he shouted over his shoulder before rounding a corner and disappearing from view. Then he popped his head back around the corner and yelled, "Don't forget to not masturbate!"

Matt Gaetz: "You know what I like about puppies? I keep getting older, but they stay the same age!"

Lauren Boebert: "The Second Amendment in the Constitution clearly shows guns are man's best friend, not dogs!"

Elise Stefanik: "If it will get me ahead in the ranks of House leadership, or get me in the running to be Donald Trump's next vice president pick, I will tear off a puppy's head with my teeth on live television, and hold its lifeless body above Kevin McCarthy's head, and let the puppy's blood drain out onto Kevin's face and into his eyes as a warning that I'm coming for his job. I will smear the blood on my forehead and cheeks like Native American war paint. I will do whatever—and I mean whatever—it takes to get ahead. If Trump will pardon me after, I will decapitate as many puppies as it takes to become politically powerful."

Jim Jordan: "I've never seen any abuse happen in a puppy mill. Who is saying I saw abuse happen at a puppy mill? They're lying! No puppy ever came to me and told me it was abused! I didn't report it because I never heard it! How can I report something I never heard? There's nothing to investigate! I don't have a guilty conscience! I never heard anything, I swear to God!"

Louie Gohmert: "I made love to a dog once in the woods behind my house. I was sixteen. Who knew how old the dog was. But its love was soft and tender. And, when we finished, it left and never came back. I've spent the rest of my life wondering, what if?"

Kristi Noem: "I call dibs on taking the puppies we need to euthanize to the shooting range!"

Mike Pence: "While I sympathize with the abused puppies, I believe prayer will save them more than adding more liberal government mandates and red tape on the pet industry. If we can just pray enough, God will change his mind about allowing puppy mills. That's why I've added puppy mills to my list of nightly prayers for God to end gun violence, school shootings, abortion, sex-trafficking, slavery, murder, poverty, and children's cancer. I think we're real close to convincing benevolent God to make those go away! So hang on, puppies, God's going to answer our prayers any day now, I'm sure of it!"

White House Staffers Say Trump Had A Visible Mushroom-Shaped Boner While Watching January 6th Happen On TV

October 24, 2021
Palm Beach, FL—

Trump staffers have reportedly told the January 6th Committee that Trump was "visibly aroused" while he watched the television coverage of the insurrection attempt for hours.

They also concur with Stormy Daniels's assertion that the visible outline of his genitals were small and mushroom-shaped.

However, Trump and his lawyers defending him have offered numerous inconsistent and conflicting excuses for why he was derelict in his presidential duty to stop the violence that day:

1. "I was praying! You know me, no one's a bigger lover of God, Jesus, and the Holy Goblin, or whatever the third one is. I had my nose deep into a *Bible* because anyone who knows me knows that every afternoon after lunch from 1pm to 4pm I'm doing intense *Bible* studying! On January 6th I was reading the book of *Prophesies*, which I remember very clearly because I found a prophesy in there that predicted the 2020 election would be stolen from a wise king with luscious gold hair and big hands, which obviously refers to me!"

2. "I was calling all my favorite charities and giving them big, tremendous donations over the phone. You never heard about it because I made all the charities keep it totally anonymous because, you know me, I'm a very quiet, modest person who doesn't like to make a big deal about myself."

3. "I was on a four-way call with Vladimir Putin, Kim Jong Un, and Xi Jinping, and they were all telling me that they were each going to give America a trillion dollars because of how strong, smart, and great at deals I am, but because Joe Biden stole the election they were going to forget about it. Unfortunately, America missed the deal of the century because Biden's such a crook."

4. "I was helping Barron with some girl issues he's having at school. He wanted my advice on dating because he knows I'm such an expert on teenage girls because of all the beauty pageants I've put together. He wanted to learn from the master, so during the riot I was away from my phone in Barron's room teaching him all my dating tricks, like sneaking into women's locker rooms by pretending you didn't see the women's

bathroom sign, and pretending to fall so you can reach out and get two handfuls of their boobs, and telling lies about your business rivals and colleagues to their wives and girlfriends so you can try to be their angry-sex rebounds, and, if all of those fail, just paying pornstars to come up to your penthouse suite for the best thirty-five seconds that money can buy!"

5. "I was talking to my guy in Kenya, who finally found out some real interesting things about Obama's birth certificate that will blow your mind when I reveal them in two weeks!"

6. "I was making love to Melania! We are so in love it's like we're teenagers. And we enjoy the art of tantric love, so sometimes we go at it for hours at a time. That's why she so often slaps my hand away when I try to hold it in public during events. After eight magnificent hours of my sensual intimacy and worship of her body she needs a break from any physical contact for several days. She tells me with tears in her eyes I'm the most sexually magnetic man she has ever seen."

7. "I was working out in the White House residence, and doing my daily routine of one hundred pushups, one hundred pull-ups, one hundred squat jumps, one thousand crunches, and a mile jog on the treadmill I can finish in under six minutes."

8. "I was having a heart-to-heart conversation with my son Eric, and telling him that, no matter what happens in life, I'll always love—ah, Jesus Christ, I can't finish that sentence. Fine! I was watching the riot on television and jerking off, and hoping the rioters would hang Mike Pence on live television, you happy? I wanted Josh Hawley, Ted Cruz, and Ron Johnson to burn all the slates of electors signed by the state governors, and instead approve the slates of electors that Rudy Giuliani schemed up to claim the state elections were full of fraud. I wanted to see the rioters break in all the windows of the Capitol Building, and break down all the doors, and defecate in all the Democrats' offices, and steal all of Nancy Pelosi's personal things, and destroy all the desks and chairs in the House and Senate rooms, and light the Capitol Building on fire, and watch it burn to the ground. I wanted to be able to institute martial law and order the military to start arresting all the Democrats, and putting them in internment camps. I wanted to fly the governors of Georgia, Arizona, Wisconsin, Pennsylvania, and Michigan to D.C. and hang them too, so their bodies could dangle as threats to anyone else thinking about not getting with the MAGA agenda. And then I wanted to go golfing. And then maybe jerk off a second time to the CNN commentary about Dictator Trump!"

All The Top Republicans' Love Languages

The five traditional love languages are words of affirmation, quality time, receiving gifts, acts of service, and physical touch, but the number of ways people can express love is limitless!

We checked in with our favorite Republicans to find out their love languages:

Donald Trump: You being willing to sign an all-inclusive non-disclosure agreement.

Donald Trump Jr.: Whispering in his ear, "Your dad told me he loves you, but he views you as too much of a threat to tell you because you're so manly and masculine."

Ivanka Trump: Planning with her the perfectly untraceable murder and dismemberment of her brothers, Tiffany, and Melania so she can inherit everything in her father's will and real estate empire for herself.

Rudy Giuliani: Giving him a 32-ounce Big Gulp cup of scotch while listening to him tell stories about his various extraterrestrial abductions, anal probings, and the time he spent nine Earth months living in a zoo on a planet several galaxies over in captivity with the actress Jennifer Lawrence, who he conceived a child with that the aliens kept to raise and make their galactic emperor. Also, not minding when he occasionally slips a hand into his pants while he's describing the sex he allegedly had with Lawrence in very gratuitous detail.

Kevin McCarthy: Texting him first thing in the morning every day telling him what MAGA-approved and Trump-endorsed opinions he should have that day.

Mike Johnson: Role-playing sex scenes from the *Bible*, such as Adam & Eve after being kicked out of Eden and learning the sin of sex, Lot and his daughters, and Noah after landing the Ark and repopulating humanity presumably with his daughters.

Matt Gaetz: Maintaining always an ambiguity regarding the fact that you are underage.

Jim Jordan: Pretending to be an FBI whistleblower, and making up unsubstantiated claims about the Biden family's supposed crimes.

Kristi Noem: Shooting puppies and kittens on her family farm.

Melania Trump: Helping her throw away Christmas decorations, transcribing speeches Michelle Obama has given in the past, and buying her expensive clothes that explicitly express her indifference to humanity.

Ted Cruz: Running away with him from the distress of his constituents to Cancún during statewide weather catastrophes. Also, whispering in his ear that he would make the greatest president in history, and should definitely run in every post-Trump election until he dies.

Mike Lindell: Helping him find evidence that Trump actually won the election because he really doesn't want to keep delaying the big reveal he has been hyping for years any longer.

Kimberly Guilfoyle: Dressing up as Benito and Rachele Mussolini with her.

Roger Stone: Wearing a Richard Nixon Halloween mask for him during the GOP coke orgies.

Stephen Miller: Digging up bodies in a graveyard for "experiments," watching his homemade horror films in his basement home theater, doing taxidermy with him, and developing new recipes for stews and soups with "mystery meat" substitutions you can't help but worry is human meat.

Eric Trump: Looking through his Pokémon card collection with him at all the cards he stole from kids with cancer during fundraisers he hosted at Trump properties that were later deemed fraudulent and exploitative by the State of New York.

Paul Ryan: Massaging his back by standing on it and walking in little circles while remarking on how soft, malleable, and spineless it feels.

Jared Kushner: Rolling around in a mountain of his Saudi cash, and telling him he's his generation's Henry Kissinger because no one but him is smart enough to realize all it took to accomplish Middle East peace deals with Israel was for America to just start screwing over and ignoring the Palestinians.

Mike Pence: Listening with him to his favorite musical artists Queen, the Village People, Elton John, and George Michael with him, and not reminding him they're all extremely gay.

Madison Cawthorn: Holding his cousin's head still for him to hump.

Marjorie Taylor Greene: Telling her you don't believe her father was a Sasquatch like people say on *Twitter*.

Lauren Boebert: Buying her a new vape, and letting her give you a handy in the theatre to own the libs.

Mike Pompeo: Flying with him to Iowa and New Hampshire every weekend and telling him he actually has a chance at someday being president.

Jerry Falwell Jr.: Cucking him with a sexy, Latin pool boy and letting him watch from the corner, and helping him pull off nepo baby real estate deals with his father's Christian university's money while thinking up new, draconian conduct rules for co-ed relations the students of the fundamentalist university have to follow.

Nikki Haley: Helping her pre-write dozens of different 2024 campaign speeches on the importance of personal principles, courage, and standing against the crowd with wildly varying content based on whether she will ultimately have to suck up to Trump if he runs for president again, shower him with compliments to be selected as his next VP candidate, beg for his endorsement if he stays out of the race, call for him to be found guilty if the DOJ's evidence of insurrection and stolen classified documents is overwhelming, or call him the greatest president is history if he dies suddenly with his Republican reputation intact.

Ron DeSantis: Leaving him unplugged so he powers down and can take a break from pretending to be human.

Tim Scott: Marrying him after a brief courtship so he has a better chance of being Donald Trump's vice president candidate.

Mitch McConnell: Letting him be alone in the turtle room at the Louisville Zoo for a half hour with the security cameras turned off.

ISIS Wants To Hire Free Agent Mike Pence To Turn The Organization Around

November 27, 2021
Rawr, Iraq—

The terror group ISIS has in recent months faced sharp losses in territory, troops, funding, and leadership, but the group's head of hiring, Mohammed al-Qaurzai, is optimistic he can recruit a new Caliph to turn things around.

Al-Quarzai reportedly compiled a list of potential candidates for caliph that ISIS is considering offering signing bonuses, and has raised some eyebrows because at the top of his list is former US Vice President Mike Pence.

"I know, I know, 'Death to America' and all that," explained Quarzai, "but we here at ISIS really need to start thinking outside the box. We're hemorrhaging staff from daily drone strikes, our money is frozen in international bank accounts, and I think it's time for an outside-hire to shake things up throughout the organization. It's no secret that we've been huge fans of Mike Pence for years, and he's a free agent now. He may not be a radical Sunni Muslim, but his brand of Christianity is really not that different when you think about it. Is Pence afraid of free, strong, independent women? Check. Personally threatened for some reason by public displays of homosexuality? Check. Confident the end times are imminent? Check. Prays several times a day? Check. All he has to do is position himself a few degrees southeast toward Mecca and you won't even notice he's an infidel! We might as well already be calling him Muhammad al-Pence! I tell you what, if ISIS was filled with soldiers half as committed to their beliefs as Mike Pence is to his, we wouldn't be in the dire straights we currently find ourselves. Pence is a devoted fundamentalist even without the motivating promise of seventy-two virgins! And he showed great courage when the Trump lovers went jihad on him on January 6th. I wish I could hire a hundred Mike Pences!"

Al-Quarzai told *The Halfway Post* that ISIS was prepared to offer Pence anything he wanted in order to convince him to switch religions.

"We'll match the salary and benefits he used to get, and throw in as many camels as he wants. We'll give him his own office cave. We'll look the other way if he wants to eat a pork chop every once in a while when he's missing home. We'll give his wife a full harem of helpers. We'll promise to keep Indiana off-limits for all our terror activities. Whatever healthcare he's getting, we'll give him even better! The best doctors we can abduct and hold for ransom will monitor his health day and night! Let me say this directly to Mr. al-Pence himself: name your price, and ISIS will meet it!"

Eric Trump And Don Jr. Have Formed An Alliance Against Ivanka And Jared

December 12, 2021
New York City, NY—

There is a civil war brewing in the Trump family over the criminal investigations swirling around nearly everything Donald Trump has ever done in politics, business, and his personal life, and the Trump kids are reportedly fighting amongst each other over who will take over which Trump-branded property if their dad is indicted and imprisoned.

According to family friends of the Trumps, they're also fighting over who will get to run for president first. Eric and Donald Jr. have agreed to form an alliance to better combat the advantage Ivanka and her husband Jared Kushner have because of their father's attraction to her.

"I'm not at liberty to disclose any information about a secret alliance," explained Eric Trump in a brief press conference with his brother this morning, "but I will say that my father has very bad taste in daughters. My half-sister Tiffany is way hotter, if you ask me, which I can say from the half of me that isn't related to her. I don't know why my father loves Ivanka so much. I personally think she's a big phony. It just so happens that my brother Don Jr. coincidentally agrees with me that Ivanka is a stuck up brat, and that her husband Jared has no business getting access to any of our family's money through Ivanka. I think he only married Ivanka to get to our dad's real estate properties because his properties, like 666 Fifth Avenue, have lost him historic amounts of money because he's an even worse nepo baby than us. I'm just saying that maybe the Department of Justice wants to investigate why Jared got that $2 billion from the Saudis, wink, wink. Ever since Ivanka married him she has turned very suspicious and scheming. I've even heard Ivanka tell Jared she was going to go change into more revealing clothing ahead of a family meeting with our dad. And Jared is always 'accidentally' dropping things in front of our Dad so Ivanka can bend down in front of him to pick them up. It's gross! And totally unfair because my dad yells at me to pull my pants up anytime I try to do the same trick. My butt cleavage isn't good enough for my father, but Ivanka's boob cleavage is? Give me a break! And then sometimes Jared sends suggestive text messages to our dad from Ivanka's phone, and then writes 'Oops, that was meant for Jared.' But it's so obvious what he's doing! And it's unfair because when I 'accidentally' send my dad suggestive texts, he texts back that I'm a loser and missing out on valuable tabloid press attention by not publicly cheating on my wife. All I can say is it just so happens to be that my brother agrees with me that this is totally unfair. And together we're going to make sure that one of us gets to run for president before one of them."

Then Eric let Don Jr. take the microphone.

"Ivanka and Jared think they're like JFK and Jackie," explained Don Jr., "but they'd be the worst power couple in American history. If Ivanka was going to be president, Jared would make the world's ugliest First Lady! He'd be even uglier than Abigail Fillmore, and she was hideous! So Eric and I have entered into an agreement to handicap them in the eyes of our father. We've even got Melania on our side. She hates Ivanka even more than we do, so she's willing to do anything we ask as long as we promise to give Barron a good job in the Trump Organization once Eric and me are made co-dictators of the company. I thought me and Eric were good at scheming, but Melania is savage. And, together, we'll make sure Ivanka can't be president first!"

"Or beat me to the presidency!" Eric interjected. "How do we know it's going to be you who gets to run for president first?"

"Sorry, bud, I misspoke." Don Jr. said, leaning toward the microphone and winking at the reporters. "You're right, it could be either one of us. But the point is that it'll be me or Eric who runs for president first, not Ivanka. I want to clarify that neither me nor Eric are anti-Semites. We will be so good to Israel when one of us is president. We'll move the embassy just like our dad did wherever they want. Over and over every year. The Israelis really seem to like that. But Roger Stone gave us some good ideas on how to combat the globalist cabal. So now we're in the middle of what we're calling 'Operation Destroy Ivanka.' A couple days ago, Eric snuck into Jared and Ivanka's house, and he stole the manuscript of her upcoming memoir. So now we're launching a website where we'll leak all of Ivanka's text so she doesn't sell more copies than my book *Triggered* sold! And we're going to leak all her secrets. Did you know Ivanka loves strangling dogs? Her favorite show is *House of Cards*, and, ever since she saw Kevin Spacey do it in the first episode, she has been keeping a journal of all the animals she has strangled. Don't get me wrong, I love hunting and shooting endangered animals, but I do it for sport. It's humane with a gun. Ivanka's spreadsheet of all the animals she has manually snuffed out of existence goes on for dozens of pages. Besides dogs, she has choked out squirrels, rats, frogs, pigeons, raccoons, stray cats, her friends' cats, a rabbit, Barron's pet ferret, an owl, and, now that she lives in Florida, a whole bunch of lizards. She keeps meticulous records of it like a Nazi! But, Ivanka and Jared are going down. And they'll be deported to Israel when I'm president."

"Or I'm president!" exclaimed Eric.

The Newest Members Of The House Of Representatives Are Revealing Salacious Secrets About Congress

January 25, 2022
Washington D.C.—

A new Congress means new House members, and this 118th Congress has added several Millennial and Gen Z representatives.

The Halfway Post asked them what they've discovered about Congress that they had not been expecting, and they got surprisingly candid, though they requested anonymity to reveal these secrets about their legislative colleagues:

"The House floor has this weird smell for which the only way to succinctly describe it is that the whole chamber just smells old and a little bit like what I imagine death smells like."

"Paul Gosar spends most of his free time drawing comics of himself as some kind of *Mortal Kombat* action hero character who decapitates all the Democratic members of the House with various weapons. And sometimes he draws these creepy, gross pictures of roadkill and other dead animals. He colors in his pictures with crayons so furiously that sweat drips from his forehead and splatters onto his drawings."

"Matt Gaetz has approached all of us freshman House members and said, 'Hey, you're young, do you know any clever strategies to get around the government firewalls on our network so we can watch porn during floor debates? The IT people keep cockblocking all of mine.'"

"Rudy Giuliani calls various House members, like, all day. Most of them are butt-dials, but some are drunken rants about UFOs. There's actually an unofficial rule in the House that's honored with rare bipartisanship where, anytime Rudy is drunkenly describing one of his alleged anal-probings by the aliens, the member has to put the phone on speakerphone for everyone else around to hear. I can't decide if Rudy is telling the truth, or is just drunk. He goes off on long tangents with real gratuitous, but amazingly specific, details about the aliens' various medical experiments, tools, and advanced technology. I'm not sure Rudy is creative enough to just be making it all up, and it's not like he's writing it down ever, or publishing science-fiction books. But he seems to really enjoy the extra-terrestrial attention. He calls Congress members so frequently that it's like he's bragging about how the aliens are so interested in his anus. Like, okay, we get it, Rudy, you get probed a lot. But that's what makes it so unbelievable. Like, really? An extremely advanced spacefaring civilization's curiosity is piqued to borderline obsession levels with

Rudy Giuliani? Look at him. His physical appearance isn't even close to normal human proportions with such a round, squat body, and a bowling ball head. Are they shocked at what a physical outlier he is or something? And he wants us to believe his brain—which must be entirely saturated with *Laphroaig* Scotch by now—is some medical marvel so spectacular that these aliens feel the need to abduct him twice a month? I don't buy it for a second. But he says he's trying to convince the aliens to let him be their lawyer. He lost all his law licenses here on Earth, so maybe that's not such a bad idea. Maybe he won't get sued as much on other planets as he gets sued here on Earth."

"I heard two different representatives in the 19th Century died at my desk."

"The least kept secret in the House is apparently that you never go into a bathroom Louie Gohmert just came out of."

"Every time I see Lauren Boebert I do an ocular pat-down to assess her current threat level. It's just a matter of time before she really brings a gun on the House floor and starts waving it around. Some members around here refer to her as 'Speaker of the Trailer Trash,' but I've met plenty of upstanding constituents who live in trailer parks, and I believe it's quite unfair and unwarranted to denigrate them as supporting Boebert's regrettable personal conduct and behavior in any way merely because of where they choose to live on account of either economic hardship or a desire for simplistic living. So I do my best to convince my colleagues that her nickname should instead just be 'Speaker of the Trash.' While I still think that's potentially demeaning to trash, at least garbage is inanimate and doesn't have feelings we can hurt by comparing it to the most belligerently ignorant representative in our current session. And that's quite an achievement in trashiness considering Marjorie Taylor Greene is also a member."

"Tomi Lahren from *Fox News* is, like, always calling Democrats' offices and leaving real nasty messages and threats between midnight and five am. She doesn't have assistants do it. She does it all personally. When does she sleep?"

"Marjorie Taylor Greene goes way out of her way to show off pictures of herself and Trump every time she goes to Mar-a-Lago. She says he wants her as his vice president, but apparently Trump has been promising that to lots of people. He makes the MAGA members rent rooms at Mar-a-Lago for the weekend where he takes them golfing and threatens them if they endorse anyone but him in the 2024 primary. And he charges much more than the market rate. He also tests them to see if they say anything when he cheats."

"In my first few weeks in Congress I was invited to three GOP coke orgies, and Chuck Grassley gave me the secret password for his f*ck dungeon."

Televangelist Joel Osteen Says He Has Never Heard Of Camels And Needles

March 21, 2022
Houston, TX—

Joel Osteen is one of the richest televangelists in the world, and his net worth is approximately $100 million.

Osteen subscribes to the prosperity gospel, a theological philosophy which argues that Jesus was just a little confused and off-topic when He would talk about money changers, the rich not getting into Heaven, and how hoarding wealth is Satanic.

Osteen raised these topics in a recent magazine interview in which he was surprised to learn from the interviewer that Jesus once said it was harder for rich people to get into Heaven than it was for a camel to get through the eye of a needle.

"Are you sure that part is in the *Bible*?" asked Osteen. "I don't remember it at all. I don't often preach about the details of the things Jesus specifically said, so my memory gets a little foggy sometimes, but I think I would have remembered something so vivid as that. It just doesn't sound like Jesus to me. The Jesus stories that stand out the most in my mind are when Jesus turned the jug of water into a jug of gold coins, and made it rain, like the young kids say, on all his Disciples. But, like, kept most of the coins for Himself, because He was running a business with his ministry, you know? I love the water into gold part. And the story of when Jesus had only three loaves of bread, but he multiplied them into dozens and dozens of loaves that He and the Disciples then sold in the market for big profits. Jesus was a real job creator. It's stories like that that I've always taken to heart. Jesus was just so good with money, you know? And of course the stories are always metaphorical. A lot of people will read the *Bible* and take what Jesus said literally, but that's a mistake because Jesus always spoke in metaphors. So when Jesus talks about sharing our wealth with the less unfortunate around us, Jesus never meant for that to be taken literally. Jesus's point was that in Heaven everyone will be rich, so don't worry about helping the unfortunate here on Earth. Jesus was metaphorically teaching us that the poor just have to muscle through a little inequality here on Earth until they get to Heaven when everything will be better for them for eternity. It takes a bit of educated thinking and theological context that goes over most people's heads."

The interviewer then asked Osteen if he thought his ministry had been behaving in a Christian manner during the COVID lockdowns when he infamously rebelled against the COVID quarantine orders, and called for his struggling, unemployed congregants to continue donating to his church regardless of their economic hardships.

"Of course I've always behaved like a Christian," snapped Osteen. "When Jesus went to the money changers in the Temple in Jerusalem, did he knock over tables or make a big ruckus? Of course he didn't! He took a cut of their profits, and demanded they tithe 10%! I'm doing exactly what Jesus did! I'm not collecting all this money from my congregants because I personally want to add new wings to my giant mansion, or buy new sports cars and private jets, or add to my collection of priceless, homoerotic Medieval art, or hire new, hot pool boys from South East Asia, or continue getting my weekly face injections… I'm doing all that because Jesus wants me to. No one was better at marketing than Jesus, and my conspicuous consumption is about one thing only: honoring God. I'm proving to all the atheists, Jews, Buddhists, and Muslims that faith in Christianity is enriching both morally and financially. That's why I customized my credit card to have a picture of Jesus. I like to be reminded of Jesus every time I buy a $10,000 bottle of wine, or a one-of-a-kind Swiss watch, or I buy a new, state-of-the-art, totally lifelike sex doll from Japan. Some of the things I buy each day costs more than a middle class family's annual income, and with my credit card I'm always making sure I'm flaunting Jesus just as much as I'm flaunting my harem of robotic sex dolls. I always put Jesus first. I even originally wanted to name my ministry after Jesus, but then I realized that for branding purposes I should really be promoting myself. One thing Jesus always preached about was personal branding. And I think Jesus is happy taking a supporting role at my church behind me. Sure, Jesus did a bunch of great things for humanity, like die for our sins or whatever, but I'm the one up on stage every Sunday morning doing the legwork for God, you know? Jesus has seen how much hard work it took getting my net worth to 9 digits. But I keep one seat on my jet always empty with a sign on that says, 'Reserved for Jesus.' Jesus is always hanging out with me on my private jet, and in my massive mansion. And Jesus really appreciates how I'm giving back to the economy by spending so much money for my extravagant lifestyle. You know how much sales tax I pay every day? More than the average American makes in a year! I'm basically crucifying my wallet on a daily basis paying so much sales tax. The Japanese sex dolls are not cheap. You really have to pay top dollar to get one that self-lubricates and has warmers inside. Jesus understands cold, dry silicone gives you a rash down there. And just like Jesus's messages of equality and love for all races on Earth, I've made sure to get sex dolls in every available skin color. I keep my sex life very fresh ethnically! I totally believe in racial equality, and with these dolls I put my money—and my penis—where my mouth is. That sounded bad, but you know what I mean."

BIG IF TRUE II

- *Disney* announced it will fight back against Ron DeSantis's homophobia by hosting the world's largest gay pride festival at *Disney World* on June 30th to make Florida the "Gayest State In America."

- Joe Biden says if Republicans can't make a debt ceiling deal, the Treasury will pay to keep the government open by recovering all the tax money Trump has stiffed the IRS over the last 50 years, with interest.

- Trump is suing a bank that won't give him a loan for slander and damages to his brand after the bank's CEO publicly explained his refusal to lend to Trump by calling him "America's biggest credit risk."

- QAnon believers are now referring to Trump as "Reverend Don," and have plans to start a compound in Guyana.

- A televangelist who regularly describes himself as "pro-life" and "pro-family" says "I'd rather see 1,000 babies starve than see one mother expose her breast in public to breastfeed where any men or boys might see."

- Rudy Giuliani claims his assistant who accused him of sexual assault is misleading people about his flagrant abuse of *Viagra*, and he was only taking those pills every two hours because he accidentally tore the label off the bottle and thought they were *Tylenol*.

- *Target* employees say they can monitor when a big group of right wing, anti-gay protesters are coming to protest their stores' gay flag products by paying attention to user's locations on the geo-locating map of the gay dating app *Grindr*'s

- Ron DeSantis's plan to give teachers guns is backfiring because now all of Florida's English teachers are forcing students at gunpoint to memorize and recite lengthy poems about the majestic beauty of gay sex, the cultural capital of turning trans, and the iconoclastic rebellion that is dying your hair blue.

- Judges in six red states have now removed *Bibles* from school libraries citing GOP laws banning books with sexual content, with one judge pointing out that almost immediately Adam and Eve's kids are doing incest, and, not much later, Lot's daughters rape him when he's drunk, and pretty soon again Noah's family all gotta do incest too.

- A leaked Russian memo shows that Trump sold several of the top secret presidential briefings he hoarded at Mar-a-Lago to Putin, but Russian officials were furious to discover how useless they are because every document is only one page, it's all written at a fifth grade reading level, and every paragraph includes his name with wildly superfluous compliments in every sentence even Kim Jong Un would find cringey.

- Trump just told *Fox News* that he checked and can verify with 100% certainty there are no classified documents at his Bedminster golf course, so there's no reason for the FBI to do a no-knock search of another one of his properties like they did at Mar-a-Lago.

- Kevin McCarthy admitted he was bested by Joe Biden in their debt ceiling negotiations saying, "Biden may be totally brain-dead, but White House staffers pulled his decaying corpse out of his formaldehyde bags and suspended it onto a system of ropes and pulleys, and flew it in circles around the Oval Office so Biden's dangling legs and feet nearly kicked me in the face, while the lights were off except for a fast flickering strobe light that was flashing, and fog machines were on behind the Resolute Desk spilling out plumes on both sides of the room, and loud, heavy-metal death music was playing somewhere from an amplifier, while AOC and Kamala Harris ran around me in circles with tribal African war masks over their faces and machetes in their hands, and they did some kind of ritual in front of me that looked like they were pantomiming giving dozens of abortions each and eating the placentas. It gave me such a spook I agreed to raise the debt ceiling just to get out of there and survive!"

- Rudy Giuliani is reportedly shopping around a sex tape to pay off his $10 million lawsuit, and is referring to it as his "directorial debut in the cinema," which he described on *Fox News* while wearing a velvet beret as "the infamous Kardashian tape meets the movie *Gremlins*."

- QAnon says if Democrats win full control of the government in 2024 Nancy Pelosi will pass into law a new healthcare law called the "Affordable Adrenochrome Act" that mandates insurance companies provide free baby blood for everyone.

- GOP Representative Huey Gobert during a hearing of the House Women's Health and Reproductive Safety Committee, for which Gobert is the chairman, to decide policy on whether tampons can be allowed in public school bathrooms shouted, "Just to be clear, how many holes do women have?" after apparently hearing for the first time that women don't pee out of their vaginas.

- Ivanka Kushner just told reporters that it's time for her to make a "conscious uncoupling" from her father.

- A MAGA country singer who claimed his music is written "to raise awareness about all the children whose blood is drank by San Francisco Democrats" just got arrested for possessing child pornography.

- The founder of the MAGA dating app "Rightward Love" acknowledged his app is used almost exclusively for gay hookups, saying, "I'm a Christian and I don't condone that lifestyle, but 3 million dollars in annual net profits is 3 million dollars in annual net profits."

- Televangelist Pat Robertson reportedly admitted he was gay on his deathbed, and had passionate affairs with Jerry Falwell.

- Trump was overheard in the Mar-a-Lago buffet line tonight telling people that if his trials didn't work out in his favor he'd "hide underground like Saddam."

- Trump's deal with the Saudi LIV Golf tour stipulates that he gets to win two tournaments per year, and all footage of him cheating will be both deleted and subject to a strict nondisclosure agreement.

- *Fox News* host Dean Fleming accused liberals of somehow brainwashing children even before they get to socialist public schools, saying, "My 4-year-old son was somehow unbothered when he saw two gay men holding hands in public this weekend, and I had to un-brainwash him by screaming, spitting on them, yelling out the f-word dozens of time, flagellating myself with a broken bike chain I found on the ground, and then masturbating behind a dumpster. The liberals are destroying our Christian society!"

- Trump has reportedly banned Rudy Giuliani from Mar-a-Lago because he can't make the membership payments anymore after being sued for ruining several Georgia poll workers' lives.

- Trump was reportedly difficult to fingerprint in the Miami federal courthouse today because of the fried chicken grease and dried ketchup coating his fingers.

- Local MAGA voter Ralph Winters just did the math, and was surprised to find out that the $11 million Hunter Biden's company reportedly made over several years is less than 1% of the lump sum Jared Kushner got from Saudi Arabia.

- After *NASCAR* tweeted in support of Pride Month, a MAGA fan in Iowa accidentally burned down his house trying to light his "Let's Go Brandon" flag on fire.

- A homophobic televangelist in Florida led a 3,000-person prayer congregation this weekend to demand God stop making rainbows after thunderstorms because it "encourages the gays."

- Jared Kushner just complained to *Fox News* about how the mainstream news attacks him for getting $2 billion in Saudi money, but never gave him any credit for donating $250 to charity last year.

- In rural Dixon, Mississippi, the town's conservatives are now sifting through trash bins for food at night to avoid having to shop at their only local grocery store they're boycotting because it put up a Gay Pride flag.

- During a campaign event in Iowa today, Ron DeSantis looked visibly furious after his wife Casey accidentally admitted that their daughter watches *Disney*'s *Frozen* every single day.

- The Saudi LIV golf tour says all PGA golfers must sign a non-disclosure agreement specifying they can never publicly accuse Donald Trump of cheating in future golf tournaments.

- Far right troll Matt Walsh excitedly claimed today in an interview, almost like he was bragging, "You would not believe how much trans porn I watched while doing research for my *What Is A Woman* movie. I must have spent the equivalent of 6 months on these sites."

- Josh Hawley just announced he's boycotting sex with his wife for the entirety of June to protest gay pride.

- The Illuminati just announced they are merging with the feminist mafia called the "Cliterati," and will work together to defeat Trump in 2024.

- After the Miami police fingerprinted Trump, his prints reportedly matched several found at the crime scene of a New York City *McDonald's* burger robbery in the early 70s.

- The FBI did DNA testing on the fecal matter collected from the top secret documents Trump stole and hoarded in his bathroom at Mar-a-Lago, and have identified seven Saudi nationals, two Russians, three Israelis, four Chinese, and one North Korean who all apparently at some point perused the files while pooping.

QAnon Just Started A Writers' Workshop For Conspiracists And Internet Trolls

April 15, 2022
Tallahassee, FL—

Sign up today to learn how to be a conspiratorial Internet troll, and get those liberal tears flowing! Check out these QWW's reviews:

"I was truly floored by how much I absorbed from the QWW curriculum in just one week! On day one, Monday morning, you hit the ground running when they help you create a dozen burner social media profiles. Then throughout the week they conduct in-depth walkthroughs of all the social media platforms' different terms and conditions agreements to show you how to avoid having your QAnon account blocked for promoting hate, harassment, and violence with hands-on exercises. I used to get locked out of my *Facebook* account every month, but now I've only been restricted once this year!" —Matt, 38

"Truthers of all kinds are sincerely welcomed, and the QWW is a perfect rebuttal against the Leftists who say we have a phobia of multiculturalism and diversity of ideas. For instance, I had never thought about the Earth being flat before, but, thanks to valuable friendships I've made at the QWW, I'm going to my first Flat Earth convention next month! Where we go one, we TRULY go all! And when I first heard the new conspiracy theory that birds aren't real, and they're all actually tiny, flying, electronic government surveillance drones, I thought it was ludicrous. But I've heard many compelling theories on the subject that really complement my suspicions that the Deep State has been spying on me ever since I celebrated American democracy and the Constitution by breaking into Congress on January 6th and taking a shit on the floor in Nancy Pelosi's office!" —Kimberly, 31

"The QWW is dedicated to making the week an adventurous potluck of truth-seeking. The facilitators and staff keep a strict 'no pedantic fact checks' rule that they rigorously maintain with dedicated 'off-the-grid hours' where everyone has to turn off their phones so our conversations can happen organically without any liberally brainwashed propaganda published in peer-reviewed studies by communist university professors. This allows for the kind of deep, brain-to-brain conversations we never get to have in public because of all the snowflake waiters, baristas, clerks, cashiers, salesmen, librarians, coworkers, kids, and ex-spouses out there in our lives who get all upset and call us 'Nazis' and 'serial sexual harassers' every time we exercise our freedom of speech to tell it like it is. At the QWW you can share all the stories full of 'locker room talk' you like!" —Franklin, 53

"I swear a janitor at the building where the conference meets is JFK Jr. in a disguise, waiting for Trump to name him as his future VP candidate. The guy denied it, but I know it's really him. I told him 'Let's go Brandon,' and he said, 'Who is Brandon?' So then I said 'Nice try, future Vice President,' and he told me if he caught me hiding in the women's bathroom one more time he was going to call the cops and have me arrested." —Zach, 23

"I was nervous about signing up for the QWW because it's natural to feel skeptical about a group claiming to teach you skepticism. When conspiracies are everywhere, it's tough to trust that other alleged Truthers aren't secretly working as Deep State governmental cutouts, or being paid by the globalist, New World Order lizard elite. But I can confirm that the QWW faculty are 100% authentic. No sign of secret cabal funding from George Soros, Bill Gates, or the Clinton Foundation anywhere, and I looked for it thoroughly! My only recommendation is to maybe not have the traditional Monday evening pizza party. When they started opening the pizza boxes I admit I freaked out a little when I pulled out my concealed firearm and started demanding to know where the baby-eating Democrats were. In my defense, every loyal QAnon follower knows that 'pizza parties' are code for child-traffickers getting together to diddle a bunch of kids! Anyway, I really hope the QWW reconsiders my lifetime ban. —Ralph, 43

"I loved the elective practicums and workshops that the QWW offers. My favorite was Racial Diversity 101, which allowed a very collaborate, comfortable roundtable setting to discuss how to use the Woke left's ideals of tolerance against them to point out how hypocritical they are by being intolerant of neo-Nazis. It gave me valuable insights into the lingo and buzzwords of Woke culture to more thoughtfully harass people with my various, elaborate fake identities online. I may be a cisgender white man, but three of my *Twitter* accounts are me posing as anti-Biden African-American women, and two more are me posing as anti-Biden Asian trans women. As far as I know, no one can tell I'm not actually Black, Asian, or trans! And the best part is that, since my alter egos are Black, my QWW counselor assured me I get to use the N-word all I want!" —Karl, 49

"One Star! The QWW is full of communists and socialists! They really think Joe Biden is president. DONALD TRUMP IS JUST WEARING JOE BIDEN'S FACE TO FOOL THE DEEP STATE! The QWW should be banned and executed when the Storm arrives any day now for going along with the Deep State lie that Biden is actually alive! THEY'RE TRAITORS AND IF I EVER SEE ANY OF THEM OUT IN PUBLIC, I HOPE MY CAR BRAKES WON'T SUDDENLY GIVE OUT AS I'M DRIVING RIGHT AT THEM AT 90 MILES AN HOUR!!! The catered lunches were really tasty though, and I am still awaiting a reply to my many emails requesting the QWW tell me what salad dressing the caterers used for Tuesday's lunch." —Ronald, 49

"Thanks to the QWW, I learned so much about each social media platform's specific algorithms! Now I know all about how to induce outrage in all my friends and family in order to increase my *Facebook* posts' engagement and enhance their digital reach. They teach you a plethora of ways to creatively reference the coming race wars, the next Capitol insurrection riot, and all the hoax Plandemic vaccines without getting automatically flagged. I feel confident thanks to the QWW that I'll be going viral in no time, and not just with COVID lol!" —Sarah, 26

"I was really looking forward to this year's QWW because Mike Lindell, the *MyPillow* guy, was this year's special guest teacher. Things got even more fun on Monday when Mike told us that Donald Trump was going to be reinstated as president on Wednesday, so we were all very excited to experience American history together. But when Wednesday came we stayed up until midnight, yet Sleepy Joe was still in the White House. Then Mike told us he meant Thursday, and we stayed up until midnight again, but it was a dud again. Then Mike swore Friday night was the big event, but, when nothing happened for the third time, he claimed he had unbelievable proof that Donald Trump really won in 2020, but couldn't show us until next year's QWW. As soon as I heard that, I bought a ticket for next year's conference. Boy, I can't wait to hear this evidence! I hope the QWW can also book Donald Trump as a special guest next year, too, because I'm still sitting on the edge of my seat to find out all about his amazing Obamacare replacement plan that is cheaper, and covers more people! And don't even get me started on his infrastructure plan! He was just about to unveil it when Biden stole the election from him, and the infrastructure deals Biden passed into law just in no way compare to the brilliant deals Trump was no doubt working on! Maybe Trump will give us a sneak peak of his amazing deals at next year's QWW. I can't wait!" —Dorothy, 71

"I love coming to the QWW. The best part is the unofficial gay orgy we have on the last day in the woods behind the cafeteria building. I'm not a white supremacist incel myself, but boy do the white supremacist incels who attend every year have some repressed sexual frustrations they need to take out on my very consenting body." —David, 29

Donald Trump Is Suing Jared Kushner For $2 Billion

May 16, 2022
Palm Beach, FL—

Donald Trump announced this morning he will not be requesting his son-in-law to work in his next administration if reelected, and will actually be launching a lawsuit against Jared Kushner to get some of the $2 billion in Saudi wealth fund investments Kushner received while acting as his adviser.

"That Saudi money is absolutely mine, and Jared knows it, quite frankly," said Mr. Trump in a press conference at his Mar-a-Lago beach resort. "He only got the money in the first place because he was supposed to be the middle man, and hold onto the money for a little bit so no one would notice when a few months later later he sent it to me. But it's been two and a half years, and he never sent it! It's so nasty what he's doing. And he thinks there's nothing I can do because it's laundered money, but I'm suing him in a civil suit. And no one knows more about lawsuits than me. I've been sued by thousands of people in business and politics. No one has ever been sued more than Donald Trump. Jared can't beat me in litigation. In fact, I've got Rudy Giuliani snooping around in Jared and Ivanka's trash bins right now as we speak. He's gonna find all of Jared's secrets. And if he finds any discarded bras of Ivanka's, he better turn them into me. You hear that, Rudy? I get the bras! That little goblin freak Rudy is going to keep her used bras, I just know it! Or only turn them over to me after he has inhaled all the good smells first. Rudy's a little rat, just like Jared. Stealing my Saudi money, stealing my daughter… You know, not many people know this, but I gave Jared's dad a pardon. His dad did some very dirty things. People think I do dirty things, but you'd never believe the dirty things Jared's dad did. He tried to get a prostitute to seduce his brother-in-law. But I pardoned his father, and this is how Jared repays me? I'm thinking I ought to hire a prostitute to seduce Jared. Then Ivanka will have more free time to lounge around the Mar-a-Lago pool. Daddy likey. Can you believe this so-called whistleblower Miles Taylor guy, and so many of my former staffers and even chiefs of staff are saying I regularly say gross, sexual things about Ivanka? What fake news! No one believes that. No one would ever believe I said something vulgar and suggestive about Ivanka in a million years. People say I used to be attracted to her when she was a teenager, but that's not true at all. It was all the other teenaged girls in my beauty pageants that I was attracted to. Some of them may have looked like Ivanka, I mean, I obviously like blondes, but so what? I have a type! Liking blondes doesn't make me some kind of sexually deviant freak. You know, the Christians, they really believe I'm morally pure. I'm bigger than Jesus with the Christians. And the Jews, they love me for moving the embassy. And the neo-Nazis love me too. The neo-Nazis think I'm their guy. They love Trump! I've always thought it was funny that zionists and Nazis both love me. How many people can say that? That the Nazis love them? Big brain. Got the Trump brain. Superior genes. My doctors couldn't believe how superior my genes were even when I was a baby. They said my DNA is off the charts. And all I'm saying is that Ivanka also has these superior genes. So is she good looking? Of course. She's like me if I were a girl. But would I ever date her? No! Even though I probably could if I really wanted to. I've already been taking her furniture shopping most of her life, you know? She kind of owes me. So these Never Trumper liars, who are total loser nobodies, and who are writing books full of the worst lies you ever heard—I mean, I've never even heard of this leaker Miles Taylor guy. I don't remember interviewing or hiring him at all. He made absolutely no impression on me whatsoever, I have no idea at all who he is. I probably only hired him out of pity. And I never saw him in the White House. I was always saying, 'Where is this Miles guy? Miles, where are you?' But it was a pity hire. He got down in my office on his knees, with tears in his eyes, and he said, 'Sir, I'm begging you. I need a job! I'll do anything!' But now he writes a book full of lies about me. I fired him. He was the worst. He had gone totally Woke like they say. It's a disgrace, really. The lowest of the low. But I'm a fighter. I fight hard. And remember that I am fighting for you. A lot of people don't know this, but I'm not on trial for me. I'm on trial for you. All of you, my faithful MAGA fans. People say I'm like Jesus holding up the Earth on his shoulders for all of eternity. Jesus did so much for us, didn't he? I just love Jesus. One of the great Jesus lovers of all time. More than Lincoln. So remember that when I'm going to be in court for most of the next year. Know that I'm not defending myself against lawsuits for sexual assaults, fraud, insurrection, and espionage... I'm defending YOU. They're really coming after you, but I'm just standing in their way to protect you. So that's why I'm going to need all my supporters to help me help you by physically forming a very thick, protective wall of bodies in front of me at all times, and around the buildings I'm in. Anywhere I go, patriots need to form an impenetrable ring around me, and bring your guns so no FBI agents can arrest me or put me in prison, even if I'm found guilty in all the upcoming trials on insurrection, rape defamation, and treason. And I'm gonna need all the Second Amendment people to bring their guns to New York, Georgia, Florida, and D.C. because those jurisdictions will all be sending arresting officers after these trials. I need some more of those stop-the-steal rallies you all are so good at. Let's do a January 6th every day until the election because America needs us to stop the steal. America needs you. We need to stop the steal of Trump! They want to steal Trump and lock him up. So, Roger Stone, if you're listening, I need you to talk to the Proud Boys and get them back on my side. Tell them I'll pay all their legal fees for committing violence and treason if they do another coup attempt for me, for real this time. And we need to really regroup because all the main guys from last time are in prison for either January 6th, abusing their wives, or public masturbation. So we need to grow a new crop of incels. Incels, if you're listening, come be patriots, and help me tear up the Constitution once and for all and be president for life. You know, forever. Because I won't die. I can't die. Donald J. Trump cannot die. You know, the incels don't get credit for how smart they are. They're some of the smartest people, maybe ever. They love everything I do, so you can tell they're really genius. I don't know why me and the incels get along so well, but it's tremendous. They remind me of me when I was their age. And for everyone else, I'm going to need you to help me fight the Deep State by really upping your cash donations. And make your donation a recurring donation. Make it monthly. These lawyer fees are bleeding me dry. And I still need to hire some new lawyers for the alleged negligence behind my hoarding of national secrets at Mar-a-Lago, and Jack Smith hasn't even indicted me yet for who I sent those classified secrets to! So I need money. Buy my NFT's! Buy the golden Trump shoes! Right now. Pull out your phones and send me cash ASAP. You're gonna have to be creative. Desperate times call for desperate measures. I didn't want to say it, but it might be time to tell Grandma and Grandpa they had big, beautiful, long lives, but maybe it's time to shove a pillow over their faces and donate the inheritances you're gonna get to help me Make America Great Again again. Your donations can bring back the greatest president this country has ever had, better than all the others combined. All the presidents. Washington… Lincoln… Obama… Martin Luther King Jr…. And I've accomplished more than all of them put together. And Biden. Biden hasn't done anything. Biden is dead. His brain is mush. A lot of people are talking about how his mushy brain leaks out his ears and nose, and his staffers have to suction it out of his ear canals before interviews or it will distractingly glisten when the stage lights are turned on. And people are saying that during those interviews, his staffers have to glue velcro strips to the back of his shirt and his chair so his limp body can stay upright. His head kind of dangles a bit and everything. It's a disgrace! And the fake news media never reports it. They only report the totally fake Russia hoax. It's always Russia, Russia, Russia, and pee tape, pee tape, pee tape, and mushroom penis, mushroom penis, mushroom penis. There was no pee tape okay? I don't do pee tapes. I'm way too smart to ever get caught in a sex sting. The Russians tried, but they gave up. They came to me and said, 'Sir, you're too smart. Your brain is too big. And you're so Christian and monogamous!' And Ivanka has that brain too. So I'm not even attracted to Ivanka's tremendous physique. The fake news is totally wrong about that. I'm attracted to her big Trump brain! But, of course, she also has some nice other big things!"

Steve Bannon's Demands For Testifying In Front Of The January 6th Committee Just Leaked!

June 11, 2022
Norfolk, VA—

Steve Bannon is reportedly offering to testify for the January 6th Committee, but has the following demands that must be agreed upon first:

- He doesn't have to shower or shave before the hearing

- He can bring a 30-pack of beer and drink as many as he wants during his testimony

- If he feels bloated, he can undo his belt, pants button, and zipper

- He can present his 90-minute slideshow presentation on "Jewish Globalist Conspiracies Going Back To The Peloponnesian War"

- He can bring his own film crew to shoot footage for his upcoming documentary "2024: January 6th Was Just The Test Run For Destroying The US Government"

- He can be barefoot to air out a foot fungus condition he's currently treating

- He can wear a prop SS Nazi uniform he bought last year from a movie studio

- Any lizard shapeshifters on the January 6th Committee have to take off their human masks and reveal themselves as extra-terrestrial reptiles

- Congress must make the Food and Drug Administration approve his brand of "Erectile Dysfunction Patriot Pills"

- Congress must name a post office in his honor somewhere

- Joe Biden must pardon him for his fraudulent "Build the Wall" fundraiser that stole tens of thousands of dollars from gullible MAGA fans who thought they were helping finance a wall project

- Congress must exempt him from paying alimony to his "bitch ex-wives"

- He will be gifted one lock of Alexandria Ocasio-Cortez's hair

- When he goes to the bathroom during his trials, he doesn't have to wash his hands

- Someone must deliver some of his feces in a bag to Dr. Fauci's porch, light it on fire, and then ring the doorbell

- Nancy Pelosi must allow Marjorie Taylor Greene to become chairwoman of a newly created "Anti-Zionist Satellite Committee" to study ways the military can fight back against globalists

- Congress must allow him to use federal land for a second storage building for his White Sperm Doomsday Vault project

- The IRS must agree not to audit any of his tax returns over the last ten years, or investigate the funding that Chinese billionaire Guo Wengui has gifted his media companies

- Hillary Clinton must agree to stop using evil liberal sorcery to sneak into his dreams and seduce him

- Congress must approve a protest permit for a demonstration he wants to lead around Congress for white supremacists and neo-Nazis on the anniversary of Hitler's birthday

- The Congressional gift store must start selling his book, *How America Can Dismantle The Administrative State And Launch A 4th Reich That Will Endure For 1000 Years*

- Liz Cheney must send him five photos of her feet, with red toenail polish, no questions asked

Dr. Mehmet Oz's Top Excuses For Why He Never Goes To Pennsylvania, The State He's Carpetbagging To Be Elected To The Senate

July 27, 2022
Cliffside Park, N.J.—

- "Where in the rule book does it say I have to live in Pennsylvania while I'm campaigning to be Pennsylvanians' senator? Besides, if I become a senator, I'm just going to buy a mansion in D.C. and live there. Whether I win or lose, I'm never going to live in Pennsylvania!"

- "Pennsylvania just has this really odd smell. The whole state gives me a migraine if I'm there for longer than an hour."

- "I'm kind of freaked out by the Amish, and they're everywhere there."

- "I'm sort of good friends with a lot of the top Turkish governmental officials. They invite me to a lot of weddings, birthday parties, campaign parties, and top secret meetings. And Turkey has a lot of elections I still vote in. It feels like I'm always flying back and forth, and flying internationally out of Newark is much nicer than Philadelphia."

- "I may have allegedly tried out a bunch of fake medical cures using Pennsylvanians as guinea pigs that maybe turned them blind, ruined their kidneys, and gave them cancer before I found which cures were less toxic to give to New Jerseyans."

- "I only agreed to run for the Senate because Mitch McConnell and Donald Trump told me I wouldn't have to work very hard to get elected. I specifically told them I'd only run as long as I didn't have to shake hands or touch any Pennsylvanians."

- "None of my friends or family live in Pennsylvania."

- "I'm afraid of John Fetterman. He's huge. He's almost 7-feet tall! I don't want to be in the same state as that ogre. Is there a scientist roaming around the Arctic right now looking for him? Plus, when I stand next to him, I look and feel like a little Oompa-Loompa!"

- "As someone who has spent a lot of time in Turkey, which isn't far from where Dracula lived, I have a natural suspicion of any places with 'sylvania' in their names."

- "The sh*tty roads in PA really f*ck the suspension of my Lamborghini."

- "I don't own a mansion in Pennsylvania that I can live in, and I haven't stayed in a hotel since 1996. I'm not a peasant."

- "I didn't realize Pennsylvania was so rural between Pittsburg and Philadelphia. All the Republicans in this state are hillbillies or Amish. I'm not trying to be a senator for a bunch of Northern Alabamians!"

- "Every time I try to drive into Philly, I get scared I'm gonna get mugged, so I turn around and floor it to the nearest bridge over the Delaware River. Philly is sketch."

- "I don't understand why Pennsylvanians are so obsessed with that big, cracked bell they have, and at this point I'm afraid it's too late and awkward to ask."

- "Philadelphia is coasting on its heyday, which was two hundred years ago. It's so annoying when cities cling to a long past prime. We get it, Ben Franklin lived here. But if he was alive today, he would 100% have set up his printing press in Jersey. He sold high-brow stuff the Philadelphians of today could never comprehend, let alone appreciate."

- "I just think Jersey chefs and cooks have innovated the Philly cheesesteak sandwich so far beyond what Philadelphians are capable of that getting one in Philly just seems poor and trashy."

- "I like going to music concerts, and all the best singers are from Jersey. Sinatra, Springsteen, Bon Jovi, Paul Simon, the Jonas Brothers. Pennsylvania is like a blackhole of musical talent where no one is talented."

- "New Jersey's beaches are way better, and I have yet to find any good caviar toast places, or any good seafood places for that matter, in Pennsylvania. The fish are as smelly and unimpressive as the people."

- "I never cared for the *Rocky* films. Each one gets worse than the last. Philadelphia owes every American the ten-plus hours it took us to watch those dumb movies. It makes perfect sense that Pennsylvanians would love movies about a sport where you give yourself brain damage."

- "I'm sorry to repeat myself so often about this, but the entire state of Pennsylvania just f*cking reeks."

Insane Texts Have Been Found On Alex Jones's Confiscated Phones That His Lawyers Incompetently Let Become Public

August 4, 2022
Austin, TX—

In the trial against the Sandy Hook families, Alex Jones's lawyer accidentally gave the opposing lawyer the entirety of the contents of Jones's phone, and didn't follow up on retracting or protecting any of the data. Now his texts, a treasure trove of insanity and possible criminal evidence in other crimes, is publicly available to read. These are the most intriguing texts found so far:

- To **Eric Trump**: "Can I get in on some of your charity fraud? These Sandy Hook lawsuits are bleeding me dry. Maybe I should switch my focus from kids in school shootings to cancer kids. Call me back, bud."

- To **Roger Stone**: "You vet your orgies, right? I don't want any secret Reptilian shapeshifters shooting their demon semen loads into my eyes. I've had enough STDs already, I'm not trying to get some extra-terrestrial chlamydia on top of the Earth one!"

- To **Rudy Giuliani**: "Hey, Rudy, if you're trying to get your hair to grow back, don't do that hair dye crap. I have some supplements on InfoWars.com that are guaranteed to reverse hair loss. But read the side-effects first. The chemicals it uses are all banned in Europe."

- To **Donald Trump**: "Hey, before you go to North Korea to meet with Kim Jong Un, I can teach you some karate moves. They all know it over there. Better to be safe than sorry. I once took on 50 Koreans by myself who Hillary and Nancy paid to make me disappear. The trick is to get naked and rub baby oil all over yourself so they can't latch onto you."

- To **Bill Barr**: "Can you investigate my bitch ex-wife to get her off my back? These alimony payments are killing me. Her lawyers have f***ed me. I think they're gay and upset I found out about their chemtrail experiments with the gay frogs. I think they paid off the judge. I'm paying alimony for kids I don't even get to see. Can you believe my bitch ex-wife called me mentally unstable? Me! Mentally unstable! I'm not even sure they're my kids. They might be government false flag plants. My ex-wife is a total globalist. Wait, you're not Jewish, are you?"

- To **Donald Trump Jr.**: "Hey bro, really loved your convention speech. Talk about passion the way you spoke so fast, and your eyes were bright red and glassy. Can you hook me up with your guy that gets you that stuff? Whatever you were on, I want a lot of it!"

- To **Ivanka Trump**: "Hey, girl, just went to the gym today. Benched two Jareds (250lbs). You ever thought about ethical non-monogamy?"

- To **Roger Stone**: "It's cool, we can talk about the January 6th coup with this number. I guarantee no enemy lawyers will ever get ahold of this phone. Oh, while I have you, when's the next GOP coke orgy? I heard Chuck Grassley put a new swing in his f*ck dungeon. Oh, will Louie Gohmert be at the next one? He lent me his Ogre Demon 3000 dildo machine and I've been meaning to return it, but I can't exactly bring it through the security checks at his Congressional office building, you know? I don't think it would fit through the x-ray machine."

- To **Donald Trump**: "I have a list of enemies I want to take out, starting with my bitch ex-wife's lawyers. If you pardon me afterwards, I'll add Pence to that list."

- To **Mitch McConnell**: "If you help the Democrats destroy Trump, I will make you into turtle soup and eat you for breakfast, Turtle Man!!! Who is paying you to betray America? I'm on to you and your little Reptilian plot! I will f*ck you up, and all your shapeshifting friends! You can't brainwash me with your fluoride water because I recycle my piss through purifiers for all my hydration. You can't control me!!!"

- To **Mitch McConnell**, two hours later: "Quick question, will you be doing a lot of oversight on the PPP loans? I'm trying to buy an erectile dysfunction pill company, but I don't want those grubby Sandy Hook lawyers to find out about the shell companies I hide my money in."

- To **Donald Trump**: "Hey, have you ever looked into Melania's past, or fact-checked her childhood? Is Slovenia real? I don't know if it's just all her plastic surgery, but she looks a little Reptilian. Thin mouth, very narrow, beady eyes… are you sure she's not a shapeshifting alien spy?"

- To **himself**: "Note for spy novel: has too many sex scenes with 1960s Nancy Pelosi… get it down to single-digits."

- To **Roger Stone**: "Dude, Madison Cawthorn is talking about the coke orgies. You said he was cool! Chuck Grassley says he's about to go strangle the little f*cker. You invited him, you have to shut him up! I've maintained a very polished reputation, and that little rat is gonna give everyone the ludicrous impression that I'm some kind of manic freak!"

Republican-Approved Remakes Of Famous Disney Movies

These ideas for *Disney* movies are 100% guaranteed to own the libs, get the Woke socialists crying, and replace the Satanic values of evil Hollywood elitists with the values of Real America:

- **Beauty and the Beast**: After getting married, the Beast locks Belle barefoot in the kitchen, and takes away all her books and burns them because they're brainwashing her to be liberal and Woke. Then Beast demands she give him ten kids over the next ten years, but, unfortunately, her first pregnancy is ectopic, and, because they live in a red state, Belle is forced to try to carry the impossible fetus to term and she dies. Beast feels sad, but is comforted that Belle died in honor of his pro-life convictions. Also, because the red state repealed its laws on child brides, Beast is excited to look for and marry a 13-year-old.

- **Cinderella**: Cinderella is kept from going out and having a social life because her good Christian stepmom knows she's a little floozie who will have premarital sex and weekly abortions. When the Prince goes door to door to meet the kingdom's single maidens, Cinderella's father gives the Prince the symbolic key to her virginity, and warns the Prince that Cinderella is a feminist so she'll need an "occasional physical reminder" that the *Bible* says women must be subservient to men at all times. The Prince chooses Cinderella, and, though at first she struggles with the trad-wife lifestyle, she realizes she's much happier doing all the daily house chores without thinking for herself or ever leaving the home without her husband's accompaniment.

- **The Lion King**: Simba trashes his father's legacy as a just ruler because his dad was a total beta cuck. Simba knows Scar is a much smarter, more respected ruler, so Simba announces he's going to Make the Pride Great Again by removing the pride from the North Africa Treaty Organization (NATO) and allying instead with the much more masculine hyenas who don't let in females or gays in their hunting packs. Then Simba shares his idea that the hyenas will be even more macho if they lounge in the sun and tan their testicles. It gets increasingly homo-erotic from there.

- **Peter Pan**: Peter gets sent to a pray-away-the-gay camp in Mike Pence's Indiana where the conspicuously homosexual camp counselor casts all the kids in a musical theatre production called "Captain Hook and the Pussy Pirates" that extols the virtues of vaginal sex for procreative purposes only.

- **Alice in Wonderland**: Alice gets arrested for having edible drugs, and her country's new hardline death penalty policy for drug dealers gets her arrested and then summarily executed by the state.

- **Robin Hood**: Robin, with his gang of outlaw socialists named Bernie, Alexandria, Barack, and Joey B. don't want to work or be productive members of society, so they slowly starve and freeze to death on the streets of Nottingham where feeding the homeless has been outlawed by the city council. The town rejoices that they didn't have to raise their taxes any to fund a safety net support system, and they thank God for cleaning up their town.

- **Sleeping Beauty**: Princess Aurora sues Phillip for kissing her nonconsensually while she was asleep, but Phillip wins the court case because the judge can tell he has such a bright future ahead of him. Also, Aurora was "asking for it" by wearing a dress that showed a little cleavage.

- **One Hundred and One Dalmatians**: Cruella de Vil successfully lobbies the federal government to cut regulations on both puppy mills and puppy fabrics used in fashion with a "Freedom For Puppies Act" she wrote herself that claims to defend the free market against Democrats' attempted communist takeover of the puppy industry. The Republicans ram it through Congress, and then celebrate with Cruella on their victory for capitalism wearing Dalmatian coats she gave them after they stopped caring about honoring the Emoluments Clause of the Constitution.

- **The Jungle Book**: Mowgli tries to reenter human society at the end, but he quickly gets arrested for being an illegal alien and deported to Mexico on account of his "cantaloupe calves" and tan skin.

- **Aladdin**: Jafar, who texts via WhatsApp with the son-in-law of the US president, finds out where Aladdin is thanks to American intelligence agencies, and lures him into the nearest embassy where Jafar's parrot Iago cuts him into little pieces with a bone saw. It's an international controversy, but Jafar later gives the president's son-in-law $2 billion for his new investment firm.

- **Lilo & Stitch**: The US president shoots down Stitch's ship with a missile in case it's another Chinese weather balloon floating over the US to spy on us.

More Texts From Alex Jones's Phone Just Leaked!

September 9, 2022
Austin, TX—

The following are more emails found on the phone of Alex Jones that his lawyers failed to keep protected:

To **Roger Stone**: "I want to start dressing like a Batman villain like you do. Got any style ideas for me? I like the idea of wearing just loincloths in public. From now on at our coke orgies will you start introducing me as 'The Beast'? Or what about 'King Dong'? Chuck Grassley's *Titan Deluxe* penis pump has given me a huge bulge. Actually, I'll get back to you, I wanna keep workshopping alter ego names."

To **Madison Cawthorn**: "Hey, bud, sorry to be the bearer of bad news, but you're no longer invited to me and Roger's coke orgies. You violated the first rule of talking about them in public, and also the second rule of nakedly humping people's heads without consent. We have a zero tolerance rule for not obtaining consent. Tell your cousin he can still come by though."

To **Donald Trump Jr.**: "Hey man, you doing okay? I'm a little worried about you. You know I love some of that Florida Snow just as much as the next guy, but you can't do it moments before you give a nationally televised address! And I've told you so many times that you need eyedrops. Your eyes were glowing so bright red I thought Hillary infected you with her Satanic zombie venom. This may sound ironic coming from me, but moderation is the key to life. You shouldn't be mixing so many downers and uppers. I'll tell you what, go on InfoWars.com and use the promo code 'HITLER2022' and you'll get a 75% discount on my Patriot Fuel energy drinks. They're great and super powerful. They help me pull all-nighters like three times a week without the drip-down issues of coke, or the big pupil issues of weed. Just the occasional paranoid hallucinations, so definitely hide your guns when you're gonna drink one. But they'll keep you going all night. Most of the chemicals are banned in Europe, so you know they're awesome. No socialism in these bad boys! Seriously, though, let me know if you need help. You look like sh*t in all the rant videos you keep posting online. Remember the rule: create f*cked up, but always edit and post sober!"

To **Matt Gaetz**: "Hey, where's the party at? The address you gave me is a house full of underage girls. Did you mix up the digits or something?"

To **Donald Trump**: "I think it was Ivanka who ratted you out to the FBI. I told you she should never have married Jared Kushner. The Jews are using her to sabotage you. I don't understand why you don't like Eric. He's got a better business mind than Don Jr. for sure. The children's charity fraud racket was the most profitable thing you've done financially since your Atlantic City casinos had a nice start before they went down in bankruptcy. The cancer charities aren't the biggest windfalls in your portfolio, but they're consistent, dependable cash! Eric was right, you guys barely have any liquid assets, so you gotta hand it to Eric for finding that little goldmine of a niche. Charity executives trying to cure children's cancer must be the most gullible dupes in the world. And because you guys jack up prices so much when hosting their fundraisers, it means less money to cure the cancer so that the racket can keep going in perpetuity! Admit it, that was genius of Eric. You should go easier on him. He's my favorite. Honestly, Ivanka gives me the creeps. I swear to God on the morning of the January 6th rally I heard Ivanka lean over to Barron and tell him that if he or Melania ever tried to sue her to get more money out of your last will and testament she would personally dismember him into little pieces and feed him to Melania in a stew. That's some f*cked up sh*t. Did you know that when Ivanka left the White House she gifted all her staffers a copy of 'The Most Dangerous Game,' that famous short story about the island where they hunt people? She told them all that if they ever write a memoir detailing secrets of what she's like as a boss, she'll hunt them all like prey and feed them to their parents or children in a stew. What the f*ck is it with her and turning people into stews?"

To **Mark Meadows**: "Tell Trump that, if he pardons me for all the school shooting parents' lawsuits, I'm willing to sneak into Hillary Clinton's volcano lair so I can rescue all the captive children there, and destroy all the shapeshifting lizards' eggs so they can't repopulate America with their demon spawn. Then I'll strip naked and rub myself with baby oil so I can fight Hillary's gay frog henchmen with karate. When I get to Hillary's palace, I'm sure she'll be hiding in her globalist bank vault full of all the Jews' gold, so I'll pretend to wait for her for several hours sitting on the side of her pool of children's blood. Real slyly, I'll drop a vial of anthrax I'll have been hiding in my mouth the whole time to poison the pool. After I've waited long enough until I'm certain she must be getting weak and desperate for another sip of the blood to preserve her Satanic flesh, I'll yell out that she must not be home so I'm leaving. As I head out of the palace, I'll know the plan worked when I hear her demonic shrieks and I feel my ears bleed down the side of my head while the anthrax vanquishes her back to the Underworld. Then I'll sprint to Hillary's spaceship as the volcano starts to shake and rumble, and the walls start to collapse, and the ceiling crumbles down all around me. I'll make it to the spaceship just in time to fly away as the volcano's steel doors are closing, and barely make it through the gap. Then I'll deliver the stolen children to their parents, and fly to the White House to accept my pardon. Mark, promise me you're gonna tell Trump about my plan this time, okay?"

To his **ex-wife**: "If you or your lawyer call me mentally unstable one more time in court I will cut the electricity from your house, sneak into your house, and hold you and the children hostage until a SWAT team mops up my blood off the floor of your bedroom! I know you're working with Hillary and Pelosi! I came by your house and I saw several frogs hanging around. The gay kind! How much money are those reptilian, fluoride freaks paying you to ruin me? I won't let Hillary Clinton steal our children and bathe in their blood! Never! Does that make me crazy? I've never been more sane about anything in my life! You don't even own a gun to protect the kids from the Democrats! If I'm the negligent parent, why am I the only one who leaves a loaded AR-15 out in every room for me and the kids to fend off Hillary if she sneaks into our house? Riddle me that!"

To his **ex-wife** (ten minutes later): "You can't send that last email to the judge in our child custody trial because I sent it to Donald Trump too so now it's protected by executive privilege!"

To **Mitch McConnell**: "Hey, Turtle Man, if Trump appointed me as a new cabinet position of Secretary of the Media in 2024, do you think the Senate would confirm me? Full disclosure, there are warrants for my arrest for public masturbation in 6 states. Let me know. I'm currently reading every biography of Joseph Goebbels I can find at every public library within a 50 mile radius of Austin... except for the libraries that have unfairly banned me for public masturbation."

To **Roger Stone**: "Hey, man, ever since we invited Marjorie Taylor Greene to Chuck Grassley's Labor Day coke orgy, it burns when I pee."

Leaked Secret Service Texts Reveal Wild Things About Trump's Time In The White House

September 17, 2022
Washington D.C.—

A leaked stash of Secret Service memos is revealing secrets about protecting Donald Trump during his first term, and the memos variously describe Trump as "needy," "fussy," "whiny," "high-maintenance," "emotionally volatile," "morally destitute," "functionally illiterate," "needlessly cruel to his underlings," and "foul-smelling like a garbage bag full of roast beef sandwiches that has been left out in the sun for a week."

The memos also revealed the following details about Trump's life behind the scenes:

- Trump never once rode in a car with Melania or Barron because Melania forbid it.

- The Secret Service had to start offering bonuses to drivers of the presidential limousine because Trump smelled so bad. The agents quietly went on strike in March of 2017 refusing to drive him without extra "stench pay." It made Trump furious because the strike made him miss a few days of golf, and he had to stay inside and suffer through the boredom of actually reading his presidential briefings.

- While being driven to campaign events, Trump would regularly complain to agents about his supporters' lackluster "star power," and accuse Hollywood of "rigging hot people against him" by brainwashing most movie stars and models to hate him. One conversation recorded in a voice memo text captured Trump saying, "The MAGA people are all missing teeth, and ugly. Yuck. I don't get enough donations from my MAGA dupes to pay any hot people to come to my rallies. I can barely afford all the 'Blacks for Trump' people I bring!"

- Trump regularly tried to choke out his Secret Service drivers when they refused to stop at the *McDonald's* drive-through citing the security risks of sitting still in line and getting trapped by other cars for five or more minutes.

- Trump was a big fan of the Swedish pop group ABBA, and on motorcade rides liked to blast "Dancing Queen" very loudly so he wouldn't have to listen to advisers read him his already abridged presidential briefings.

- The floor mats in the back seats of the presidential limousine had to be replaced monthly because of how much fried chicken Trump would eat messily on his way to rallies and coat the fabric with grease. On long drives, Trump would sleep and always leave orange stains on the seats and seat belt straps.

- Trump used to once a month go on a drive with Kevin McCarthy 45-minutes into the middle of nowhere in Virginia farm country, and leave him there to walk back to D.C.

- Trump would often fart, and then blame the driver.

- The cloth seats of the vehicles Trump rode in were regularly stained with blue *Adderall* dust. Sometimes Trump would throw burgers he brought for snacks against the windshield when he'd hear bad news. The Secret Service found this to be an incredibly reckless, potentially catastrophic security threat given that they'd have to stop the vehicle and wipe off the smeared ketchup.

- Following every meeting with an Asian diplomat or leader, Trump would talk with an exaggerated Asian accent for fifteen minutes.

- Every Secret Service agent has heard Trump recommend they spend their next vacation in Moscow because "Russian girls are into some crazy stuff."

- During international events and global summits, Trump would always "accidentally" walk into the women's bathrooms, which was always really awkward for Secret Service agents to have to witness.

- The Secret Service had to triple its golf cart fleet and pay for storage space in foreign countries to store them because Trump refused to walk anywhere, even when attending ceremonial events outside with other leaders, including female leaders wearing heels.

- Trump repeatedly asked Secret Service agents in the week leading up to January 6th if, hypothetically, it would be possible to "pull a Princess Diana" on Vice President Mike Pence.

- After every motorcade ride for four years straight, Trump told his drivers "I'd tip you but I don't have any cash, so I promise I'll tip you big on the next one." The Secret Service also heard him say that to every Mar-a-Lago employee who served him, his golf caddies, and various hotel staff members when staying in foreign countries.

- 95% of Secret Service agents' COVID infections were directly linked to Trump demanding no one around him wear a mask, and half of them were directly or indirectly related to the infamous car ride he took while staying at the hospital with a nearly fatal COVID infection so he could pretend he wasn't about to die.

- Trump once ordered a Secret Service agent to run over his son Eric after Eric revealed he had given a children's cancer charity a 1% discount for booking consecutive fundraisers at a Trump property.

- When playing golf, Trump made every Secret Service agent carry three of his golf balls in their pockets for him to cheat with.

-
- Trump often told his generals they should watch more WWII movies about the Nazis to understand the military vibe he wanted to see.

- The Secret Service had to regularly invent excuses for why women Trump invited to ride alone in a car with him couldn't in order to save the government millions in under-the-table hush money payouts.

- A few times when Trump was napping on long car rides, Secret Service agents could tell from Trump mumbling in his sleep that he was having a sex dream about Nancy Pelosi or German Chancellor Angela Merkel.

- Trump watched porn a lot on his phone during car rides, and typically played it at full volume.

- Trump asked a few SS agents in his first month of his first term if they could "make Eric disappear."

- Trump would occasionally make suggestive comments to agents like, "You know, in Russia and North Korea, their security agencies will push the leaders' political enemies out of windows…"

- Trump would regularly make long phone calls where he'd listen a lot, and say things like, "NATO is ripping us off, you're right," "Ukraine is ripping us off, you're right," and "the US should tell Poland, the Baltic states, South Korea, Japan, and the European Union to fuck off, you're right," and then announce after he hung up, "That wasn't Putin I was talking to by the way, it was—uh—Barron, yeah, Barron was asking me questions about his homework."

- Trump once asked the head of the Secret Service, "Why do we call you the SS if you won't do any of the stuff Hitler's SS did?"

Don't Let The Facts That I Only Criticize Democrats And Always Defend Donald Trump Confuse You, I'm An Independent Centrist!

By Tommy Poolman

I've done it! I've climbed the media ladder and joined a cadre of independent pundits like Joe Rogan, Ben Shapiro, and Tucker Carlson, and I did it with just an insatiable appetite for trolling liberals!

Of course I've made a lot of enemies along the way—the socialist Democrats, the thought-police, and all the blue-haired feminists who are too high on their own supply of DEI to keep a rational, emotionally uninvested, bird's-eye, macro view of political issues like me—but they're all just snowflakes who hate how a straight, white, cisgender guy like me can amass a huge following online by mocking their civic rights, socio-economic grievances, and pathetic obsession with democracy.

But remember, I'm not actually committed to any of the things I say or do that provokes them into Wokesplaining conniptions, I'm just asking questions! Or playing devil's advocate. Or trolling for the lolz.

Life would be much easier for the Woke if they remembered that at the end of the day virtually no contentious pieces of legislation or civil rights issues ever affect me personally. Politics, government, and public policy are just games for me, and I play to win. So, when I throw out a what-about-ism here and a "both sides" there, I'm just tossing curve balls to strike out the libs who get so mad they start yelling. When they quit the debate and block me online, I win!

Although, sometimes, when I'm in danger of losing an argument, I say I used to be a Democrat myself years ago, before Democrats took a hard left turn to Commie Town. I even voted for Obama in 2008. There's no way I can verify that for my haters on *Twitter* who point out that my earliest tweets when I started my account in 2009 regularly hashtagged the Tea Party, and featured the anti-Obama "NOPE" poster as a profile picture, but that just proves how much of an open mind I keep. I'm a CLASSICAL liberal. It's the liberals who have abandoned liberalism, not me!

I also sometimes claim I'm a demisexual or aromantic so I can demand liberals support me and accept my opinions as facts because I have LGBTQ+ membership, and am therefore just as much an oppressed victim of the capitalistic, white, cisgender, heterosexual patriarchy as any of them. Isn't pedantic trolling fun?

Which is why I laugh so hard when the Woke mobs try to cancel me. Making liberals upset is exactly why my fans love me, so I can't be canceled! And I tally up all the times I get called a "Nazi" online because I'm a neo-Nazi at best on my most fascist days. Do I think the Nazis may have had a few good ideas? Of course! Not every single idea they ever had was about genocide and world-wide race wars, you know?

For instance, I love the VW Beetle. The autobahns weren't so bad, were they? The Hitler Youth taught girls how to cook. Hugo Boss pivoted from the SS, and now makes wonderfully fashionable suits for everyone—even Jews. So, see? The Nazis were full of ideas, many of which we should adopt. Only a handful of them were, quote, "evil." I want America to have a fun, affordable "people's car" just as much as I want America to start up a few concentration camps for social undesirables.

But there is one downside to being an anti-Woke Internet troll, and it's that the liberal elites just happen to coincidentally be involved in almost all this country's good art, cultural innovations, and social fun.

I'll admit it's ironic that I spend ten hours a day calling the cosmopolitan, globalist, coastal metropolises "baby-eating communist shitholes where everyone is mugged and murdered by marauding gangs of Black thugs every day" when there's no way in Hell I'll ever leave my big city and move to some flyover country mining ghost town or farming county I spend all day on my podcast celebrating as "Real America." I'm not happy saying this, but elitist liberals shitholes are somehow where all the cool celebrities and parties are, where all the artists and tech geniuses live, where all the skinny and pretty people live, and where all the money, economic growth, and GDP come from in spite of how deranged the liberals are.

But because I get unfairly tarred as a Republican—remember, I'm an independent centrist!—I don't get invited to any of the good parties or media events. I may defend everything Trump does, and excuse everything he says, but I'm barely on the political right at all. I'm very much in the middle, no matter how high I am at the top of the Y axis into the "Authoritarian" end of the 4-way political compass.

I just want to stop the libs from ruining America, and that might mean Trump will have to become a dictator and settle on a Final Solution to rid America of liberals. Just kidding, I'm only being ironic!

The Most Shameless GOP Responses To The Allegations That Georgia Senate Candidate Herschel Walker Paid For At Least One Abortion

October 5, 2022
Washington D.C.—

Republicans all over the Hill are showing off their trademark political hypocrisy in their responses to the news that Herschel Walker paid for an abortion.

The following are the most craven examples:

Mitch McConnell: "If aborting every fetus in America would get me one inch closer to getting the Senate majority back and becoming majority leader one more time, I'd do it in a cold-blooded heartbeat."

Donald Trump: "If I had a dollar for every abortion I paid for, I wouldn't have to lie and beg Forbes to pretend my fraudulent financial records are accurate so they'd put me on their list of billionaires! I only regret I didn't have more abortions in life. You know how many illegitimate Erics are running around out there? I lost count after 20!"

Marjorie Taylor Greene: "No one is talking about the fact that the Jews can do abortions from space with lasers from their satellites. How do we know it wasn't the Jews who aborted Herschel Walker's baby? The Jews can do all kinds of things from space. They made me cheat on my husband by shooting gravity beams at me from their satellites. One moment I was praying to Jesus, and thanking God for my pure and monogamous marriage, and, the next thing I knew, the Jews were flinging naked men at me with from every direction. I tried fighting them off to stay faithful to my Christian values, but the Jews had flung too many penises at me and one got me! The Jews caused my divorce and betrayed my marriage, not me. Now I know just how the Germans felt at the end of WWI!"

Alex Jones: "Folks, you know me, I'm no crackpot conspiracist. I tell only the truth, and the truth of the matter is that no one can verify Hillary Clinton's whereabouts on the day Herschel Walker allegedly paid for that abortion. Did she forge that 'Get better soon' card that supposedly has Walker's signature on it that was mailed to his mistress? Did she write the check he appears to have sent her to pay for the abortion? Was Hillary in the hospital that day? Did she use chloroform to render the doctors and nurses unconscious so she could be put on a white coat and be alone with that little zygote doing who knows what kind of horrifying, Satanic, communist rituals and spells to end it's little life? Folks, Hillary absolutely refuses to tell us where she was on that day, and the liberal media is helping her cover it up!"

Dr. Mehmet Oz: "I want every Pennsylvanian to know I may have been involved in some sordid medical studies that murdered a few hundred precious, adorable puppies, and threw their lifeless bodies into garbage bags, but I'd never pay for an abortion. Unless Pennsylvanians approve of that kind of thing. Ah, d*mn, I can never keep track of the weird sh*t Pennsylvanians think, and the gross sh*t they eat, and the ghetto sh*t they say, and how the whole state smells like sh*t. Why can't Pennsylvanians be more like New Jerseyans? New Jerseyans are sensible, rational people. Pennsylvanians are f*cking savages. Philadelphia is like the goddamn, feral, Hobbesian state of nature. It's a lawless wasteland of primitive anarchy and terror. Running for the Senate in Pennsylvania was the biggest mistake of my life. I give up pretending to respect these barbarian Pennsylvanians! The entire state is full of vulgar, miscreant, philistines!"

Kevin McCarthy: "What do I think about the Herschel Walker situation? Uh, what was Trump's response? Has Trump given a response? Let me just take a look on *Twitter* at what Trump said. Whatever Trump said I'm for. Abortion is bad. Unless Trump says it's okay. Then I'm for abortion. Stop it with this 'Gotcha Journalism,' okay? My opinion is the same as Donald Trump's opinion. There is no daylight between him and me whatsoever. Trump supports me for Speaker, and I support him for President. So all his supporters in the House have no reason not to vote for me to be the Speaker if we Republicans end up taking back the House. A vote for me is a vote for Trump, because I am 100% a Trump guy. You hear that, Donald? I'm loyal. I've always been loyal, Donald. Please don't put me back in the dog kennel for being disloyal. I don't want to go back in the kennel. You leave me in there for days at a time, and I have to go to the bathroom in the corner. It's dehumanizing. I hate the kennel! You told me to do whatever you say, and that's what I'm doing. I'm being a good boy, Donald. I mean Mr. Trump! Mr. Trump! I said mister! Everyone heard me say mister! Aw, Jesus Christ, it's back in the kennel for little Kevvy!"

Donald Trump Jr.: "Ha! Take that liberals! Herschel Walker owned the libs so bad by paying for that abortion. Liberal tears, am I right? The libs are crying so hard. Aren't they, Dad? Aren't they? Dad. Dad, did you hear me? Dad, did you hear me own the libs? Dad. Dad, I owned the libs. Dad! Oh, big deal, you can see Ivanka's nipples poking through her shirt. We all have them. Honestly, Dad, it's 2022, you shouldn't objectify your daughter like that. Dad, stop staring. She's not even hot." *[Donald Trump, talking over him: "I paid for them, I get to stare at them all I want."]*

Donald Trump's Strategy To Win His 3rd GOP Presidential Primary Just Leaked!

October 20, 2022
Washington D.C.—

Fool-proof steps to defeat Ron DeSantis, Nikki Haley, Chris Christie, and the rest of my primary challengers:

- Hire goons to go through the trash bins outside the homes of Liz Cheney, Kamala Harris, Nikki Haley, Kristi Noem, and any other potential female critics and rivals, and look for tampons and pads to try and track their menstrual cycles to know when they're about to get totally nasty.

- Pick a new ethnic demographic to call rapists and drug dealers to keep my next campaign fresh… maybe the Irish this time? Puerto Ricans? Maybe trade that island with some other country for an island with white people? Trade it to Denmark for Greenland? Maybe just sell Puerto Rico for cash? China and Russia would probably pay top dollar for an island so close to America to put some nukes.
    And I could probably get an off-the-books finder's fee

- Send Rudy Giuliani to San Francisco to search around for any laptops Gavin Newsom may have left at a computer repair shop just in case Biden dies and he takes over as the presidential candidate

- Find out if Tiffany's new husband wants to be my next executive adviser since Jared Kushner is going to be busy with his $2 billion in Saudi money.
    First find out if Tiffany's husband is Jewish
        (The QAnon people won't like me having another globalist)
    Demand Jared give me some of that $2 billion Saudi cash ASAP

- Get more body-doubles for Melania because I'm not sure she'll do any more campaign appearances with me, or agree to spend another four years in D.C.

- Hold an intervention for Don Jr. about the drugs. The Bidens did one for Hunter, and it straightened him out. Maybe I should try being as good a dad as Joe is to his troubled son.

- Make a fake treasure map that occupies Eric for the next two years of campaigning, and keeps him away from media attention.

- Get Stephen Miller a makeover, personal stylist, or PR coach so he stops looking like Nosferatu had a kid with Joseph Goebbels and then locked it up in a shed for the first 18-years of his life.

- Find lawyers and media spokespeople with bigger breasts, blonder hair, and better lying talents. My defense arguments aren't so innocent, so I'm gonna need to distract my fans with lawyers hired straight out of Babe Town.

- More litigation:
    Sue the RNC for failing to stop Biden from winning
        (And causing billions of dollars in damages to my brand!)
    Sue the enemy of the people secretaries of state who let me lose
        (GA, AZ, WI, MI, and PA)
    Sue the 81 million voters who voted for Biden
        (Can Rudy get drunk enough to argue this in court?)

- Figure out an Obamacare replacement plan that will cover more people and be cheaper.
    Ask around if Obama had other infrastructure ideas he never used

- Make all my hotels and golf courses switch to cash-only transactions because the IRS and DOJ are getting so nosy about my accounting.

- Find a darker shade of orange foundation makeup: new campaign, new Donald Trump whose facial glow looks younger than ever!

- Find longer red ties, taller shoe lifts, more absorbent diapers, and stitch more of my taint hair into the gaps of my head hair so I can refresh my look for 2024.

- Go to a doctor and find out if 50 years of eating fast food and never exercising was bad for my health, and if there's anything I can do to ensure I live the whole four years of my next term. What a joke I'll be if I die in office! The last president I want to be grouped in with in the history books is Zachary Taylor or William Harrison!
    Remember to clear my Internet browser history more frequently

- Find one military general somewhere who will sign an affidavit verifying the truth of all my "Sir" stories, and pay him whatever it takes to break his oath of honor.

- Stick my peepee in between my legs after a shower to see if I'd be hotter than Ivanka if I was a woman.

Some Of The Insane Things Kevin McCarthy Has Promised To Earn Speaker Votes

November 27, 2022
Washington D.C.—

Thanks to Republicans' surprisingly narrow majority in the House of Representatives, aspiring Speaker of the House Kevin McCarthy is struggling to get all the votes he needs to be elected.

Some of the most MAGA members of the House are threatening to withhold their votes unless McCarthy promises them favors. These are the wildest:

- Lauren Boebert—Wants to be able to bring a gun onto the House floor and in Congressional committee meetings, and be allowed to vape on the House floor.

- Marjorie Taylor Greene—Wants McCarthy to vow he'll fund the launch of Christian space lasers to defend against all the Jewish ones.

- Herb Williams—Wants to be able to wear his grandpa's Ku Klux Klan outfit on the House floor.

- Morgan Clinedell—Wants the House to install "gay-dar detectors" and "trans-dar detectors" next to all the metal detectors at the Capitol's entrances so he knows how many gays and trans are visiting each day.

- Matt Gaetz—Wants the House to pass a bill lowering the age of consent to 16, and to have no Friday morning votes so he can fly to his weekend drug parties in time to pick up his girlfriend from high school.

- Clay Higgins—Wants to become the chairman of a new subcommittee "focusing on foreign policy with regard to the Mole People."

- Jim Jordan—Wants the House to lower the statute of limitations on whatever crimes are involved in hearing about sex abuse on your wrestling team and then trying to sweep it under the rug.

- Thomas Duncan—Wants the Friday "casual day" dress code at the House to include wearing no pants, because that's casual for him.

- Karen Trechus—Wants gift cards to Applebees for when she dines there and they don't comp her food after she complains about every dish even though she ate almost everything.

- John Lupin—Wants McCarthy to institute a new rule that no men can "go commando" on the House floor so that with pants and underwear there's always at least four layers of fabric protecting his penis from other male House members' penises accidentally touching his.

- Paul Goshaar—Wants the House to pass a resolution officially declaring that Hitler and the Nazis had "some good ideas."

- Madison Poshey—Wants the House to mandate all Smithsonian Museums and other federally funded museums put wax models of Jesus riding all the dinosaur fossils to promote Creationism and Jesus.

- Ralph West—Wants McCarthy to have the House Sergeant at Arms arrest his ex-wife and imprison her in a room in the basement of Congress for reporting him under his state's red flag law, and getting his AR-15 confiscated by the police for getting drunk and threatening to kill his family on tape.

- Bob Harris—Wants something to be stocked and available for free in the men's bathroom since women get free tampons.

- Louie Gohmert—Wants to be the chairman of a newly created House subcommittee on Female Anatomical Truths because he's sick and tired of hearing women claim that they have a clitoris, a G-Spot, brains equal in size to men's brains, a hypothalamus, a pelvic floor, or that they're capable of having orgasms.

- Richard Drowning—Wants McCarthy to let him put a couple hidden cameras in each of the women's bathrooms "to do surveillance for protecting women from creeps in the bathrooms."

- Andy Riggs—Wants McCarthy to pass a bill to send to the Senate that would hire unemployed veterans to stand guard in the bedrooms of gay people across America to ensure they don't have any gay sex.

- Chip Normen—Wants McCarthy to fire the Senate pool lifeguard for wrecking his family values credentials by publicly accusing him of trying to grope him in the locker room.

- Elise Stefanik—Wants McCarthy to gift her a sword with which she has vowed someday she will literally backstab him with for the Speakership.

- Albert Schweizer—Wants McCarthy to get him an invite to one of Senator Chuck Grassley's underground f*ck dungeon coke orgies.

A Dispatch From The Frontlines Of The War On Christmas

December 1, 2022
North Pole—

My Dearest Samantha,

I regret to write that the generals have revoked our furloughs to come home at all before Christmas, and it's back to the trenches for me and my 101st Snowborne Division brothers in the forests around the liberals' heavily fortified trenches at the North Pole. Things haven't been progressing well for us here on the Northern Front. The liberals have taken Santa hostage, and are forcing the Elves into forced labor day and night building weapons to use against our men. They also conduct airs raids from above with Santa's reindeer against their will so our conservative platoons can't get close to the liberals' trenches. The liberals have an unshakeable, Satanic resolve to end Christmas once and for all. But we are holding onto hope that we can make a breakthrough somewhere along their trenches, and free Santa and the Elves in time for Christmas. Millions of good little children across America are depending on us conservatives.

But, Samantha, oh how I miss snuggling with you at night. I haven't been getting much sleep at all these weeks because the liberals probe our defensive lines all day and night looking for weak points to push through. We are on high alert always, and we're bombarded several times daily. The liberals will fire volleys of metal menorahs, then copies of the Koran, and then Black Santa dolls. They try to force us underground while they creep up underneath their cover fire barrages to get close enough to our trenches to toss in hundreds of coffee cups that say "Happy Holidays" on them instead of "Merry Christmas." It's terrifying when one lands right next to you. They also toss in smoke bombs that shoot out smoke in the Kwanzaa colors of black, red, and green. Worst of all is the glitter bombs that explode homosexual glitter and confetti all over us. We try to quickly throw them all back out of our trenches, but the liberals outnumber us, and we lose good men every day to these diversity attacks, bombs of tolerance, and reminders of America's religious multiculturalism.

It's very tough to stay positive, and our officers struggle to keep up the morale. Sometimes the liberals fly over us on Santa's sleigh, and drop propaganda leaflets to discourage us. The leaflets will say things like how Jesus really wasn't born on December 25th, and that He wasn't blonde or blue-eyed, and that Christmas trees are a pagan tradition, and that corporations have a financial interest in being inclusive of all religious faiths and December holidays, not just the Christian Christmas.

But we commit ourselves to keeping the Christmas spirit alive in our trenches. Sarge has an advent calendar, and every morning we get together and watch him reveal another little candy cane that means we're hopefully one day closer to saving the North Pole from the liberals' secular invasion. It's a small daily ritual, but, amidst all the liberal godlessness and Satanism, it's the only Christian reminder we have. Sarge gave me one of the candy canes yesterday after I jumped on one of the glitter bombs to save some of my friends. It got glitter all over me, but so far I haven't been turned gay. Unfortunately a good friend of mine did turn Muslim after he got hit by a Koran and read it.

Oh, Samantha, I hope everyone back home appreciates the sacrifices me and the boys are making here in the trenches. I regret to think about the magical Christmas memories I'm missing out on this year. I can't even remember what eggnog tastes like. The only thing we have to drink is vegan almond milk that our patrols find in abandoned liberal stashes. We of course never take any of their jars of baby blood they've left behind. I shudder to think you might not even recognize me if I somehow manage to get through this war alive. My red and green sweaters have been torn to shreds, my Santa hat has bullet holes in it, and my rosy red cheeks are covered in dirt and mud. But at least I'm still alive, and I promise you I'll never let the liberals take away my Christmas cheer. To keep Christmas alive in our hearts, we spend the time in between the liberals' barrages singing Christmas carols, and acting out scenes from *A Christmas Carol*. We had a good laugh because my buddy Tommy makes the perfect Tiny Tim since he's on crutches after he got hit in the knee by a Jewish dreidel sniper a couple days ago.

I miss you so much, Samantha. The nights are very lonely. We must maintain a total blackout at night, so we can't have any light strands, candles, or Christmas-themed inflatables at all. We've had to blacken our gold and silver cross necklaces so they don't reflect moonlight or flare light and give away our positions. It's the saddest December you've ever seen. What I'd give to come home just for one day and sit next to our Christmas tree and fireplace with some festive Bing Crosby playing.

But someday we will defeat the liberals, and be free to celebrate Christmas the way we want again. Religious liberty will return to America, and everyone will have to celebrate Christmas the way we Christians want them to. We'll never again have to see any evidence there are other religions practiced in America besides Christianity, or there are other holidays in December besides Christmas. That's what we're fighting for: the freedom to force our Christmas traditions upon everyone else in America.

Much love to you always, Samantha,
John

BIG IF TRUE III

- "I was fooled by Rudy Giuliani's manly charisma and sexual magnetism," said one of the fake Georgia electors involved in the scheme to submit fraudulent electoral college votes in 2020.

- Melania Trump has been wearing her "I really don't care, do u?" jacket every day since her husband got arrested.

- A group of QAnon fans in Idaho who committed various felonies so they could go to prison and be ready to protect Trump from other inmates in case he gets incarcerated just got sentenced to a prison Trump would never be sent to.

- CHRISTMAS MIRACLE: Only 2 GOP House members accidentally shot themselves this year photographing their families' Christmas cards where everyone is holding guns.

- Trump claims his gag order in his New York trial means he isn't legally allowed to reveal his tax returns this election either.

- The political group "Blacks 4 Trump" is reportedly offering $150 on *Craigslist* for any Blacks who will show up to Trump's arraignment and hold signs that say "Trump is being treated worse than a slave."

- A local conservative says that every time a character on a TV show or movie he's watching with his kids is gay, "I'm forced to play them an hour of straight porn to undo all the gay grooming."

- Don Jr., Ivanka, Eric, and Barron are all reportedly upset with their dad for saying multiple times that immigrants are "poisoning the blood of America" because their moms are immigrants.

- Nikki Haley says she believes she can convince the racist conservative voters who call her "Nimarata Randhawa" every chance they get to vote for her instead of Trump.

- Eric Trump just asked his father, "Daddy, am I a nepo baby? Did I earn my job at the Trump Organization on my own?"

- "Republicans are the party of Lincoln!" just yelled a man holding a confederate flag and wearing a shirt that says "The South will rise again."

- To celebrate Christmas and unify the country, Joe Biden has offered to pardon Trump for one of his 91 criminal charges.

- A new viral *TikTok* trend is called "Deprogramming 2024," and involves kids going on their conservative parents' social media accounts and unfollowing all the political content that keeps them debilitatingly enraged, conspiratorial, and racist.

- The "Melania Trump" who celebrated at the Mar-a-Lago Christmas party with Trump had no accent.

- Trump is reportedly threatening to sue Supreme Court justices Brett Kavanaugh, Neil Gorsuch, and Amy Coney Barrett if they don't vote to give him presidential immunity after he appointed them to the Supreme Court.

- A new survey of Gen Z girls shows their biggest fear in life is getting pregnant in a red state.

- A hospital in the "most MAGA town in America" just bought 20 iron lungs because of an outbreak of polio after the mayor declared vaccines were a "socialist plot to inject people with Satan's mRNA semen."

- A new report on *Fox News*'s sexual harassment lawsuits finds that over 1,071 women have become millionaires from successfully suing and settling with *Fox* producers, executives, and show hosts.

- A viral *TikTok* video uploaded by GOP Senator Ralph Masters's kids features them opening their Christmas presents and then screaming at him, "How many times do we have to tell you we don't want guns? We have enough guns! Stop getting us guns for Christmas, you psycho! We all fucking hate guns!"

- A lottery event held at Mar-a-Lago that raised $25 million this weekend just announced its winner: Donald Trump.

- A Montana televangelist claimed, "Jesus is rolling in His Heavenly grave that Democratic prosecutors won't let Trump be a billionaire while president!"

- A Florida judge just ruled that Trump's excessive makeup use qualifies him as a drag queen according to the rigid text of the state's strict anti-drag law, and from now on official pictures of Trump are to be banned from all school social studies textbooks.

- Donald Trump is reportedly depressed because his New Year's Eve party opened his eyes to the reality that he has no deep personal connections with any of his friends or family, and they all only want the political influence that proximity to him brings.

- At the NYE party at Mar-a-Lago, several Gen Z kids who aren't MAGA fans like their parents took a ketchup bottle and smeared the phrases "TRUMP & EPSTEIN BFFS 4EVR," "TRUMP LOST," and "DARK BRANDON WUZ HERE" on the wall of the pool shed.

- A televangelist from Georgia who was recently caught in a police sting soliciting truckers for sex outside a rural gas station has blamed Taylor Swift for feminizing America and turning straight Christian men like himself homosexual.

- At his Mar-a-Lago NYE party, Trump brought a confused boy who was not Barron up on stage with him before leading the crowd in a toast to Barron's health.

- Trump reportedly just asked his lawyers, "How come all our legal defense arguments focus on presidential immunity, and we never try to argue that I'm innocent?" which was followed by a long, silent pause where his lawyers just stared at him.

- Trump reportedly just asked his lawyers whether, hypothetically speaking, presidential immunity would protect someone for selling nuclear secrets to Saudi Arabia in exchange for, again purely hypothetically, hosting annual LIV golf championships at his resorts.

- Arkansas Republicans say that since children can now be employed throughout the state, they ought to be allowed to buy AR-15s and enjoy the freedom granted by the Second Amendment before they die or are maimed for life in workplace accidents.

- A group of diabetic MAGA fans in Louisiana are demanding their pharmacists charge them more than $35 for their insulin so they don't have to acknowledge Joe Biden did something good for them with his executive order ending insulin price gouging.

- A guy in Florida who got "TRUMP" tattooed on his face says he can't help but notice that no Democrats ever got a Biden face tattoo.

- BREAKING NEWS: Henry Kissinger, who died several days ago, was just reanimated by scientists and is alive again.

- The conservative Freedom Network's upcoming show "Christian Housewives" has paused production because two of its main stars have begun a lesbian romance.

- After hearing Nikki Haley refuse to condemn slavery, an impressed Stephen Miller says he won't kick her out of America in Trump's next term until at least the third round of deportations.

- Trump told everyone at Mar-a-Lago last night that Biden's stock market records are fake news, that Kim Jong Un called earlier and says hi to everyone, and that if anyone sees Rudy Giuliani sneaking in they should call security because Rudy can't pay his membership dues anymore.

- Trump has reportedly been wearing so much cologne the last couple days following "#TrumpSmellsLikeShit" trending on *Twitter* that Mar-a-Lago members' eyes water when he walks by.

- A New Hampshire primary voter asked Nikki Haley in her town hall if she'd still pardon Trump if, hypothetically, it turned out he sold nuclear secrets to Saudi Arabia in exchange for hosting a LIV golf championship at one of his golf courses, and she replied that she would not be answering any "gotcha questions from secret Democrats."

- The RNC is now mandating all GOP state party chairmen to begin paying 2% of their salaries into an insurance fund to help offset the cost of their inevitable sex scandals.

- A new poll finds that 97% of Democrats want Bill Clinton to go to prison if he had sex with underage girls, while only 27% of Republicans want Donald Trump to go to prison if he had sex with underage girls. However, of those Republicans, 100% want Bill Clinton in prison.

- Lauren Boebert just bragged that the new district in which she registered to run for reelection has a lower literacy rate than her previous district so she has a better chance of winning.

- *Disney* says it's dropping its feud with Ron DeSantis out of mercy after how low his presidential campaign has sunk, and will not release their animated film project about a sassy drag queen Florida governor named "Rhonda Santis."

- Trump claims his slavery deal with the South "would have been way better than Lincoln's deal, and cheaper."

Jesus Just Returned To Earth, And Demands To Know Who Decided All The "Christians" Didn't Have To Be Jewish

December 4, 2022
St. Louis, MO—

Jesus Christ miraculously returned today 2,000 years after His crucifixion, and, following a brief look around Earth, His first question stunned many of the Christian fans He had gathered around Him.

"Who the f*ck decided these so-called 'Christians' didn't have to be Jewish?" Jesus reportedly exclaimed. "When did I say you didn't have to be Jewish? Oh, that's right, I didn't! I'm a Jew! I ate boring kosher food, skipped out on shrimp and pork, and I took great care to never sit anywhere near where a menstruating woman might have sat, which the *Old Testament* specifically forbids many times! Seriously, who made up this absurd, ludicrous, preposterous rule that you don't have to be Jewish or do Jewish things? Was it Judas? I bet it was that asshole Judas!"

Several bystanders didn't know what to say, and one of them muttered, "Saint Paul did."

"Who the f*ck is Paul?" continued Jesus. "And what's a saint? I don't remember a Paul among My Disciples. There were only twelve! If he had been there, I think I'd remember him! And what's all this Catholic stuff? When did I do any of that bullsh*t? What the f*ck is a Pope, and who gives a sh*t about them living in Rome? Did I ever live in Rome? No! And why aren't any women involved? Trust Me, every crew needs a prostitute. And what's with all those gaudy hats and robes, and all the gold everywhere in the Vatican? If you're all allegedly trying to be like Me, why aren't you styling yourselves according to My homeless-chic fashion! These Catholic bishops and popes wear the gayest sh*t I've ever seen! And speaking of gays, when did I ever say to persecute them? Did I ever persecute anyone? The only people I said to persecute were money-changers and selfish, greedy assholes. And look who you all elected president! I was painfully clear that you couldn't be rich if you wanted to be My follower. So what the Hell is the Catholic Church doing with so much art and global treasures stockpiled in their giant, elaborate palaces and castles? And why are all the people in their paintings white, blonde, and blue eyed? Do I look white to you? I spent a lot of time wandering around in the f*cking desert! If these Catholics were actually anything like Me, they'd be selling all of their treasures to help the poor! Like I did! How many times do I have to tell you all to spend literally all your time and money helping out the poor? I said it a thousand times! All the stories you recite about Me are about Me being utterly selfless! And what are all those creepy rituals you Catholics do? I never said you were literally eating My flesh! It was a metaphor! You think I literally transform your dumb little crackers into My literal flesh? And that cheap wine and juice into My blood? I died and ended My materialist existence 2,000 years ago! I've been metaphysical for millennia! And what the f*ck is Latin? You think I was going around Judea talking in Latin to a bunch of uneducated, illiterate ancient Jews? If you 'Catholics' are going through all this trouble to pretend to preserve ancient traditions and rituals, why are you not even doing them in the Aramaic I spoke, or at least Hebrew? I am so insulted. I don't know who came up with all this dress-up pomp and pageantry, but it seems to Me to be getting in the way of sharing everything with the less fortunate, doesn't it? And why do devout Catholics dislike crossdressing trans people so much? Is there much of a difference between a random dude putting on a dress and the Pope? And why do priests apparently think I went around diddling kids? At no point in the Gospels is it ever written I fondled little boys! None of My miracles involved pedophilia, or life-long sexual repression! And this confession business has really gotten out of hand. What is that about? At no point did I ever say in the entire *New Testament* for everyone to have to tell dirty, old perverts every little sin they ever committed so priests can use people's greatest guilts and most repressed memories to create a psychotic power dynamic where they can get away with diddling kids for decades! I need a shower just thinking about it. Why do so many cults pretending to follow My path inevitably turn into sex cults?"

The Catholics in the audience shuffled their feet.

"And don't even get me started on Evangelicals. You Evangelicals are seriously Biblically illiterate. I don't remember saying that the kingdom of Heaven was only obtainable if you stopped using your brain, and went around claiming the *Bible* means whatever you want it to mean! And, for the record, Donald Trump was a test by Me for all of you Evangelicals, and you failed. You guys fell for the Antichrist, way to go. You know who didn't fall for Donald Trump's idiotic demagoguery? Black churches. All you white Evangelicals who are racist—and I know who every one of you is—can think about that while you burn in Hell. Just kidding! The idea that God just allows Satan to exist and torture people forever for finite sins makes literally no sense. But maybe We'll make it exist for all these racist white churches! You know what? From now on, the Kingdom of Heaven is Blacks only! Whites need not apply. Ha! You like that? Do you? F*cking racist gentiles! And can someone please explain to me what all this Christian rock music nonsense is about? You Christian rockers don't need Me to save your souls as much as you need Me to save your musical taste! Yuck! And what's with all the capitalistic Christmas conspicuous consumption? Remind me, did I ever suggest that economically secure families should spend hundreds of dollars on gifts every year for their douchey little kids? No! I said to give it all to the poor and homeless! And when it comes to diddling kids, you all are even worse than the Catholics! It's like every day I read an article about a youth pastor somewhere in the US getting arrested for touching or grooming kids. Seriously, the early Roman and then medieval power angling that kept women shut completely out of church leadership and positions of authority really made churches fill up with pervs! And you think things are bad now? Just imagine how f***ed up the church and its leaders were back when lay people were way less educated, more superstitious, and church leaders had virtually unimpeachable power in their communities. Honestly, I've been telling God for practically forever that Earth is long overdue for a new flood."

The Evangelicals in the audience started to tear up.

"I swear to Me," Jesus said. "Oh, and by the way, evolution is real, so quit it with creationism. It's like you idiots don't believe Me and God are capable of coming up with natural selection. You think We're too dumb to design a self-sustaining system of biology? Is that it? Some reverent children you are. And let's get one thing straight... I never rode a dinosaur. If Romans were going around riding dinosaurs, don't you think they'd be drawn on temples, vases, and mosaics instead of just a bunch of boners, sex positions, and references to the gods' drunken orgies? Christians just don't use their brains critically anymore. And for real, start doing a bunch more Jewish stuff or Me and God will send down more pestilence. Think We won't? Try Us! So no more shaking hands with women who are on the rag! They need to be untouchable and shunned by society for a week like the *Bible* says, and stay inside their homes in impure exile reflecting on their filth until the full seven days are up, and then only come out once they've burned a couple turtle doves in offering to Me and God. One as a sin-offering acknowledging their terrestrial putrefaction, and the second as a burnt offering to honor Me and God's Heavenly magnificence. The two turtle dove offerings are both individually very, very important to Me and especially God. There's literally nothing He cares more about than having millions of turtle doves sacrificed to Him every year. That's why He f*cking included it in the *Old Testament*, and Jews did it for millennia! Though We can't help but notice that the turtle dove sacrificing practice has severely waned. Seriously, if menstruating women don't wait the full seven days before going out in public, and they don't burn the two turtle doves, you're all going to really regret it. Trust Me on this one. Oh, and quit it with the polyester clothing, that wasn't a f*cking suggestion! And how in God's name does *Red Lobster* think it's okay to offer deals for unlimited shrimp? What the f*ck?! Does anyone read *Leviticus* beyond the one random bit about dudes railing other dudes? There's a lot more important stuff!"

Trump Says He Knows The Election Was Rigged Because His Campaign Cheated Way Too Much For Biden To Have Won Fairly

December 11, 2022
Palm Springs, FL—

Donald Trump is again alleging fraud in his election loss:

"I know for a fact the Democrats cheated, and it's because we Republicans snuck in a whole lot of fraudulent votes ourselves. But only to test the system and make sure it was fair! I had my team print thousands of extra votes in Georgia, Arizona, Wisconsin, and Pennsylvania, more than enough for me to win! There's just no way Georgia went blue, or Joe Biden got 81 million votes! We threw tens of thousands of the Blacks off the voter rolls, we passed unnecessarily difficult voter ID laws, we made sure the lines in Black communities were hours long, we outlawed giving food or water to voters in those long lines, and we even got Kanye West to run for president as a distraction for the Blacks. So either Democrats cheated, or Governor Kemp is being paid by Hillary Clinton and George Soros to betray the best president America has ever had: me! Even worse, all my lawyers' lawsuits got thrown out of court. I wasn't given a fair chance in court, and I think Hunter Biden slipped some crack into Rudy Giuliani's morning Scotch whiskey to get him sloppy before each court hearing because I don't know how else Rudy let himself become such a giant embarrassment to the legal community. He was once a respected mayor! The Democrats must have paid off the judges, even the ones I appointed who should have been loyal and taken my side instead of the evil Democrats. It should be illegal for judges to double-cross the president who gave them their jobs! The judges in Arizona were the worst. They totally refused to look into Mike Lindell's Chinese bamboo fiber claims. But I know for a fact there were bamboo fibers everywhere because I personally paid several guys to go get the bamboo from China, shred it up, and throw it all over the place in dozens of Arizona voting locations. And the judges refused to look at any of the thousands of affidavits we had, but those affidavits were totally real! I had Eric and Don Jr. write hundreds themselves! And don't even get me started on the media! There's no way America actually chose Biden after years of *Fox News* and all the other conservative media outlets ignoring every negative story about me, defending my every statement and action, and convincing their audience of all kinds of made up conspiracies like QAnon, hydroxychloroquine, ivermectin, Black Lives Matter demolishing every major city to rubble, and so many more! *Fox* even shared the Biden campaign's TV ads and debate strategies with my campaign. There's absolutely no way Democrats could have cheated more than me!"

Twenty-Five Donald Trump Jokes Written By A Precocious First-Grader

December 15, 2022
St. Louis, MO—

The Halfway Post's newest staff writer is a six-year-old named Claire who gets the tone and style *THP* is going for more than any adults:

1. Why did Trump wear a toupee? Because he was bald and orange!

2. Why did Donald Trump always have a scowl on his face? Because he was constipated from eating too many *Big Macs*!

3. Why does Donald Trump always deny being in love with Ivanka? Because incest is still illegal in most states.

4. What does Donald Trump use for birth control? His face.

5. Why was Donald Trump's inauguration the shortest in history? Because no one showed up.

6. Why was Donald Trump's face red? Because he was embarrassed to be seen with his own hair.

7. Why did Donald Trump get a DNA test? To see if he's a human or a pile of garbage.

8. Why does Donald Trump always wear a suit? So he can look like a professional con artist.

9. Why was Donald Trump banned from *Twitter*? Because his fake news smelled worse than his dirty diapers!

10. Why did Donald Trump's advisors give him a mirror? So he could at least try to see how stupid he looks.

11. How do you know if Donald Trump has been in your fridge? Because everything is gone, and there's a small piece of crap on the door handle.

12. Why does Donald Trump always wear a red tie? Because it hides the ketchup stains from his *Double Quarter Pounder*.

13. Did you hear about the new Trump fragrance? It's called *Eau de Covfefe*.

14. Why does Donald Trump always wear a tie? So he can have something to hang himself with when he finally goes bankrupt.

15. Why was Donald Trump's presidency like a roller coaster? Because it was full of ups and downs, twists and turns, and plenty of vomit.

16. Why was Donald Trump's presidency like a toilet? Because it was full of crap.

17. Why did Donald Trump always talk about Eric in a negative light? Because he was jealous of his son's full head of hair!

18. What's the difference between Donald Trump and a creepy old man? A creepy old man doesn't stare at his daughter like she's a piece of meat.

19. Why did Donald Trump's hair catch on fire? He was too busy staring at Ivanka to notice the iron.

20. Why did Donald Trump start a trade war with China? He was jealous of all the trademarks the Chinese were giving Ivanka.

21. Why did Donald Trump always roll his eyes whenever Eric spoke? Because he was annoyed by the sound of his own genes!

22. Why was the Trump family always a laughing stock? Because they were a bunch of buffoons who didn't know how to behave like normal human beings!

23. What's the new Trump hair salon? It's called *The Comb-Over*.

24. Why did Donald Trump get impeached? Because he was a bad orange!

25. What's the difference between Donald Trump and a raccoon? One's a trash-picking, disease-spreading nuisance, and the other is a raccoon.

Thanks, Claire!

Donald Trump's Call With The Saudis Begging Them To Buy His NFT Trading Cards Just Leaked

December 20, 2022
Palm Springs, FL—

A source at Mar-a-Lago just leaked a recording he or she secretly made of Donald Trump calling an unknown government official named Abdullah from Saudi Arabia the day before his NFT trading cards went on sale.

Trump made the phone call in the middle of the buffet restaurant at Mar-a-Lago between repeat trips to load up his plate with fried chicken, which made secretly recording the conversation very easy:

"Hi, Abdullah. Donald Trump here. Just calling to let you know the NFT deal we discussed is all ready to go, and we'll reveal all the NFTs tomorrow. I think you, and Muhammed bin Salman, and everyone else are all going to be very impressed by these NFTs. Everyone around the world is going to be talking about them. This is the deal of the century. You're not going to believe how great my NFTs are… No, the depictions of me as Jesus lying on big piles of cash and jewels were an earlier idea we had, but we went with the superhero aesthetic instead… Yeah, a lot of people don't know this, but apparently Jesus was like homeless or something, and he didn't like rich people… Yeah, the Christians take Jesus pretty seriously. I see you Muslims don't have too much of a problem with rich people—your royal family is loaded! But these superhero cards really good. They're the best presidential cards of all time. Even better than the cards Lincoln and Washington had. You're going to love them. … Oh, there are so many for you and Muhammed bin Salman to choose from. They basically represent me and all the amazing things I've done throughout my life. So there are cards of me being president, an astronaut, an ancient relics collector, an Air Force pilot, a sheriff, a boxer, and all that… No, I didn't really do all that stuff, but I could have. I would have been the best boxer or astronaut of all time. … So they go on sale tomorrow, and they're all $99 each. But be fast, because I'm sure they'll sell out real quick. Putin's gonna buy a whole bunch. … Even the evil Democrats will be wanting to buy them because they're such a fool-proof investment. I should have thought of NFTs a long time ago. … Trust me, everyone in America knows that when I license the Trump name to a third-party product or service, it's going to be extremely great quality and never go bankrupt! My brand is kind of a bankable commodity here in America because I never let business partners or investors down. … That's the thing, though, all those lawsuits are just me doing good business. It's way cheaper to not pay any contractors, fees, bills, or taxes, and just slow down the lawsuit deadlines in court for years to get everyone to finally just settle at a much lower price than the original price I signed my name to at the beginning. It's my greatest dealmaking talent. ... No, it's not immoral or unmanly, it's good business! I can't believe no one else has thought about just never paying any of their bills or taxes again. Am I the only genius in the world or something? ... Trust me, everyone here knows that the Trump name is the safest luxury brand in the entire world. ... Trump Steaks don't count because they didn't sell them right! I told them a million times Trump Steaks had to be pre-cooked well done and have ketchup freeze-dried on them to be a real Trump Steak. But what did they do? Sell them uncooked with no freeze-dried ketchup! We needed the ketchup to mask the fact they were extremely low-quality meat so we could save on costs. So that one wasn't my fault! ... Trump University doesn't count either! No one knew universities could be so complicated, and have so many regulations! ... Well, no one told me! ... It wasn't even fraud. That's fake news! I was very clear within the contract I had my lawyers write up that I'd only ever personally teach a course there if I felt they had enrolled enough hotties who liked to party—at least 9s out of 10. The whole idea was to have a girls-gone-wild annual spring break kind of vibe at Trump University, but apparently the dumb government says accredited universities can't do that because it's sexual harassment. But the administrators I hired turned out to be total morons who knew nothing about attracting a sexy student body. The only women they enrolled were well past middle-aged. They said old people were easier to trick into signing the predatory loans, but it was awful for my brand. I hid out in the bathrooms for an entire week and never saw one woman younger than 40. So walking around campus ended up being a big waste of my time. ... The casinos weren't my fault either! ... Stop listing all my companies that went bankrupt! ... It's an NFT, of course the value is going to go up. The value of crypto only goes up! ... I don't know what 'NFT' stands for, but, trust me, it's the deal of the century. ... Where is this coming from? A deal is a deal—remember all those nuclear secrets I gave you? And you have to buy all these NFTs tomorrow. ... And pay fast. These federal investigation are killing me, and none of my lawyers do anything until I pay a full year of their retention salary up front in cash. It's like they don't trust me to pay them! ... No, you have to buy at least 10,000 of these! You owe me for all the military support I gave you in Yemen, and helping with the palace coup that gave Mohammed control, and the Qatar blockade, and ignoring the murder of that journalist, and the secret stuff I let Jared do... Okay, fine, let Biden get another term, and bother you about your human rights violations. ... See? You need me, which means you need to pay me, and buy thousands of digital pictures of me looking like Superman with a big T on my chest. Trust me, you won't regret these cards. They'll be a big hit. And, you know, it's a pump and dump, so just—you know—don't wait too long to sell them. ... I know! My fans just never stop falling for all the crypto scams, it's crazy!"

Donald Trump Says Three Christmas Ghosts Visited Him Last Night, And He Now Understands The True Meaning Of Christmas.

December 25, 2022
Palm Springs, FL—

Former President Donald Trump called into *Fox News* today to share a wild story in which he claims he was visited by three Christmas ghosts last night:

Last night the strangest thing happened to me, and it totally changed how I want to spend the rest of my life! It started yesterday morning as I was busy doing my "Executive Hours" at Mar-a-Lago, and Eric was complaining how I was making him work on Christmas Eve, and how he was freezing because I wouldn't turn up the heat, and how he wasn't comfortable signing all the financial disclosures that the Trump Organization was submitting to the IRS solely by himself.

So I started yelling at him about how easy he has it in life, and how my dad was way tougher on me than I've ever been on Eric. He started tearing up a little so I told him I was docking his paycheck $100 for being a pussy.

Then my son-in-law Jared Kushner came into my office and invited me to a Hanukkah dinner. I have always worshipped my daughter Ivanka, and of course her body full of sexy, dominant Trump genetics, but Jared has been real stingy with the $2 billion he got from the Saudis that I deserve a cut of because he got the deal while working in my administration. It was only because of me letting him use government-owned airplanes that he got to go to Saudi Arabia so many times for free throughout my presidency. But he's hogging all the money, and it's not like I can sue him because then everyone would find out the details of the deals we made with Mohammed bin Salman that were maybe not as squeaky clean as we've claimed.

So I screamed at him to get out of my office, and never invite me to a "globalist" party ever again because it makes me look bad in front of my most committed supporters like Kanye West and Nick Fuentes. The 2024 election looks like it will be real close, so I can't afford to lose the Nazi vote by breaking bread with a bunch of Jews, even if one of them is my incredibly smoking hot daughter Ivanka! I need to keep my Nazi fans' enthusiasm high because I may just need them to try another coup if I lose to Biden again, or if a few trials don't go my way!

Finally I went home and got into bed, cracked open a *Diet Coke*, and fell asleep to the soft, relaxing sound of *Newsmax* hosts calling for all my political enemies to be tried for treason. But then I was suddenly awakened by the sound of chains dragging around on the floor, and discovered it was my father, Fred Trump, somehow back from the dead!

At first I assumed I was imagining him, perhaps because of some indigestion from eating too much fried chicken at lunch, or maybe the late-afternoon snack of two *Big Macs* and two *Filets-o-Fish* had upset my stomach. But he shook my bed, slapped my face, and called me a loser in the same way I had called Eric a loser earlier that day. He then told me the chains he was wearing were forged throughout his lifetime of sociopathic greed and selfishness, and he warned me the chains I was currently forging were much longer and heavier than his own. He warned me that I would be visited by three ghosts throughout the night, and that, if I didn't learn the lessons they'd offer, I was doomed to wander forever carrying chains in the afterlife like him. He then vanished, and I passed out onto my pillows from the fright!

The first Ghost to wake me was the Ghost of Christmas Past, and he took me to a Christmas morning many years ago. It was when Don Jr., Ivanka, and Eric were all little, and I was still married to Ivana. We were all playing games, and laughing with joy.

I sat there with Ivanka sitting on my lap, smiling the biggest smile as she told me she wanted to someday marry someone just like me, and Don Jr. was showing me the *D.A.R.E.* pledge he signed at school vowing he'd never do drugs, and Eric was sitting on the floor precociously playing with a science experiment kit involving thermometers and various elemental substances I had picked out for him because all the teachers at his school agreed he was the smartest student in all of his classes. It was the best Christmas of my life because it was before Ivanka started puberty and became interested in boys other than me, before Don Jr. stopped "giving the cold shoulder" to drugs, and before Eric put one of those thermometers in his mouth, accidentally broke it, and then swallowed all the mercury forever poisoning his brilliantly developing, gifted brain.

Then the Ghost of Christmas Past snapped his fingers, and took me to a different place, an apartment where I was having an affair behind Ivana's back. It was the first sexual liaison me and this woman had that didn't take place in the dark of night with the lights off, and she shrieked when she saw me naked in the light of day. She screamed, "Ew, get that mushroom thing away from me! Is that some kind of freaky STD? Aw, Jesus! Have you infected me with it?" Then the Ghost kept rewinding and replaying her screaming at me over and over, at least fifteen times, until I yelled out for him to take me back home! In a deep, haunted voice, the Ghost reminded me, from that night on, I never had sex again without having to pay for it in cash upfront to get the woman to sign a strict non-disclosure agreement.

After that, I was visited by the Ghost of Christmas Present, who took me to Jared and Ivanka's Hanukkah party to which I had been invited. They were with their friends, and everyone was having a great time eating and laughing, and they began playing a game of "Twenty Questions." I got really into it, and shouted out questions and guesses—though no one could hear me—until it slowly dawned on me that the answer to the round of the game was me! Once they figured out the subject was a politician, they started asking questions like "Is he racist and divisive," "Did he lose reelection?" and "Are his hands the size of a toddler's?"

They all laughed at me, even Ivanka, who raised her glass for a toast and announced they should drink in honor of her and Jared retiring from politics, and no longer having to make up excuses for my behavior—like my having dinners with Nazis, or my scamming my supporters with trading card NFTs, or my turning every happenstance into a culture war battle. It made me a little sad to see my beloved daughter didn't respect me, or think of me as the paragon of patriarchal authority anymore like she did when she was young.

Then the Ghost of Christmas Present took me to Eric's house, where his family was eating a meager meal because I dock his pay every time he acts like a loser, which is about every forty-five seconds. Eric was telling his kids one at a time how much he loved them all, and how he wanted to break his family's generational cycle of paternal abuse. Then his kids started asking lots of questions about why Grandpa was so mean to him all the time.

One asked, "What's an abortion, and why did Grandpa tell you you should have been one?"

Then another asked, "Why does Grandpa always put blue candy sugar in his nose and snort it? I've heard of a sweet tooth, but not a sweet nostril!"

Then one more said, "When Grandpa took me golfing, I saw him kick his golf ball into the pond when no one was looking, pull a new ball out of his pocket, and toss it much closer to the hole than where the first ball had landed!"

The first one asked, "Grandpa's hands sure are small for a grown man, aren't they?"

The second asked, "How come we never see Grandpa and Grandma Melania in the same room together?"

The third said, "Grandpa has had three wives, and I've heard him say bad things about all of them!"

And the first said, "I'm not going to fetch Grandpa any more *Diet Cokes* until he pays me. He says he'll give me a dollar for each can that I go get for him, but he never pays! He just says a check will come in the mail in two weeks. But a check never comes!"

Eric told his kids that Grandpa had been abused emotionally as a child by his dad, and that's why he can't help himself but be a mean jerk to everyone in the same way. "It's all he knows how to do, unfortunately," Eric said. He explained that it wasn't Grandpa's fault that he didn't get enough love as a child, but the lack of parental affection did leave him unable to empathize with others or feel love like a normal, emotionally stable, and psychologically healthy person. Then Eric opened up his arms to hug all his kids, and told them he'd always love them no matter what, and he'd never be mean to them like Grandpa is to him, no matter how much the mercury in his bloodstream fogs up his brain.

I was silent while watching, and sniffed a little, at which point the Ghost of Christmas Present asked me what was wrong. I told the Ghost it was nothing, but that maybe, possibly, I had been a little cruel to Eric earlier in the day. The Ghost began to laugh at me with a low rumbling chuckle, and I commanded him to stop, but he wouldn't for quite a while.

The Ghost then removed me from Eric's house, and I found myself in a cold, dark alley. In front of me in the shadows I heard some footsteps getting closer, and discovered two emaciated children creepily shuffling toward me. The Ghost told me their names were Treason and Insurrection, and I should beware them. The children were growling terrible, guttural sounds, and I tried to run away, but the alleyway led to a bricked dead-end. I turned around to see the children sprinting toward me like crazed zombies, and, right as the children nearly got to me, I blacked out and woke up back in my bed.

My nerves were still rattled, so I got up to grab my bedside can of *Diet Coke* to calm myself and wait for the third specter. I tried to turn on *Fox News* to cheer myself up, but the TV's power went out immediately! Finally the Ghost of Christmas Future arrived. His face was obscured in his great, big, black cloak, and he didn't say a word to me. I shouted out for him to show his face, but he just raised his gaunt skeleton hand and pointed at me. I demanded again he show himself, and asked if he was Stephen Miller playing one of his famous "I'm-a-serial-killer-and-I'm-gonna-murder-you" pranks on me, but he walked toward me with his bony fingers raised until he touched my forehead.

Suddenly I found myself at Mar-a-Lago, but the resort was abandoned, empty, and in an alarming state of disrepair with dust everywhere. I asked the Ghost to explain what happened to all of my belongings, but he just pointed again, this time down the main staircase to the lobby where I discovered Melania and all my kids talking together.

"It's too bad he never actually was a real billionaire, and all the ritz and golden gilding everywhere was cheap, gaudy, and fake," said Ivanka.

Then Don Jr. said, "After the estate pays off all his debts, sells off the money-losing properties, and makes all the back payments due from decades of tax fraud, we won't even inherit enough to buy a single dime bag of coke!"

Melania spoke next, and said, "You think you're disappointed, I spent two miserable decades married to that disgusting, orange slob waiting for him to die and leave me my share, but clearly that money never existed. I wasted my best years pretending it didn't fill me with revulsion and fury every time he tried to hold my hand in public."

"Oh, everyone could tell," said Tiffany.

Then Ted Cruz and Steve Bannon walked into the lobby, and Ted explained that I had made him do "some Sodom and Gomorrah stuff" in exchange for me endorsing him in his next election, and that he was hoping they all would honor his humiliations by giving him the family's endorsement. They refused.

Steve Bannon announced he had only come by to grab the signed-by-Hitler copy of *Mein Kampf* he had let Trump borrow. Bannon then warned them that he had used the toilet, but had managed to both miss a little and clog it.

Then the Ghost snapped his bony fingers again, and transported me to an unkempt gravesite. It was foggy, but, as I walked closer to inspect the gravestone, I was horrified to find my name etched into the stone. It said *"HERE LIES DONALD TRUMP, 1946–2027, WHO EVERYONE LAUGHED AT DURING HIS FUNERAL!"*

I let out a scream, and grabbed the Ghost's cloak. "Tell me it isn't true!" I demanded. "Ghost, tell me I'm not a joke! A loser! Tell me the elections were rigged, and I was cheated! And the low approval ratings were fake news! Tell me I'm a winner!"

The Ghost said nothing at first, but then began to laugh the most terrifying cackle I've ever heard, worse than all the other ghosts. He roared with a howl that shook my bones, and bellowed out in a cavernous voice the word "loser" over and over until I cupped my ears with my hands to stop hearing it. It wouldn't end, and I began to sob. I collapsed to the ground, and rolled around in the mud begging to go back home and have a chance to change things. I yelled out to the Ghost that I would change, and, in between sobs, I pledged to become a different man. If only I could be allowed to prevent the prophecies I had seen!

At last, I woke up in my Mar-a-Lago bed, and was relieved to discover it had all been a dream. My beloved Mar-a-Lago wasn't dusty and empty. But how vividly the dream remained in my mind! Then I remembered Christmas. I wasn't sure what day it was. Had I missed Christmas? I jumped out of bed, and ran downstairs to the breakfast buffet where I found an oddly youthful servant I hadn't remembered ever hiring.

I said, "Boy! You, boy there! What day is it? Tell me at once!"

The boy said, "Dad, it's Christmas morning," and I giggled like a child. So I hadn't missed Christmas!

"There's still time!" I shouted.

The boy said, "Dad, are you okay?" and I reprimanded the servant for calling me "Dad." I told him he was fired, and demanded to know who had hired such a young child for my house staff.

He yelled out, "Mom, I think Dad did too much *Adderall* this morning, or huffed too many *Sharpie* markers!"

But I was too filled with relief that I hadn't missed Christmas to further admonish this disobedient, suspiciously juvenile waiter. There was so much I had to do to make good on my promise to the Ghost of Christmas Future!

So I picked up my phone and made several calls to ensure the vision of the unkempt gravestone recording for all of history that I was a loser would never, ever come true. I called Don Jr. and told him I was suing him for $5 billion for damages to my brand tarnishing my name with his drug habits.

I called Ivanka and told her that because she was now over 40 and was Jewish, my new favorite daughter was Stephanie, or Bethany, or whatever her name is.

I called Eric and told him to stop being so soft and loving with his kids because he was going to turn them into even bigger failures in life than he was.

I called Melania and told her I was divorcing her because she was over 50, and that, while I had thought for a while the plastic surgery was making her hotter, I could now see she had done too many operations, and was getting a creepy alien look in her eyes that made me worry Alex Jones was right when he once whispered in my ear that she might be a reptilian shapeshifter.

I called Ted Cruz and told him that, even though he had done so many disgusting, violating, and criminal things for my endorsement, I was still never going to give it to him because his desperate attempts to curry favor with me were the most pathetic displays of self-emasculation I've ever seen, and made me respect him even less. Then I reminded him that his wife was ugly.

And, finally, I called Steve Bannon and told him that, as long as he promised to bathe at least once a week, I was ready to agree to his plan to publicly deputize all the Proud Boys, Oath Keepers, 3 Percenters, and QAnon conspiracists as "MAGA Knights" and "Trumpler Youth" to do another coup, fight against the US military, and make me Dictator of America at any pyrrhic cost, even if I have to go into exile and hide underground in a hole for years like Saddam Hussein.

So thanks to all the Christmas Ghosts last night for showing me the horrible future that could have awaited me in 2025 and beyond had I not changed my ways, and committed myself to making sure no one will laugh at my funeral for failing to overthrow America's democracy and make myself a dictator. They will one day fear my name after I achieve my vengeance upon everyone who ever laughed at me, or called me a small, little man, or shouted out loud when they got close to me that I smell like shit, or screamed when they saw me naked, or won a sexual assault lawsuit against me, or didn't vote to elect me in 2020, or give me the popular vote in 2016. All America will pay!

Because Donald J. Trump is a winner! The Christmas Ghosts showed me that throughout my life I've been far too soft, generous, humble, charitable, kind, and obedient to the law, and I very nearly was going to go to my grave letting such magnanimity ruin my legacy!

So I vow now to do whatever it takes to make myself Dictator of America, and etch "WINNER" myself on my future gravestone with a pressure washer using as much blood of this nation as it takes!

With the Ghosts of Christmas as my witnesses, I will destroy all my enemies!

God damn them, every one!

Things Donald Trump Doesn't Know, And At This Point Is Afraid To Ask

- How the nuclear triad works.
- Whether we fought the Nazis or the British in the Civil War.
- Why America ever gave women the right to vote.
- If New Mexico is an American state or a Mexican state.
- Why everyone throws a fit if you try to blackmail a foreign country by withholding military aid until the country's leader gives you manufactured dirt on your political opponent.
- Where in the Constitution it says the president doesn't have the power to use the military to arrest and imprison his political opponents.
- The difference between Catholics and Protestants.
- Why Christians like Jesus if he died. (He once told Mike Pence, "I like messiahs who DON'T get crucified").
- Why Christians think God is pro-life after God destroyed almost all of humanity with the Flood.
- Why Abraham Lincoln didn't take the South's slaves for himself, make himself dictator, and become the richest person in human history.
- Why George Washington would voluntarily give up power after only two terms, and not rip up the Constitution and make himself dictator.
- Why Harry Truman didn't take the opportunity in the 4-year window while only he wielded nuclear launch codes to threaten every country, nuke a couple capital cities to show he'll do it, and make himself dictator of the entire world.
- Who Bill is, the guy from Bill of Rights.
- How people in previous centuries ever thought any of the First Ladies and First Daughters prior to the 1950s were good looking, because they look plain at best and hideous at worst in those black and white photos with their big, cumbersome dresses not showing any skin at all.
- Why Stephen Miller has requested from him the privilege to do medical experiments on his brain after he dies.
- If anyone knows or has seen which of his phone numbers are in Jeffrey Epstein's black book so he knows which phones to smash, burn, and bury.
- How he ever let himself ruin his awesome, simple, relaxing life of winning his own golf tournaments, cheating on his wife with apathetic pornstars, casually shushing sexual assault victims with hundreds of thousands of dollars and non-disclosure agreements, and getting paid to pretend to be a real billionaire on TV by running for president in 2015.
- Which character from the *Old Testament* Moses is, which one Noah is, and which of the two got to bang Cleopatra.

How Donald Trump Spent Christmas Morning Yesterday

December 26, 2022
Palm Springs, FL—

6:03am—Woke up from raging symptoms of *Adderall* withdrawal muttering "How's my hair?" and reached for a mirror to see how many of his implants slipped out from his scalp while sleeping. He gathered them up on the bedside for his hairdresser to re-implant later.

6:04am—Rang the bell for Lindsey Graham to bring him his first daily can of *Diet Coke*.

6:05—Logged into *Twitter* from his David Dennison account to search "Donald Trump," and see what people had been saying about him all night. Started drinking *Diet Coke* while Lindsey crushed up an *Adderall* into lines.

6:06—Replied to tweets by the White House's *Twitter* account with "Remember the time Biden fell off his bike? Donald Trump never falls off his bike! Trump's the most fit president of all time, except maybe Lincoln, but he'd totally beat Lincoln if he biked against him!"

6:09—Got filled with rage everyone was still mocking his NFT trading cards. Snorted the *Adderall*. Told Lindsey to write him a post-it note about having another dinner with Nazis to get back at all the liberals who say his NFTs are a giant scam. Lindsey wrote it down, but hoped Trump would forget.

6:11—Started crafting a *Truth Social* post about the Constitution being the worst trade deal America ever signed, and how it should be torn up.

6:13 — Yelled at Lindsey for not turning on *Fox News* yet.

6:14—Calmed down a little after seeing *Fox & Friends* discuss how Trump was the greatest president for Christmas in US history.

6:21—Deleted *Truth* post draft about tearing up the Constitution, drafted a new post about how Joe Biden was making being Christian illegal again "like Obama all over again," and posted it. Watched more *Fox & Friends* praise. Softly masturbated under the sheets.

6:24—Got a text from Eric saying "Merry Christmas, Dad, I love you!" that totally killed the boner. Yelled at Lindsey that his *Diet Coke* was 2/3rds gone, but he didn't have another in his hand yet. Thought about texting Eric with an insult, but decided it would hurt him more to just leave him on "read."

6:25—Lindsey returned with a new *Diet Coke*. Chugged the rest of the first one, opened the second. Lindsey asked what he got his family for Christmas this year. Told Lindsey he gave Don Jr. and Eric promotions at the Trump Organization as Co-Chief Financial Officers so they can have the amazing privilege of signing all his tax documents from now on; he gave Barron and Tiffany each a signed portrait of himself; he gave Melania a gift card to a plastic surgeon; and he gave Ivanka a gift card for a boudoir vanity photoshoot.

6:26—Gave Lindsey his Christmas present of a homemade certificate that can be redeemed for Trump making Ted Cruz do any one thing—no matter how humiliating, disgusting, immoral, or illegal—Lindsey wants.

6:28—Called the designer for his NFTs, and left a long voicemail explaining his ideas for the next batch of trading cards, including a series of himself being depicted as various Biblical figures like Jesus, Noah, and Lot with two scantily clad Ivanka-looking daughters.

6:34—Called Melania, but she doesn't pick up. Asked Lindsey if he thought the facts that Melania hadn't been to Mar-a-Lago in two years and never responded to any of his texts or calls meant she left him.

6:35—Told Lindsey about the weird dream he had while sleeping about three ghosts visiting him, and taking him on a journey through various times in his life starting with his father calling him a "regrettable loser" at age 6; then to various moments in the 80s when he refused to pay his businesses' contractors, their companies went bankrupt, and their families had sad Christmases with few gifts for their children; then to several moments when he berated, slapped, and insulted Donald Jr. and Eric just like his dad did to him; then to his own future funeral in 2027 to which no one attended, not even Ivanka, and he screamed when he saw marked on his gravestone, "Here lies the worst President of all time, who was a convicted felon, had small baby hands, and everyone could tell all along his hair was fake."

6:38—Lindsey asked if he wanted to buy a big turkey. Told him, "That's a great idea, let's send Ron DeSantis a big one as a peace offering and apology for calling him 'Ron DeSanctimonious,' but fill the turkey with pudding!"

6:39—Called Stephen Miller and told him there's a job he can do, and explain the turkey idea. Stephen Miller asked if he could kill the turkey himself, but said he doesn't care how the turkey dies. Hung up after Stephen asked if he could call dibs on Ron's corpse.

6:41—Rang the *Diet Coke* bell again. Changed the channel to *Newsmax*.

7:01—Started putting on orange foundation makeup.

7:09—Used a whole can of hairspray to mold hair into place.

7:13—Snorted a second line of *Adderall*.

7:14—Changed into golfing clothes.

7:18—Hid nine golfballs in underwear for cheating and to make his package look less small and mushroom-like.

7:19—Rang the *Diet Coke* bell, and yelled to Lindsey that he'll take the next *Diet Coke* can "to go."

7:21—Walked through Mar-a-Lago. Passed by Barron, but mistook him for an employee and yelled, "Boy, what is this ketchup stain doing on the wall still? If it's still here when I get back from golfing, you're fired!"

7:45—Got to the golf course, said hello to Nick Fuentes, and asked him if he had ever seen a golf course more beautiful. Took first golf shot that went wide. Yelled out, "mulligan." Hit a new shot that wasn't much better, then got into golf cart to drive right up to the hole.

7:47—Took a ball out from his underwear and dropped it next to the hole. Hit it in, and told Fuentes he always finishes rounds of golf under par, and often even beats Tiger Woods.

7:56—On the third hole he sh*t his pants bending over to pick up his ball and had to go back inside and change.

8:14—Decided to stop exercising for the day, and just go to the Mar-a-Lago cafeteria and eat all the fried chicken.

8:58—Sh*t his pants again and had to go up and change.

9:09—Turned on *Fox News*, took off all his clothes, slipped into bed, and softly masturbated to an energetic, masculine-looking weekend news host who was passionately ranting about how the military needs to stop hiring women and stop following international laws on warfare and human rights.

9:13—Thought to himself, this guy should be my next Secretary of Defense if I get reelected.

The Halfway Post Nominates Dada Genius George Santos For Speaker Of The House

January 6th, 2023
Washington D.C.—

Serial liar and US Representative George Santos is somehow the most contemptible person in the House of Representatives, a legislative body that includes Kevin McCarthy.

So we here at *The Halfway Post* nominate him for Speaker of the House! Swing for the fences, George! We've taken the effort to write you a handful of inspirational slogans and persuasive arguments for you to use:

- "I heeded the call for public service after my mother's death on 9/11!"
- "Goldman Sachs has no record of me working for them so let me come clean: I was on the SEAL Team 6 that killed Osama bin Laden, and a mild-mannered career in banking was my cover story."
- "I've been evicted by two different landlords, so conservatives can rest assured I have the guts to let America default on the federal debt the next time we do a government shutdown!"
- "I'm not just Jew-ish, I'm also Speaker-ish!"
- "I've just heard great things about the coke orgies, and want in!"
- "I'll be as bipartisan as I am biracial like I've claimed! So, very little!"
- "Kevin McCarthy is too principled and high-minded to be Speaker!"
- "I lied about college degrees from universities I never went to so Republican voters can be confident I haven't been brainwashed by any of the liberal elite socialists in higher education!"
- "I've stolen funds intended for charitable causes, so I'm actually therefore the most Trumpy, MAGA candidate in the race for Speaker!"

Why not you, George? You could be the member of Congress we've been waiting for, the one who unites both parties and ushers in a new US Era of Good Feelings and Pax Americana!

Meanwhile, Kevin McCarthy has barricaded himself in the Speaker of the House's office, and has reportedly taken on a somewhat Gollum-esque appearance wearing only a loincloth and muttering, "My precious" to himself while cradling the Speaker's gavel in his hands and petting it profusely. According to eyewitnesses, McCarthy has torn out much of his hair, and hasn't bathed since the beginning of his string of Speaker vote failures. The #2 Republican in the House, Steve Scalise, says he recognizes the "unmistakable, putrid scent" emanating from McCarthy's office, and confirmed in a press conference it's three-day old urine.

Famous Presidential Quotes Throughout History... If It Was Donald Trump Who Said Them

A juxtaposition of former presidential quotes with Trump's sense of morality, written in Trump's sociopathic vernacular:

- "The only thing we have to fear is all the people we paid to sign non-disclosure agreements revealing our secrets at the same time because there's no way I have enough lawyers to sue them all for $5 billion at the same time." (Franklin Delano Roosevelt)

- "Associate yourself with men of good quality, if you esteem your own reputation; for 'tis better to be alone than in the company of the evil, demonic, enemy of the people Whigs." (George Washington)

- "Try to fail, but don't fail to try because, afterwards, you can always claim it was rigged against you anyway." (John Quincy Adams)

- "What counts in alleging voter fraud is not necessarily the size of the dog in the fight, it's the size of the fight in the dog." (Dwight D. Eisenhower)

- "Never waste a minute thinking about people you don't like, unless they're totally unfair and mean to you, in which case run for president to obtain power to destroy them and enact total vengeance" (Dwight D. Eisenhower)

- "It is amazing what you can convince people you've accomplished if you don't care at all how it gets done, but work obsessively to take all the credit afterwards." (Harry S. Truman)

- "A house divided against itself cannot stand, so lock up all my political opponents and be rough with any protesters!" (Abraham Lincoln)

- "Change will not come if we wait for some other person, or if we wait for some other time. We are the ones we've been waiting for. We are the change that we seek. So hang Mike Pence!" (Barack Obama)

- "We will not waver, we will not tire, we will not falter, and we will not fail… But tee-time is in an hour. (George W. Bush)

- "There is nothing more corrupting, nothing more destructive of the noblest and finest feelings of our nature, than the exercise of unlimited power… but still I alone can fix it!" (William Henry Harrison)

- "Any man worth his salt will stick up for what he believes right, but it takes a slightly better man to acknowledge instantly and without reservation that he is in error, so thankfully I know more about every subject than everyone and was right about everything!" (Andrew Jackson)

- "One of the tests of the civilization of people is the treatment of its criminals, so I'll pay for the legal fees of anyone who fights the people who protest me, and my election slogan for 2024 is to give the death penalty to all drug dealers!" (Rutherford B. Hayes)

- "You can fool all the people some of the time, but your closest fans you can fool all the time to buy your crypto meme coins, NFT trading cards, gaudy tennis shoes, and hats made in China." (Abraham Lincoln)

- "An honorable defeat is better than a dishonorable victory, which is a lesson my tough dad and my psycho lawyer Roy Cohn showed me is total BS because who cares about being honorable?" (Millard Fillmore)

- "No president who performs his duties faithfully and conscientiously can golf more than every other day." (James Polk)

- "Yes we can... in two weeks!" (Barack Obama)

- "I'll never tell a lie. I'll never make a misleading statement. I'll never betray the confidence that any of you had in me. And I'll never avoid a controversial issue... So trust me when I say COVID is going to disappear like magic, and you need to keep all your money in the stock market, and keep putting those UV wands up your butt, and chugging ivermectin smoothies!" (Jimmy Carter)

- "No man has a good enough memory to be a successful liar... so don't worry about being a successful one. Who had the biggest crowd sizes of all time? Me!" (Abraham Lincoln)

More Of Kevin McCarthy's Secret Deals To Win Votes For Becoming Speaker Of The House Were Just Revealed

January 7, 2023
Washington D.C.—

Before becoming Speaker of the House, Kevin McCarthy agreed to a secret three-page addendum to the official House rules in order to earn the votes of the House's most MAGA members in the House Freedom Caucus, including Lauren Boebert, Marjorie Taylor Greene, and Matt Gaetz.

Eyewitnesses claim several Freedom Caucus members forced McCarthy to eat the document to dispose of the evidence as soon as they agreed on its terms. Gaetz later bragged to reporters about the fact that he had jerked off onto the document several minutes before starting the crowd's chanting that coerced McCarthy into eating it.

However, one moderate Republican House member, who requested anonymity, leaked some of the rules he could remember from the list because the Freedom Caucus members' ongoing threat of a government shutdown has disgusted him over how much McCarthy has let the MAGA members of the caucus walk all over him:

- All Freedom Caucus members get to kick Kevin McCarthy in the testicles every first Tuesday of the month.
- The House will show off Hunter Biden's dick pics live on C-SPAN.
- The House will institute a new rule that all members have to say "merry Christmas," and, if they say "happy holidays," they will be fined $100.
- The House will start hosting monthly tours of the Capitol for Proud Boys and Oath Keepers.
- Every morning the House will formally apologize to billionaires and corporations for taxing them.
- The bathroom signs that say "Employees must wash their hands" will all be removed for being an "infringement on Constitutional rights."
- All paintings of Jesus in any House member's office must depict Jesus as caucasian.
- Matt Gaetz can hire interns and staffers who are seniors in high school.
- Democrats must take random drug tests to see if they have any adrenochrome in their system from ritualistically murdering kidnapped children in sacrifice to their pagan gods. Republicans are exempt from all drug tests because they're good Christians.
- QAnon will be invited to give a speech on the House floor and accuse all the agents in the FBI and CIA of being pedophiles.
- Immunity will be granted to House members in all future abortion laws.

- The second order of House business every day must be an out-loud reading of the Second Amendment, and the third order of House business must be an impeachment vote against Joe Biden.
- A "Special Committee Against Wokeism" will be formed consisting of Elon Musk, Kanye West, Alex Jones, Tucker Carlson, Aaron Rodgers, Donald Trump Jr., Andrew Tate, and Nick Fuentes.
- The House will issue a resolution reaffirming that the first rule of the GOP coke orgies is, "You do not talk about the GOP coke orgies."
- Lobbyist campaign donation checks can be passed out on the floor following votes again like the "good ol' days."
- The House will bring up a vote allowing international campaign donations in presidential elections, but only from the following nations: Russia, Israel, and Saudi Arabia.
- Vladimir Putin will be invited to address the House and insult NATO.
- The House Ethics Committee will be shut down because, as one member phrased it, "The Ethics Committee is made up of a bunch of RINO boy scouts who ask too many questions about why so many GOP super PAC donations are in Russian Rubles and Saudi Riyals."
- The House Committee on National Security will designate the IRS as a "State Sponsor of Terrorism" for terrifying billionaires, and put all IRS agents on the no-fly list so they can no longer fly to any corporations' headquarters and do any audits.
- C-SPAN cameras cannot zoom in on Lauren Boebert while she's sitting in the House gallery with dates in case she wants to get a little handsy.
- The House will formally apologize to Trump for his two impeachments.
- The House will recommend new ethics rules for Supreme Court justices that authorize the creation of a "Big Brother/Big Sister" program where each "Little" conservative justice is matched with a "Big" billionaire who buys them real estate and takes them on vacations via yachts or private planes.
- Jim Jordan's district will be redrawn to be even more absurdly gerrymandered than it already is.
- Congressional Republicans will get their own cafeteria Democrats can't use where the chefs ignore all the FDA's regulations on food sanitation, preparation, storage, and service to prove that cutting all health and safety regulations will make food taste better and be safer thanks to the free market.
- The next budget will include a loophole that makes all trips to Mar-a-Lago or other Trump properties for members of Congress tax-exempt.
- The government's Internet firewalls will start allowing gay pornography to be viewed on GOP Representatives' computers so they can do "surveillance" on the Gay Agenda.
- The Congressional investigation into Chuck Grassley's GOP coke orgies in his subterranean f*ck dungeon will be defunded.

- There will be an annual "Bring-Your-Mistress-To-Work Day" where C-SPAN will be turned off so that family values representatives can show off for their mistresses.
- Matt Gaetz gets to spit in Kevin McCarthy's food, coffee, or open mouth at any moment of his choosing.
- The House will try to force the US to default on its debts because, as Rep. Sally Moerthe explained, "Donald Trump never paid any of his debts, and his career turned out great for everyone!"
- The House will allow messaging votes on legalizing polygamy, legalizing child marriage, and banning women from being able to own property or take out bank loans without written permission from their husbands.
- Signs will be placed on all Congressional bathrooms that feature Senator Josh Hawley's frowning face on it with a caption that says "NO MASTURBATING ALLOWED INSIDE."
- The House will vote to defund all the Postal Service stamps featuring Harriet Tubman, Rosa Parks, Louis Armstrong, and Martin Luther King Jr. because "racism is over."
- The House will debate a national ban on the following *Disney* characters for allegedly grooming children to do drag or be gay: Ursula (drag), Mulan (drag), Lefou (gay), the 7 Dwarfs (gay), Tinkerbell (lesbian), and Lumiére is on probation because it's unclear whether he's gay or just European.
- The House will hold impeachment hearings on Barack Obama, even though he's not in office anymore, and Hillary Clinton, even though she was never president.
- The House will fund a $2.5 million grant to Steve Bannon for his "Doomsday Vault of Caucasian Semen."
- Rudy Giuliani will no longer be allowed to come into the House of Representatives during working hours, sit in a bathroom stall, and try to conduct lobbying deals by promising, "I know a guy who can make both of us a lot of money on this one." Also, the suspicious hole he drilled into the stall wall at about waist-level that he claims is "just for talking business" will be fixed at Rudy's expense.
- The day before Juneteenth will also be made into a federal holiday called "Thank You, White People, For Freeing The Slaves Day."
- A new ethics rule about sexually harassing female staffers will be relaxed from zero tolerance to a "5-strikes-and-you're-out" policy.
- The House will reimburse all expenditures for ammunition that House members use in their campaign videos where they shoot various objects that have the words "socialism," "communism," "science," "Nancy Pelosi," "Bidenomics," or "vaccines" written on them.
- The House will spend $1 billion on testicle tanning machines for the military due to the repeated recommendations of Tucker Carlson that they increase testosterone, masculinity, and alpha male energy.

Republican House Majority BINGO! 2023–2024

George Santos declares he was elected Speaker of the House	A televised House committee hearing shows off Hunter Biden's dick pics	Vaccinated House members accuse Dr. Fauci of killing people with the vaccines	Lauren Boebert brings a gun onto the House floor	The House raises taxes on poor people
Big intra-party fight over whether Russia is America's enemy or best friend against Wokeism	Matt Gaetz votes against a bill that combats human trafficking	The Freedom Caucus demands white people get a federal holiday the day before Juneteenth	First impeachment attempt of Joe Biden	QAnon is named as an "Honorary House Member"
An anti-gay representative is found on Grindr	Someone references the GOP coke orgies again	Kevin McCarthy is held hostage in the House basement **(FREE SPACE)**	A representative claims women's vaginas have teeth that can chew up sperm to prevent any unwanted pregnancies	A representative takes a family Christmas card photo with his infant children holding AR-15s
Second impeachment attempt of Joe Biden	Marjorie Taylor Greene demands Space Force funding to combat Jews' control of space	The RNC tweets support of Elon Musk a week before Musk praises Hitler	Representatives threaten to withhold funding for the military until it gets less woke, gay, female, and socialist	Vladimir Putin is invited to address the House
The House debates a bill mandating corporations tell Hindu, Muslim, and Jewish customers "Merry Christmas"	A House commission on voter fraud exclusively cites Rudy Giuliani and Mike Lindell	The House funds a "0 A.D. Project" that claims Jesus was white and a libertarian	Third impeachment attempt of Joe Biden	Donald Trump starts a new party after losing primaries to Ron DeSantis and poaches members, ending the GOP majority

Behind The Scenes, The Primary Battle Between Donald Trump And Ron DeSantis Is Getting Savage

March 7, 2023
Miami, FL—

With the primary season getting closer, the rivalry between Donald Trump and Ron DeSantis is heating up! Here are the latest details of their efforts to sabotage each other:

- Donald Trump says Ron DeSantis is paying Palm Beach state troopers to blare their cop car sirens next to Mar-a-Lago dozens of times a day.

- Trump just gave DeSantis a lifetime ban from Mar-a-Lago.

- Trump says he's going to reveal a "huge announcement" about DeSantis's birth certificate "in two weeks."

- Florida state troopers keep pulling over cars that Trump is riding in to check for unprescribed *Adderall*, and Trump believes DeSantis has directed them to do it.

- Trump told all his MAGA fans to boycott Florida elections so Democrats win majorities in the FL legislature and stop DeSantis from achieving any accomplishments as governor.

- Trump has directed Stephen Miller to live in the sewer outside the FL governor's mansion, and to go through DeSantis's trash every night to collect dirt on him.

- The Trump campaign is offering $1 million to anyone who can find one of DeSantis' old laptops.

- DeSantis is selling hats that say "Make Republicans Win Again."

- DeSantis just banned *The Art of the Deal* from all Florida schools and public buildings.

- Trump says he'll let people say "gay" all they want if they don't vote for DeSantis in the 2024 primary.

- Vladimir Putin just accidentally said on a hot mic during a Russian press conference that Trump is too stupid to collude intelligently,

- and Russia's social media trolling will now be for the promotion of DeSantis instead.

- Trump is threatening the RNC that if they allow DeSantis or Nikki Haley to win any primaries he'll start a new MAGA political party and "wreck the GOP worse than he wrecked the Trump Taj Mahal Casino."

- With top GOP donors and officials considering DeSantis for 2024, Trump just realized he has no real friends.

- DeSantis is encouraging the Florida legislature to act on the 14th Amendment by banning Trump from any future ballots due to his involvement in the January 6th insurrection attempt.

- Trump is reportedly paranoid that Ron DeSantis is paying the state's *McDonald's* employees to poison him.

- DeSantis has been delivering a bottle of Scotch whiskey to Rudy Giuliani every morning for months so that Rudy gets drunk every day and does a terrible job as Trump's lawyer.

- Trump is reportedly making all Mar-a-Lago guests sign a pledge saying they won't vote for DeSantis in the GOP primary when checking into their hotel rooms.

- The reason Trump is always complaining about low water pressure is because DeSantis has directed the Palm Beach municipal water utilities department to halve Mar-a-Lago's water pressure.

- Trump has asked all the Evangelical pastors to pay him back for giving them three Supreme Court justices by praying for a hurricane to hit Florida and make DeSantis look bad.

- DeSantis, in an apparent attack on Trump, says if he is elected president he'll arrest all users of unprescribed *Adderall*, and adopt Trump's idea of executing them.

- Trump says he's going to host a rally called "Stop The Primary Steal" outside Ron DeSantis's governor mansion in Tallahassee, FL, and says for everyone to come because, "It will be wild."

- Trump says it's suspicious that Ron DeSantis is so anti-gay "because a lot of anti-gay people turn out to be gay."

The 21 Worst Laws Red States Are Debating This Month

March 9, 2023
Washington D.C.—

- The Mississippi legislature is currently debating a bill that would fine Mississippians $75 "every time they think gay thoughts."

- Oklahoma Republicans are trying to ban science and anthropology teachers in public schools from ever saying "Homo erectus." Another proposed bill would legally change the scientific classification of "Homo erectus" to "Hetero Jesusus."

- The Texas legislature is debating a bill that would fund an after-school program to send children into coal mines and oil fields to help stockpile fuel in case the Texan energy grid collapses again. "I'm up for trying anything to help our energy crisis in Texas, except raising taxes on billionaires," said Governor Greg Abbott.

- Several Republicans in the Idaho state legislature are sponsoring a bill that would force all the state's school textbooks to say that female orgasms are a liberal hoax, and that the only "G-Spot" is in Heaven where God is.

- Ohio Republicans are debating a "hail mary" bill where high school kids who identify as gay or trans must sit in detention one hour a week to watch heterosexual pornography to try and turn them back cisgender and straight.

- The North Carolina legislature is debating a bill that would mandate every mall Santa carry an AR-15 in the event of a mass shooting at the mall. It would also give them legal immunity for any bystanders they accidentally shoot with a "Good Guy With A Gun" clause in their Santa contracts. *[This bill is currently facing intra-party challenges from Republicans who object to the original bill's mandate that all Santas must have a permit or proof of training as an infringement on the Second Amendment.]*

- Missouri Republicans are debating a bill that would mandate all female members of the state legislature report their menstrual cycles so male members "know when to take their amendment proposals or Congressional votes seriously."

- Montana Republicans have proposed a new law that would mandate women have to pay for concealed-carrying permits for their vaginas.

- Alabama Republicans are debating legislation that would require all parents to burn the books in their homes, and raise their kids illiterate to "own the libs" and "prevent Woke brainwashing."

- Arizona Republicans are calling for putting lead back in gasoline "to bring back our energy freedom."

- Wyoming Republicans are debating a bill that would ban "all forms of female cleavage" in public, including both breasts and camel toe, and fund a commission to study the effectiveness of Muslim nations' morality policing of women's fashion choices.

- Kentucky Republicans are debating a bill to take away women's right to drive alone without a male chaperone.

- Utah Republicans are debating the legalization of polygamy as a "laboratory of democracy" experiment with a tax-free-for-life incentive for women who birth at least 10 children "to defeat America's enemies whether Islam, Chinese, Woke, feminist, or Democratic." *[Much debate is ongoing over how to write this bill to ensure only white conservative women are getting through the process obstacles to obtain required "Mother Permits."]*

- West Virginia Republicans are debating a delicate bill that would legally make daughters' virginities the property of their fathers until age 18.

- Arkansas Republicans are proposing a "Groomer Tax" on *Froot Loops* and all *Cheerios* branded cereals for looking too much like little buttholes.

- North Dakota Republicans are debating a bill that would ban school cafeterias from serving sausages, bananas, corn dogs, or any other phallic-shaped foods for lunch.

- Iowa Republicans are proposing an "Anti-Spinster Law" that would force every woman to get married by 30 or the state will intervene and arrange a marriage for her with a self-identified incel.

- Kansas Republicans are debating a bill that would make it illegal for women to tell jokes about men's penis size *[Though there is considerable disagreement over whether the punishment should be a fine, two weeks in prison, and/or the loss of voting rights.]*

- South Dakota Republicans want to buy new textbooks for the state's public schools that claim slavery abolitionists were the "real racists."

Ivanka Trump: "Unemployed People Should Just Get Jobs In Their Dads' Companies Like I Did"

March 12, 2023
Palm Beach, FL—

Former presidential adviser Ivanka Trump today offered brief remarks to a reporter about the Biden Administration's record-breaking job growth and stock market numbers:

"These numbers are nothing compared to the number of jobs my father and I created while in the White House," Ms. Trump said. "But, to be honest, I don't understand why there is any unemployment in the first place. What are all these jobless people doing? It's not like there aren't jobs. Like, why don't they just go work at their dads' companies, or their dads' governmental administrations until they figure out other options? Working at your dad's company isn't such a bad thing. When I graduated from college I didn't know what kind of career I wanted to pursue, so I just got a temporary summer job as executive vice president of the Trump Organization. And you know what? It turned out to be a great fit. I found it very gratifying to get involved in the family business. We were doing all these amazing events with charities for kids' cancer benefits, and making big business deals with Russians, and I learned all these great accounting tricks from my dad, who is a total genius at taxes and marketing. He taught me the very valuable lesson that if you're having trouble getting a loan from a bank, or if your taxes on a certain project are higher than you want to pay, you can just make up numbers and report whatever financial disclosures you want. Your numbers don't even have to be consistent! That's just one of the many amazing lessons I learned from my dad. Like how you don't actually have to pay taxes. A lot of people don't realize this. I don't think I've ever paid taxes. I've always gotten paid either off the books, or with my dad writing off my salary as a business expense like I was a contractor or something instead of an employee. Our Trump brains are always coming up with awesome ideas to save a ton of money and get our operating costs very low like that. And learning from the greatest businessman ever was hardly the only benefit I had working in the family company. My dad gave me a credit card from the Trump Foundation to buy whatever I wanted on the side and treat myself if I was feeling down or depressed about anything. The account was always flush with cash because our Trump Foundation was always getting lots of donations from people for the kids' cancer charities. We made so much money off those kids. Children's cancer really gets people motivated to donate a lot of money to fundraisers. We make so much money off these kids that I hope they never cure children's cancer! But, anyway, I don't understand why so many young people complain about jobs and internships being difficult to find, or say that they're exploitative in nature. My first internship at the Trump Organization was very easy to find, and it was a breeze. And it paid amazingly well. There are tons of amazing opportunities like I had everywhere out there, I promise! Sometimes you just have to open your eyes, you know? And after my day-long internship, my dad signed me on for a long-term job. Take it from me, if you put in a little hard work and stick with it, great things are possible!"

The reporter stared with her mouth open, so Ivanka continued.

"And it's not like you have to commit for life, you know? After several years of working at the Trump Organization, I found myself getting bored and thinking about switching my career path. A lot of people don't have the courage, nerve, or willpower to make big changes in their lives like that, but determination has always been my best trait. I wanted to try out politics, but I was nervous about jumping into the deep end of a whole new industry. It can be very uncertain and risky to try to get hired at a new job when you don't have much experience, but I decided to go for it! So I applied for my dad's presidential administration, and got hired thirty seconds later. See? You'll find out that following your dreams is not as hard or scary as you might think. I got another great salary, I met tons of interesting people around the country and world, I got to travel, I made $640 million with my husband in personal business deals on the side, I registered a bunch of new personal trademarks in China, and I even eventually got a $2 billion kickback from the Saudi government for whatever my husband was doing on all his secret trips to the Middle East. All because I had the ambition to start a brand new career in government with just my brains, work ethic, and a verbal recommendation from my dad. So I'd love it if my story of struggles, achievements, and overcoming adversity inspired all the unemployed people out there. And to all the women out there, I want to tell them not to ever let sexual harassment in the work place ever bother them or get in their way. I sure didn't! I faced sexual harassment from the boss every day at both the Trump Organization and the Trump Administration, but I kept my head down, ignored it, and thrived in both workplaces! So take it from me, hard work always pays off. People down on their luck don't have to squander their time sitting at home feeling sorry for themselves and collecting unemployment, you know? More people should just stop being poor. It's so easy. There's no excuse not to pick yourself up by your bootstraps, and call your dad to get you a job in your grandpa's company, or ask him to let you work in his political administration. Trust me, if I could do it, anyone can!"

Ivanka then looked down at a notification she got on her phone.

"Oh, yay!" She exclaimed. "China just gave me another trademark on my latest product of '*Ivanka*' branded child coffins!"

Marjorie Taylor Greene's Online Dating Profile Was Found!

April 4, 2023
Washington D.C.—

Marge Green
—49 years old
—Washington D.C.

You may know me from helping incite an insurrection, but on here I'm only trying to incite an erection, if you catch my drift…

REQUIREMENTS

- **THE PERFECT LOVER FOR ME** is a mix between Vladimir Putin, Donald Trump, and Benito Mussolini, with a dash of Heinrich Himmler. MUST have strong authoritarian tendencies. I want a man who wants to be a dictator in the country AND in the bedroom, and nothing gets me hotter than a man willing to try a coup.

- **UNVACCINATED ONLY.** I won't date any sheep who don't do their own research, and just blindly trust medical professionals. I only get my medical advice from websites with the word "Freedom" in their URLs.

- **MUST BE ACCEPTING OF AN OPEN RELATIONSHIP.** I just got divorced, and I'm not ready to settle down anytime soon. Plus, I get invitations to the hottest coke orgies in the D.C. area, and they're a blast. However, if you want to join, you must have a strong stomach and not be too squeamish because Chuck Grassley eats more ass than the rest of Congress combined.

- **MUST KNOW WHAT "FJB" MEANS.** I don't know how, but that's what I involuntarily shout when we're knocking boots. You also must be cool with the fact that I have a LOT of Hunter Biden revenge porn on my phone that I need for my House floor speeches, and will NOT be deleting anytime soon.

- **FAITH!** I'm a good Christian girl who is pure for Jesus, so Christians only! But no Lutherans, Methodists, or Episcopalians because they're too liberal and Woke. I am looking for a fundamentalist Evangelical man, who will never apply critical context to the *Bible*, or even read too closely into the things Jesus actually said. A man who knows that

God never intended for Jesus's commands to love your neighbors, take in refugees, turn the other cheek, forgive your enemies, and focus all your attention on the needy and poor to be taken literally and adopted by the government. If I hear you repeating any of the Woke propaganda in Jesus's Sermon on the Mount, or the fake news Beatitudes, we're immediately breaking up!

- OBVIOUSLY NO LIBTARDS, or Jews, Muslims, Asians, Blacks, or Hispanics. The only people getting in me are the people the Founding Fathers intended to get in America: agrarian-minded Christian whites who didn't graduate high school, and are tolerant of the economic benefits of owning other people.

- DOESN'T READ BOOKS! No socialist college graduates, Stalinist masters degrees, or full on communist doctoral theses! Education is a Trojan horse for the liberals to sneak Critical Race Theory into your brain, so I prefer men who dropped out of high school and get by with the common sense of a farming hillbilly (previous bestiality experiences are a dealbreaker for me though).

- MUST LOVE GUNS. My house is filled with tons of them hidden everywhere in case Hillary Clinton or Nancy Pelosi ever try to sneak in at night to suck my blood! Full disclosure: during fights with my ex-husband I occasionally pulled out an AR-15 and aimed it at his head, but I'm currently in therapy addressing my anger issues.

- MUST LOVE BOYCOTTING THINGS. I'm currently boycotting over 200 companies and businesses that the liberals brainwashed to be Woke and socialist. This is an always-revolving list, so you must be an organized person capable of staying up to date on *Fox News* outrage segments and Donald Trump's social media posts to know who or what we're supposed to hate each day.

- LOVING CONSPIRACIES IS A BONUS. I not only have seen Bigfoot with my own two eyes, I made love to one in the woods in the late 90s. I like to role-play in the bedroom, and I have a full-size Sasquatch costume you should get comfortable with the idea of wearing.

- A GENETIC TEST IS MANDATORY. I want to make absolutely sure you're not Jewish. I am not interested at all in helping the Jews spread their globalism by raising Jew babies, and, if we break up, I don't want to be zapped by any Jewish space lasers. Upon completion of a DNA test, I'll share mine with you. (Just a heads up, I have about double the Neanderthal DNA as the average human.)

- **BONUS POINTS IF YOU'RE FROM RURAL GEORGIA, OR AT LEAST THE SOUTH.** My ex-husband has a Confederate Flag tattooed on his taint, and it really turned me on seeing it appear to wave back and forth when I'd peg him.

- **MUST BE REVOLUTION READY.** And be willing to abandon your life, move into the sewers, eat garbage, disguise your body scent with feces, and wage guerrilla warfare against the libs outside their urban, city strongholds for years when QAnon announces that The Storm has officially begun, and Joe Biden will tear off his face revealing he has really been Donald Trump in disguise all along.

- **MUST ALWAYS TAKE MY SIDE IN MY FEUD AGAINST LAUREN BOEBERT.** She's like my total opposite in every way: loud, uneducated, unprofessional, ignorant, and turning Congress into an impossibly dysfunctional workplace.

- **MY TURN-OFFS:** *Disney*, *Bud Light*, Hollywood, evolution, climate change, vaccines, the numbers 44 and 46, *Nike* shoes, Critical Race Theory, Mexican restaurants and food trucks, rap and hip-hop and jazz and R&B, the *NFL*, the *NBA*, fact-checking, grammar, spelling corrections, historical accuracy, contextual understanding of the *Bible*, most of biology and all of math, traveling outside of America, electric or hybrid vehicles, cities, immunologists, the media, reporters, "Gotcha Journalism," plant-based foods, Ukrainian democracy, American democracy, democracy, diversity, renewable energy resources, anthropological musings on Jesus's likely skin color, Never Trumpers, RINOs, rhinos that remind me of RINOs, anything German pre-1933 or post-1945, fair elections, 95% of the US government and particularly the FBI, and the majority of Americans who have voted for Democratic presidents in the national popular vote 7 times in the last 8 elections.

- **MAGA IS MANDATORY.** And I get a free hall pass if Donald Trump ever wants to grab me by the you-know-what.

If you meet these requirements, DM me with a "Let's Go Brandon!" and I'll hit you up the next time Chuck Grassley schedules a soirée in his subterranean f*ck dungeon! But if you talk about it in public like Madison Cawthorn, we are immediately over!

Mitch McConnell Reportedly Worships And Prays Multiple Times A Day To A Turtle God

April 13, 2023
Washington D.C.—

Senate Minority Leader Mitch McConnell is looking increasingly infirm, and is reportedly preparing himself for the afterlife he believes in by only eating lettuce now, a diet he says will prepare his mortal body for the "Great Pond," the metaphysical destination of our souls at the end of our lives and our materialist existences.

Afterwards, McConnell has faith in the "Great Shelling," a transcendental event in which all righteous human souls will be gifted their spiritual shells and flippers to swim through the gentle, serene Great Pond ripples at the edge of the Universal Garden where they'll float peacefully and eternally, basking in the warm, sunny goodness of the Ur-Turtle, Tort-Ler, the herpetological god and creator of the universe, whose ancient wisdom and omnipresence preserve justice and balance to all matter and existing beings.

McConnell claims he has seen unambiguous signs that the Great Shelling will take place any day now, and he has begun sneaking breaks during the Congressional workday to go outside and lie down on the lawn in front of the Capitol Building and take a sun shower to purify his soul's cold-blooded veins in prayer and meditation. He then confesses his sins to Tort-Ler, who absolves him, and blesses him despite his original sin of having a warm-blooded circulatory system that can thermoregulate itself.

While basking in the sun, McConnell reportedly recites softly to himself under his breath Tort-Ler's Prayer over and over until he reaches a zen-like state of meditation:

"Our Turtle Lord in the Great Heavenly Pond of the Beyond, hallowed be Your name. Your kingdom come, Your will be done, on Earth as it is in the soft ripples of Your aquatic salvation. Give us this day our daily lettuce, and forgive us our sins of warm blood, hair, and sweat glands, and lead us not into the mammalian temptations of uterine womb hedonism, but deliver us into reptilian oviparous piety."

McConnell has also reportedly begun digging several giant holes in the lawn around the Capitol Building into which he says he will soon lay hundreds of eggs.

Mike Pence's Presidential Campaign Has Gotten Off To An Odd Start

April 21, 2023
Indianapolis, IN—

Former Vice President Mike Pence is hitting the campaign trail early for the 2024 Republican presidential primary by attending as many GOP events as he can, and giving political speeches in several of the early voting states to measure support.

It remains to be seen if Pence has any appeal as a presidential contender after four years of quiet, mindless loyalty to Donald Trump's bombastically demagogic presidency, but he insists his character and faith will offer a sharp contrast with Trump's personality flaws for GOP voters.

However, Pence appears to be unsure of how he wants to present himself and differentiate his campaign from Trump's third presidential campaign. He has experimented in the following ways to brand himself:

- Pence floated several potential campaign slogans, including "Getting hard on socialism," "Penetrating the Left's radical agenda," and "Cocky For America."

- At a College Republicans event in South Carolina, Pence had the announcer introduce him as "Mikey." Also, a young campaign staffer tried to get the crowd of college students to chant "Hang WITH Mike Pence," but they stuck with chanting "Hang Mike Pence" anyway.

- To date, a fly has landed on Mike Pence's head at eleven separate events.

- Pence is giving out unusual freebie campaign merchandise at his events, including pocket books of *Leviticus* and "gay whistles" to carry on you and blow when you see a gay person to alert good Christians in the vicinity that a homosexual is nearby.

- Pence is selling odd merchandise as well, including coffee mugs, t-shirts and water bottles depicting Jesus on the cross with unnecessarily defined abs, pecs, and an adonis belt.

- During a speech in Iowa, Pence spent fifteen minutes ranting about how girls and women these days are flaunting their knees and ankles too much in public.

- At a GOP fundraiser in Los Angeles, Pence wore a 1950's-style sailor outfit for some reason.

- Pence treated one audience during an event in Wisconsin to an excerpt from a screenplay he was writing entitled, *A Streetcar Named Repentance*.

- After so many flies kept landing on his head with videos of it going viral, Pence now brings jars with dozens of flies in them to each event to let them fly all around him as it's the only way he gets any media attention for his campaign rallies.

- Pence vomited all over himself onstage in Iowa when someone told him that his favorite song to play as he takes the stage, "Y.M.C.A." by the Village People, is about gay men cruising for libertine hookups.

- Pence vowed that if he gets elected president, he'll start a new, updated version of Hollywood's old Hays Commission that will ban all female nudity in films, ensure the male superheroes in the Marvel movies no longer have bulges in their spandex, and mandate all movie theaters stop showing previews prior to films starting, and instead mandate fifteen minutes of silent prayer.

- Pence said he wants to sign a Congressional bill that renames California as "Sodom," and renames New York as "Gomorrah."

- Pence promised that prayer will finally start working once he's elected president, and claimed that the only reason prayer so far hasn't stopped children's cancer, mass shootings, abortion, terrorism, Democratic presidents from getting elected, poverty, world hunger, diseases, and violence is that no US president in history has ever prayed as much as he promises he will.

- Pence was asked what he'd be doing if he wasn't in politics, and he answered that he has always wanted to launch a *Bible* adoption agency where he'd take in abandoned and lost *Bibles*, and find them good homes with loving families to adopt them.

- During a roundtable discussion about how he might utilize the strength of the US military, Pence said that drone strikes and even nukes were still on the table to combat "Ru Paul's drag caliphate."

- Pence is allowing guns at his events, but he has banned glitter, not because of environmental concerns, but because glitter bombs are the gays' weapon of choice for terrorism.

BIG IF TRUE IV

- Marjorie Taylor Greene says she has been studying Hunter Biden's nude photos "for weeks" to discover new incriminating information about him no one else has noticed yet.

- Local QAnon followers say the conspiracies around the Jeffrey Epstein files just aren't as much fun since photos and videos of Donald Trump hanging out with him were publicly released.

- Trump, potentially in danger of having to sell Trump Tower to pay off his massive fines to New York, claimed, apparently preemptively, that he had no idea what all the Russians who lived there were doing.

- The ethics report on Matt Gaetz's sexual delinquency reportedly details that he snorted so much erectile dysfunction medicine at one 2017 party that his penis "turned inside out," and he had to go to the hospital to flip it back, but we won't know if it's real or not until the House releases the report.

- Mitch McConnell has reportedly been drinking formaldehyde smoothies every morning to keep his organs from rotting long enough to survive until the next election to see if he can be elected Senate Majority Leader one last time before he retires to volunteer at the turtle room in the Louisville Zoo.

- Ralph Hardlebee, GOP chairman on the House Committee of Health and Human Services, said, "Women who complain about the 'pink tax' on tampons should just stop using them if they hate paying for them because my butthole bleeds a lot more than once a month, and I get by just fine without any tampons at all!"

- Mitch McConnell reportedly died four months ago, but everyone in the Senate is pretending he's alive because they all know the GOP is too dysfunctional for Republicans to elect a replacement Majority Leader without an embarrassing weeks-long fight between MAGA radicals and normie conservatives.

- Texas power utility ERCOT says the state's grid is about to blackout, but they can't fix it because, three months ago, Republican state senators passed a bill forcing them to throw away every copy of the repair manuals after it was discovered one of the pictures depicting happy customers featured a gay couple.

- Lauren Boebert honored Martin Luther King Jr. Day by reminiscing on the first handjob she ever gave in 10th grade while listening to her teacher read aloud *Letter From Birmingham Jail*.

- Texas power utility ERCOT says the state's grid is about to blackout, but they can't fix it because, three months ago, Republican state senators passed a bill forcing them to throw away every copy of the repair manuals after it was discovered one of the pictures depicting happy customers featured a gay couple.

- Texas Governor Greg Abbott says his state's power grid issues are from "the gays plugging in too many strobe lights during their drag shows."

- Marjorie Taylor Greene and Mike Johnson argued with each other today over whether God wanted Johnson to be Speaker of the House, with Greene saying God told her it was time for him to resign from Congress, and Johnson saying God told him Greene was a "hussy."

- Vivek Ramaswamy said he couldn't believe how many GOP primary voters were opposed to him merely because of his name, ethnicity, skin color, and religion, "especially after Republicans treated Barack Obama with so much civility and respect."

- A televangelist in Tennessee claims Satan has possessed the Internet because all the advertisements he ever sees online when surfing the Web are for gay dating apps, dildos, and LGBTQ swinger cruises.

- Texas Governor Greg Abbott says the ERCOT power grid is in severe danger of collapsing, but he wants to assure all Texans that the state has "more than enough detained migrants to ensure no Texan on his watch will ever starve."

- Chuck Grassley, 91 years old, has opened up invites for his previously exclusive GOP coke orgies to everyone in Congress, and says he wants "to eat as much ass as the farming state senators used to eat in the 50s."

- At Trump's recent campaign rally in Iowa the temperature was so cold that eyewitnesses said they could see Trump's infamous stench steaming off his body, and not just smell it.

- Following Donald Trump's $83.3 million decision in the E. Jean Carroll defamation lawsuit, the bigger New York fine, and his ongoing legal fees for his other trials, Mar-a-Lago has reportedly switched to using single-ply toilet paper despite members paying thousands of dollars a month.

- Trump is reportedly beginning to think his strategy of picking lawyers based on physical attractiveness was a mistake.

- Mike Lindell says he won't reveal any of his evidence the election was rigged until *Fox News* starts running his *MyPillow* commercials on credit again.

- Mitch McConnell accused several MAGA Republicans in the House, including Marjorie Taylor Greene, of mailing boxes of dead turtles to his Senate office to threaten him not to let the bipartisan immigration and border deal pass in the Senate.

- Ron DeSantis says, now that his presidential campaign is over, he'll "no longer worry about hiding his reptilian shapeshifter form."

- Texas Governor Greg Abbott reportedly really wants to invite other states' national guard members to showboat at the border and score political points against President Biden, but he's afraid the extra people would cause a blackout in the state's teetering energy grid.

- Marjorie Taylor Greene and Lauren Boebert are reportedly feuding again, and will fight each other in the Capitol Building parking lot at 5pm today.

- The judge in Trump's New York trial says he'll be instituting a zero tolerance policy for smeared ketchup on the walls of his courtroom.

- Nazi groups across America say they're conflicted because they want to support Taylor Swift because she's a blonde, blue-eyed Aryan, but they don't approve of an unmarried woman being successful or liberal.

- Mitch McConnell is reportedly done trying to deal with MAGA Republicans in Congress, and is increasingly spending his work days lying on the floor of his office creating obstacle courses for his pet turtle Franklin, and timing how fast Franklin can finish them, and having lettuce parties with Franklin.

- Mike Johnson said today, unprompted, that Trump "definitely doesn't have a folder of blackmail on me," and that's "definitely not why I'm going to kill the bipartisan immigration reform and border deal."

- Eric Trump says he can no longer defend his father. "I'm my own man," he said, "and my dad has to pay a woman $83 million for defaming her over sexual assault. It's despicable and indefensible."

- Top national security officials in both the US and Israel are reportedly worried Trump will "fall in love" with Iranian dictator Ali Khamenei like he fell in love with Kim Jong Un if he's reelected and sees the violence Khamenei is directing against the Mahsa Amini protesters.

- Trump told *60 Minutes* that he got all his crimes out of the way in his first term, and won't do any more in a second term if he's reelected.

- Trump's lawyers are requesting his trials be postponed because he refuses to read any of the documents, evidence, or court filings.

- The House GOP is hosting a book burning tonight in front of Congress at 7:30pm with light refreshments available. Kids are invited, and Marjorie Taylor Greene requests everyone bring at least five liberal books each.

- A televangelist in South Carolina says he was wrong about the gays being the biggest threat to the institution of marriage because it's actually Taylor Swift."

- Trump says he needs presidential immunity, "just like Jesus got."

- GOP Representative James Comer says it's an "unfortunate coincidence no one could have foreseen" that, once again, another Biden impeachment investigation has turned out to be based on Russian disinformation, and he's going to try even harder than ever to make sure it doesn't happen again.

- A Secret Service agent testified today that Trump did try to choke him in the presidential limousine on January 6th, but Trump's fingers were so covered in fried chicken grease and ketchup that he wasn't able to get a good grip on his throat.

- Trump says his statement on Vladimir Putin's murder of his political rival Alexei Navalny is coming "in two weeks."

- Mitch McConnell has created in his office what he calls "Turtle City," an elaborate series of variously themed kiddie pools filled with water and decorations for his pet turtle Franklin to play in while he has long phone calls negotiating prices and delivery dates with exotic reptile salesmen.

- Florida Republicans passed a bill that would ban Americans from looking at nude paintings in European art museums when on vacation.

A Day In The Life Of Elon Musk After Buying Twitter For A Ludicrous $44 Billion

April 24, 2023
Austin, TX—

5:30am—Elon wakes up in a makeshift bed at the *Twitter* HQ in sheets he hasn't washed since taking over the company.

5:31am—Elon opens his *Twitter* app to see if @Catturd2 tweeted anything while he was asleep. Then he checks Stephen King's page. Then he searches "Elon Musk," and responds to random verified users with 6 followers for an hour. His most used emoji is the cry-laughing emoji. He posts his first of 13 pictures he'll post today of AI art of himself looking like Iron Man.

6:37am—Elon opens up his Reddit app to start perusing good memes he can steal without giving credit. After finding one, Elon posts it, and then switches through several burner *Twitter* accounts he maintains commenting iterations of "Elon Musk should do stand-up," "Elon Musk is the Dave Chapelle of tech bros," and "*Netflix* should give Elon Musk an hour-long comedy special."

6:56am—Elon switches to another burner account and tweets, "As a gay Black Democrat, I totally agree that the liberal Woke mind virus is ruining society." Then he switches to his real account, and retweets it with "True."

7:30am—Elon goes to the bathroom and monitors the near translucency of his pale skin while washing his hands. His barrel chest looks like it's still getting bigger. He contemplates various tattoos he could get that would totally own the libs. He writes down "My pronouns are Rich/Bitch" into his "Tattoo Ideas" note on his phone.

8:01am—Morning meeting with his "hardcore engineers" who depend on their jobs at *Twitter* for American visa status, and have no choice but to essentially be Elon Musk's 24-hour tech slaves if they want to stay in the US:

- Elon tells them he wants them to shadow-ban all tweets referencing his father's emerald mine, his weird jumping, his previous balding, his technically illegal immigration to the US, or his companies' dependence on federal subsidies.

- Elon asks if there's a way to retroactively change the results of his *Twitter* poll from a year ago that proved a majority of *Twitter* users want him to stop serving as the company's CEO. Elon asks if it would be believable if he tweeted out that the poll was rigged by employees bitter about him firing 80% of the company, and he actually won the poll significantly.

- Elon looks at the three funny meme ideas he forces every *Twitter* employee to find each night and print out as "evening homework" to bring in the next morning for Elon to consider tweeting out.

- Elon asks the *Twitter* head of PR if @Catturd2 tweeted anything while they were conducting the meeting.

9:04am — Elon tweets about how his blue checkmark system has made *Twitter* a level-playing field. Then he claims freedom of speech is terrifying Woke journalists at legacy institutions because X is the place for real, legitimate citizen news now. Then he retweets a "that's what she said" joke followed by a cartoon photo of himself as a Roman emperor.

9:06am — Elon gets a call from an Indian government official who wants a tweet critical of the Modi government taken down, so Elon takes it down.

9:10am — Elon retweets a tweet from @HistoryBuff1488 about how Democrats are deranged socialists.

9:12am — Elon calls his team of *Diablo 4* players and tells them to get him to #1 on the international leaderboard.

9:15am — Elon ignores a phone call from a *Tesla* board of directors member.

9:16am — Elon listens to a voicemail from that board member begging him to stop alienating and attacking liberals with *Twitter* toxicity, and stop doing childish and juvenile things like changing logos to the *Dogecoin* dog that makes his companies look unprofessional.

9:17am — Elon texts *Tesla*'s PR director to change the profile picture on *Tesla*'s *Twitter* account to the *Dogecoin* dog.

9:19am — Elon texts *Tesla*'s PR director to make the *Dogecoin* dog picture go live at 4:20 Pacific time.

9:21am — Elon texts *Tesla*'s PR director to announce that *Tesla* will be unveiling a special edition *Model Y* to be sold for $69,000 on June 9th.

9:22am—Elon goes to the bathroom, and spends 45 minutes sitting on the toilet looking for a meme to steal until his legs go numb. Searches "Musk emerald mine" and "Musk illegal immigrant" on X, and is furious to find the tweets have not been successfully shadow-banned yet.

10:07am—Elon decides *Twitter* is spending too much money on toilet paper while it's still losing millions of dollars every day, and he thinks up a new rule where every *Twitter* employee gets only three squares of toilet paper per day. Elon drafts a quick, company-wide memo detailing this new policy, and reminds every employee they all signed pledges to be "hardcore."

10:10am — Elon sends a second company-wide memo reminding all employees they also signed NDA's restricting their privilege to discuss internal company policies with the media.

10:16am—Elon wonders briefly if his abandonment-style parenting of his kids is continuing a toxic family cycle.

10:26am—Elon searches "Elon Musk" on *Twitter*, and responds to random verified users with 6 followers for an hour. He finds a few memes he can steal and post later. Forgets to un-like those tweets with memes so it's obvious after he posts them who he stole them from.

10:32am — Elon calls his *Diablo 4* players and says he wants to film himself beating a boss right now.

11:27am—After losing to the boss 16 times, Elon finally beats the boss.

11:31am—Elon uploads a video of the *Diablo 4* global scoreboard showing him at #1 because his desperation for adoration makes him want to make people think he's a super-genius video game player for some reason.

11:42am — He gets upset for a moment when he reads a tweet from a prominent fellow billionaire asking why the richest person in the world, who is CEO of 3 of the biggest companies in America wants to be on the leaderboard of a video game.

12:00pm—Elon starts a 2-hour video meeting with the Trump team where he's made painfully aware Trump is an ignoramus because he changes his mind constantly based on what the last thing someone said to him was.

1:27pm—Elon tries to delicately interrupt Trump, who had been ranting about using the Air Force to destroy wind turbines, and using the US Navy to kill all the sharks around America's beaches for the last fifteen minutes.

2:12pm — Elon wanders around his office building trying to find furniture pieces or appliances he could take a picture of himself holding to post with a pun.

2:19pm — Elon writes down in his "Ideas" note in his phone, "Picture of me holding a toaster with burned bread in it with the caption 'The liberal Woke Hive Mind is toast.'"

2:23pm — Elon retweets a tweet from @SiegHeilFan1933 claiming Elon Musk and Donald Trump are the biggest geniuses in world history.

2:28pm — Elon tweets several AI photos of himself as various superheroes.

2:24pm — Elon takes a phone call with a Chinese government official regarding which Chinese *Twitter* accounts he should censor in exchange for the right to someday build another *Tesla* manufacturing plant in China.

2:52pm — Elon calls a tech bro buddy, and asks if he has any ideas for another company he can buy his way into, fire the founders, get federal grants for funding, and then pretend he started the company and made it successful all with his visionary mind.

3:00pm — Elon conducts his afternoon meeting with his chief X engineers, in which they brainstorm a weekly list of X updates they can push out. Engineers cheer and yell out, "Genius!" when Elon suggests that at 4:20 every day the "like" heart button turns green when you push it instead of the usual red. Elon struggles to think of a way to incorporate a "69" themed joke for 43 minutes, but obsesses over it until one engineer eventually says they could make it so a little sound effect of a moan plays out loud when tweets' numbers of likes or retweets reach the number 69. Elon loves that, and then finally moves on to the next topic of whether every one of Elon's tweets on X should send a push notification to every X user's phone, and have it be that there's no way to turn off that notification permission.

3:43pm — Elon asks his coders to tell him truthfully what they think about the democratized blue checkmark policies. After a long silence, one coder asks to confirm if Elon truly wants an honest, constructive opinion, and any opinions expressed won't in any way affect the opinion expresser's job security. After Elon says yes, "of course," the coder suggests that *Twitter* should publicly admit the changes to the verification process, terms of agreement, and conduct rules did not work out as intended, and that, because famous and viral users understandably have no interest in paying the world's richest person to create most of the viral content for his increasingly toxic and militantly abrasive social media platform, *Twitter* will reverse the changes Elon made, and go back to the old policies that, while not perfect, did ensure *Twitter* was the world's premier source of legitimate breaking news and professional commentary with minimal but necessary censorship designed to prevent the platform from becoming a swamp of racist and sexist, trollish bullying at best and a cesspool of racist genocidal propaganda of totalitarian dictators oppressing their people and disrupting global stability at worst.

3:45pm—Elon fires that coder.

4:06pm—Elon returns to his nest of dirty sheets, and spends the rest of the night responding to verified users with 6 followers the cry-laughing emoji and quote retweeting various conspiracy theories with words like "concerning."

8:53pm—Elon texts Dave Chappelle, "What's up?"

9:07pm—Elon posts several more AI photos of himself as superheroes, and switches to his burner accounts to like them and comment that he is like Thomas Edison, Nikola *Tesla*, and Tony Stark combined.

10:15pm—Elon texts Dave, "Remember when I said I'M RICH BITCH onstage to all your fans? You should bring me onstage again sometime lol."

10:19pm—Elon notices his Dave texts are on "read."

11:13pm—Elon checks one last time to see what @Catturd2 has tweeted tonight, and sees that @Catturd2 is angry at him because he's paying the $8 but all the comments under his posts are for porn accounts. Elon sighs, and wonders if he needs to just step back and take himself out of the public spotlight for a while, put his head down and focus, and start letting his actions speak for themselves rather than talking too much about everything and subjecting everyone to his every thought injecting himself into every topic in the national discussion with a self-destructive impulsiveness reinforced by delusions of grandeur approaching dangerous levels of hubris alongside a big group of brown-nosing fake friend opportunists hoping to ride his coattails and profit from his proximity and connections.

11:16pm—Elon retweets a post that claims Nancy Pelosi's husband sucks dick for crack.

11:39pm—Elon checks the *Diablo 4* leaderboard, and is furious to find out he has dropped down in the rankings to #4. He calls and wakes up his players to get to work immediately or he'll send them back to India.

A list Of Things More Dangerous Than Drag Queens and Trans People

- Kyle Rittenhouse's mom driving him across state lines
- Donald Trump taking you furniture shopping
- A gun lover going anywhere near an elementary school
- A youth pastor hanging out with pre-teen girls
- Partying with Brett Kavanaugh in the 80s
- Hunting with Dick Cheney
- Matt Gaetz trying to *Venmo* you money for something
- A QAnon follower going to a pizza restaurant
- A MAGA fan being asked to put on a mask in a grocery store
- Going bowling with Lauren Boebert and her husband
- Jim Jordan coaching you on a wrestling team
- Being pregnant and giving birth in a red state
- Believing Trump when he says the election was rigged
- Going into a hotel room alone with Rudy Giuliani
- Being married to or interacting with a cop
- Being married to Herschel Walker
- Living in a rural area in a red state that turned down free federal Obamacare and Medicare money that would fund a hospital within 100 miles of where you live
- Being in the same room with Trump's infamous stench
- Serving as Trump's vice president and upholding the Constitution in a purely ceremonial role while counting electoral votes
- Riding in a *Tesla* and hoping it won't catch fire
- Watching *Fox News* for decades and living in constant fear of brown people and immigrants
- Living next door to Rand Paul
- Attending a GOP coke orgy
- Being Madison Cawthorn's cousin
- Depending on Joel Osteen or any other televangelist opening up their mega churches during a hurricane or other natural disaster
- Standing between Trump and a *Big Mac*
- Taking medical advice from *Fox News* hosts
- Living through the surge of a easily transmissible disease in Florida
- Waiting for guidance or assistance from Ted Cruz during a snowstorm in Texas
- Being an endangered animal when Donald Trump Jr. is around
- Being a child with cancer and hoping Eric Trump will raise enough money to cure it
- Living in a state prone to natural disasters and depending afterwards on Congressional Republicans voting for federal relief funds
- Stephen Miller walking behind you at night

The Governor Who Cried "Woke"

There once was a governor named Ron Desantis, who was bored as he sat in his governor's office eating pudding with his fingers. One day to amuse himself, after licking his chocolatey fingers clean, he took a big, deep breath and shouted out, "Woke! Woke! Woke is coming to groom the children and turn everyone gay!"

The town people of Tallahassee immediately came running up the Florida Capitol building steps to help the governor drive the Woke away. But when they arrived at the top of the stairs, they found no Woke anywhere, just the governor laughing at the sight of their alarmed faces.

"Don't cry 'Woke', Mr. Governor," scolded the town people of Tallahassee, "when there's no Woke!" Then the town people went grumbling back down the stairs.

Later that day, the governor shouted out again, "Woke! Woke! The Woke is coming to make white people feel bad about slavery and convince our women they should have bodily autonomy!" To his nasty delight, Ron watched the town people of Tallahassee run up the stairs again to help him drive the Woke away.

When the town people found, again, no Woke, they sternly told Ron, "Save your frightened cries for when there really is a Woke mob coming! Don't cry 'Woke' if there aren't any Woke around!"

But the governor just giggled and watched the town people walk grumbling down the stairs once more.

Later that afternoon, Ron saw a real Woke mob coming to groom the children. Some two dozen drag queens swinging used condoms, waving around school textbooks on Critical Race Theory, and swinging baskets full of birth control pills they were throwing out like confetti. Alarmed, Ron began shouting and screaming as loudly as he could, "Woke! Woke! Woke is here! Help!"

But the people of Tallahassee thought Ron was just trying to fool them again, so they didn't bother trying to help him.

At sunset, after he never came home, everyone wondered where the governor was so they walked up the Capitol stairs to find him, but he was gone. The only evidence of what happened was a trail of glitter that led north toward the liberal states.

"There must really have been some Woke that time!" said one villager.

"Looks like some drag queens snatched him," said another.

"Should we follow the glitter trail and try to get him back?" asked a third villager.

"No," said another. "A Woke mob can groom a grown man in under an hour, I've seen it before. The last time Ron called out was hours ago. I wouldn't be surprised if Ron was already dolled up and tucking his penis around his balls and taped to his taint dancing on a stripper pole in a San Francisco gay bar, and having a train run on him during his breaks in a bathroom's stall by coked-up, leather daddy bears."

"Let this be a lesson to all of us," said the last villager. "Nobody believes a liar, even when they're telling the truth. If governors like Ron keep calling everything Woke, it won't be long before everyone starts ignoring them completely."

Ron DeSantis's Weirdest Food And Eating Habits

1. He eats pudding cups with three fingers in lieu of a spoon.
2. He eats spaghetti with just ketchup for the sauce, and also uses no utensils for this meal. He just grabs handfuls of noodles, and smashes it into his mouth flinging ketchup all over his face and clothes.
3. He eats little cups of applesauce by taking off his shoes and socks, and then using three toes as a spoon that he then lifts toward his mouth with his two hands. He struggles mightily because he's not very flexible, and the exertions often make him fart at the same time.
4. He pours soups into one of his cute, white rain boots, and then holds it up to his mouth and sips at it.
5. For a guy who is really anti-gay, he suspiciously eats lots of raw hotdogs with no buns or condiments. He likes to pinch one end with his fingers and see if he can poke his uvula with the other end, and sometimes enjoys just swallowing the hotdogs whole.
6. He eats raw onions like apples.
7. His favorite snack is celery, and his staffers say he munches on it not unlike a rabbit.
8. On Fridays for lunch, he brings in sandwiches with just an inch-tall layer of mayonnaise in the middle.

Shady Gifts And Deals America's Supreme Court Justices Accidentally Forgot To Disclose On Their Government Forms

May 3, 2023
Washington D.C.—

Clarence Thomas was gifted by his billionaire best friend and benefactor Harlan Crow several authenticated hairs from Adolph Hitler's mustache, a signed copy of *Mein Kampf*, and a full SS uniform. Thomas had to confidentially ask Crow to stop gifting him Nazi-related gifts.

Amy Coney Barrett makes $5,000 a month licensing her name and image to a brand new, allegedly non-profit, Christian charity that spends its donations transporting typically elderly volunteers to gay bars around the nation to stand a legally-specified 25 feet away from the front doors on the public sidewalk to yell at all the people walking in and out, read out loud with bullhorns cherry-picked excerpts from *Leviticus*, and call the cops if they see anyone using poppers.

John Roberts owns a 33% stake in a Korean pop music record label that was recently accused in a class-action lawsuit of forcing its teenage stars into exploitative contracts and physically abusing them.

The owner of **Samuel Alito**'s favorite restaurant lets him eat free every day. It's an extremely upscale establishment called "The 1%." Alito promises his relationship with the owner in no way influences his opposition to federally raising the minimum wage of restaurant servers. The restaurant's most famous dish, keeping with its 1% theme, is a stew made up of A-List celebrities' nepo babies' placentas, and it costs $150,000 for a small bowl. This is the dish Alito orders on Mondays, when he says it has the most flavor because of extra placentas procured over the weekend. Alito regularly critiques how the soups smell "on the nose," and he lowers his nostrils to just above the rim of the bowl, takes a big whiff, and then tells his dining companions that his biggest life regret is he never got to taste his own placenta.

Brett Kavanaugh belongs to every conservative country club in Washington D.C., and pays no fees for any of the memberships. He regularly annoys the staffs of these clubs because he crashes their private events, helps himself to the catered buffets, and then gets drunk at the open bar and dances aggressively while yelling over the music to random guests, blowing heavy beer breath in their faces, about whether there are any cases they might want to "grease the wheels on" by paying off one or more of his credit card debts. He always requests the DJs play summer themed songs from the 1980s.

Ruth Bader Ginsburg was revealed posthumously to be the American cocaine cartel boss even the Sinaloa Cartel was afraid of known only by her street name, "La Justicia."

When **Anthony Kennedy** agreed to retire and let Donald Trump replace him, Trump promised he could come to Mar-a-Lago any time and stay in the penthouse, but Trump now says the promise never happened. Kennedy claims Trump also promised to donate $1 million to the Anthony Kennedy Foundation, but Trump keeps saying the check is coming "in two weeks."

Throughout his life, **Antonin Scalia** was a committed participant in Civil War reenactments. He only ever chose to be on the Confederate side because slavery was specifically protected in the original Constitution so he believed the Confederates were the righteous originalists and textualist moral victors of the Civil War. He only was paid for the reenactments under the table in cash so he skipped thee taxes on it, and he sometimes accepted antebellum belongings of slave-owning Confederate generals in lieu of cash, which he never disclosed. He also was credibly accused of skipping taxes on lucrative private performances at his alma mater, Harvard, with his barbershop quartet named "The Three-Fifthers."

William Howard Taft, the only former president to be a Supreme Court justice as well—and the court's chief justice—used to eat 40 hotdogs a day, and threatened to send the court's police officers to "shake down" any hotdog vendors that wouldn't give him one of their products when he'd walk by and shout out, "Weiner me!"

Elena Kagan gets free baby blood smoothies from her local Planned Parenthood in exchange for her votes protecting abortion rights.

Sonia Sotomayor gets free coffees made from beans roasted with baby blood at her local Planned Parenthood in exchange for her votes protecting abortion rights.

Ketanji Brown Jackson gets free baby blood Arnold Palmers blended at her local Planned Parenthood in exchange for her votes protecting abortion rights.

Oliver Wendell Holmes Jr. mysteriously got a 50%-off lifelong discount on women's lingerie from his local Woolworth's store.

Josh Hawley's New Book Talks A Lot About Masturbation

The following is a sneak peek preview excerpt from Senator Josh Hawley's forthcoming book, "Manhood: The Masculinity Men Must Erect," which critics say is a surprising, avant-garde tour de force that frames its narrative within an exhaustive exploration into how much gratuitous detail of sexual perversion an author can ask readers to endure, which several academics said was reminiscent of "Lolita," Nabokov's literary masterpiece:

I care so deeply about manhood, masculinity, and the struggles boys and men face in our decidedly anti-men era because I've struggled too. I know firsthand how easy it is for males in this society to succumb to the temptation to waste their lives watching pornography for hours every day, and commit the sin of masturbation over and over from morning to night.

I was once a serial masturbator myself. When I hit puberty, Satan tested my soul for over a decade by raising my libido beyond what seemed natural or even possible. No matter how much I prayed, no matter how much I begged God to purify my thoughts, and no matter how much I tried to focus 100% of my attention on the suffering of Jesus during his crucifixion, I could not stop myself from masturbating 5, 10, as much as 15 times a day.

Jerking off consumed my almost every waking second and thought, regardless if I was in school, at church, at the dinner table with my parents, or even in the graveyard at my grandparents' funerals. I planned and strategized every hour around sneaking away to a bathroom or my bedroom.

I did the deed constantly until my hands were so blistered and raw I needed to wear gardening gloves. I did it until my penis was calloused over completely, with my skin as hard as (no pun intended) oak tree bark. I did it until the only thing that could get me off was literally hard, scratchy tree bark, and I'd drill holes into trees in the woods in the park behind my childhood subdivision to hump. Or concrete bricks I'd stack up and make a little hole in between to go to town on for 45 minutes until I could finally coax an orgasm from my poor, mangled, almost sensation-less penis.

I literally could not help myself. So wholly was I trapped in the heartless, shackled prison of addiction that I could think of almost nothing else.

I'd sneak my hand into my pants during math class and fondle myself while imagining my 70-year-old teacher Ms. Kasselstein slowly taking off her thick lensed glasses, letting her hair down out of her tight, austere buns, and provocatively stripping off her winter cardigans.

During Sunday school I'd ignore the lessons, and flip to the Genesis pages about naked Eve, or Lot's daughters, and imagine them making craven love to me. I'd hide my erection under my *Bible*, and vigorously rub it up and down on myself. Unfortunately, I ruined dozens of *Bibles* when I'd stain them, and make the pages stick together. I hid from my parents just how many *Bibles* I defiled, and had to save up my allowance and lunch money to replace them so they wouldn't notice. It got expensive as I began having to buy a new *Bible* on a weekly basis, and it led to me getting my first job at 15 and a half.

That summer after 9th grade I got hired as a lifeguard, but I of course got fired on the first day. There I was, a serial masturbator, standing up on the side of a pool watching upperclassmen girls in bikinis frolic with each other and swim around right underneath me. I was at full-mast three minutes into the first shift, and lucky I could hide it behind my buoy tube! It's a miracle I wasn't put on the sex offender list!

Thankfully, I found a second job as a paperboy, which allowed me the freedom to take breaks whenever I wanted to ride my bike into the woods in the park to relieve myself like a savage, wild animal, or hide underneath the bushes in the yards of some of the houses to which I was delivering newspapers and fertilize their lawns, so to speak.

In my junior year of high school I made the JV baseball team, but I volunteered to play the position of right field to make sure the ball came to me as little as possible so the game wouldn't interfere with me flexing my penis muscles against my cup until I'd climax. I always wondered if I even needed to wear a cup after jizzing into each pair of my underpants so many times they were as hard as a rock.

I have little memory of seeing my parents between the ages of 12 and 17. I'd get off (no pun intended) the bus, and go right to my room to close and lock the door and start beating off—after first beating off on the bus underneath my backpack, of course. I was like an alcoholic blacking out years of my life in the sharp taloned clutches of the disease—the disease of masturbation.

And in my masturbatory deliriums, I would forsake God and Jesus, and commit some of the more depraved of the 7 deadly sins. I was slothful in that I didn't do my homework, or much of anything else while incessantly pleasuring myself. Wrath because I found myself getting more and more angry as my penile tolerance raised higher and my shaft's callouses were hardened, and orgasms became exceedingly grueling. I was flooded with rage at my acute sorrow and omnipresent guilt over my powerlessness to win just one battle against my addiction, or go a mere two hours between "sessions."

But the only object at which I could direct my overflowing fury was my penis, which I did with sadistic vigor.

Lust was an obvious sin I daily committed because of the pornography to which I was addicted, and a spectacular envy accompanied my lust as I watched all those men giving in and acting out their naturalistic sexual urges with big bosomed women, whereas I was just alone in my bedroom, a perverted, damned creature like Gollum, making a mockery of the righteous, Christian virtues my parents believed they had instilled in me. They remained utterly in the dark regarding my wretched existence in the shadows of their house as I slowly drenched practically everything they owned with my seed. When they were at work or doing errands there was no room I wouldn't desecrate with my disgusting acts. I'd probably be ashamed if I walked through their house today, all these years later, with a blacklight.

However, I, and everyone, can rest assured, despite the degenerate depth of my years-long, rock hard (no pun intended) bottom, that I was chaste and successful in preserving my virginity for my wife. I never pre-cheated on her with a real-life woman, though I own up fully to the fact that I was a thoroughly debauched, libertine hedonist with myself. I may have watched hundreds of thousands of naked, Woke, liberal women worshiping at Satan's vaginal alter, and I may have routinely imagined my savaged hands' leaking blister juice lubricant was the warm moistness of those godless, soul-sold jezebels, but I never, ever did the kind of sex that counts for God.

I couldn't begin to estimate the number and variety of inanimate objects I've violated, and the women I have perversely imagined making love to in my mind. I even took a few glances at some gay videos just to make sure I didn't have to add homosexuality to my long list of deplorable sex sins, and I can verify with certainty I am certifiably heterosexual. I did watch one gay video that made me realize my stereotype impression of gay men as sassy dandies might not adequately convey the full spectrum of variety in which gay men are merely trying to find their own little slices of happiness in individual and uniquely valid ways living lives almost wholly outside my knowledge of their existence anyway, but it doesn't change the fact the *Bible* says homosexuality is an abomination. Or the fact that I was a pure virgin for my wife, which I was, and I'm definitely going to get right into Heaven because of that.

So remember that I understand the struggles of being a young man in our society grappling with manhood. And what America needs is a revival of masculinity. And I will lead this crusade! So help me run for president in 2028. Get signed up now, and register to make recurring monthly campaign donations. America needs strong men again, and America needs a strong man. I am that strong man who conquered the trials and tribulations of masturbation, and will lead an emasculated, porn-addicted nation into the promised land of chastity and handjob independence.

So join me, and help me help you help me become president. In 2028. Not this year, Hell no—I'm not trying to get in the mud with Donald Trump. With my masturbatory past his sex-related nicknames would obliterate me in the primary. But by 2028 he'll definitely be disgraced and in jail or have a heart attack, and be out of my way. And for all his fans out there, I totally love him, and he was the best president in my lifetime. So only I can continue his MAGA mission. I raised my fist on January 6th, remember? But if the DOJ is reading this, that was only to remind all those rioters that one great trick for holding off the urge to masturbate is holding your hands in fists up above your head to keep them as far away from your penis as physically possible. It really works. It's what I had to do to not get fired at my third job back when I was desperate for money to buy all those *Bibles* I was desecrating.

The only job I could find after word got around my town that I was the kid fired for getting a four-plus hour boner at the summer pool and had to go to the hospital to get it flaccid again—and also the kid fired from his paper route for getting caught jerking off into the rolled up newspapers—was a gig as an elementary school bus driver a couple towns over. But talk about difficult. You definitely can't go to town on yourself when you're around a big group of children. Being a bus driver though makes reaching your hand into your pants so tempting because you have to keep your hands down near your crotch while handling the steering wheel. And sometimes your hand brushes your crotch when you're spinning the wheel all the way around, and it creases your pants in a way that puts just a little pressure on your member, and it wiggles a teeny-tiny bit, and then it grows just enough to press against the fabric of your pants, and then it gets tighter and you get harder, and now you can't think of anything else except jerking it, and you relapse back into the exhausting, sisyphean cycle of craven sexual appetite derailing your life until you briefly satiate it for a fleeting moment of respite from its eternal siren call of torment, and you pull over at a gas station, lock the kids in the bus so no one can abduct them, run into the gas station bathroom and lock the door, and then relieve yourself of the carnal urges with which your personal, penile, hell-spawned, teenaged libido tortures you. Then you have to arrive at the school late so all the children are tardy by thirty minutes, and you must invent increasingly elaborate lies for the superintendent about why your bus route is so consistently behind schedule.

So heed my call for action, America. We must save manhood. I've written this with graphic honesty to warn all the men out there who, like me, suffer from addictions to pornography and masturbation that they can still beat it (no pun intended) like I did, and become honorable men. Men's lives matter!

BIG IF TRUE V

- The political gambling app *Degenerate Politics* is offering a $1 million parlay bet if Lauren Boebert does the following during President Biden's State of the Union speech: vape, give someone a handjob, yell out "Let's go Brandon" at some point, and get escorted out by security.

- With Donald Trump as the GOP presidential nominee, he will soon begin getting presidential briefings again, and he is reportedly already offering a "Platinum+" membership level at Mar-a-Lago that advertises the return of the "Classified Docs Bathroom Club" for the 2024 fall season.

- Merrick Garland says he will direct the DOJ to begin investigating the Smirnov scandal implicating top House Republicans James Comer and Jim Jordan in collusion with Russian propagandists, and he will formally launch the investigation 16 months from now, followed by appointing a special counsel a year after that, and then subpoenaing several various witnesses and accomplices six months after that.

- A televangelist in Louisiana claims Taylor Swift is "brainwashing an army of women and girls into sleeper agent feminist freedom fighters to conquer the US and enslave all the men so they can peg them."

- MAGA fans are furious that Trump is reportedly considering naming Tim Scott as his 2024 vice president running mate, and would "turn the next MAGA administration Woke."

- Local MAGA fan Ralph Henderson is beginning to suspect that none of the hundreds of dollars he has donated to Trump's campaign has been spent on anything except legal fees, state-mandated fines, and non-disclosure agreements.

- A televangelist from Georgia is now commanding his congregation to pray in the direction of Mar-a-Lago five times a day.

- Trump claimed today, "Prosecutors have now taken more money from me than Rome ever took from Jesus. This is worse than crucifixion!"

- A televangelist from West Virginia claims Satan is engineering Taylor Swift's relationship with football star Travis Kelce so Swift can give birth to the antichrist and ignite the apocalyptic thousand-year war against Christ.

- Trump interrupted a wedding rehearsal dinner today at Mar-a-Lago to ask the wedding guests if they loved America enough to donate all their gifts and checks to his campaign instead of the bride and groom.

- Republican National Committee Co-Chair Lara Trump is following the Trump family playbook by demanding the RNC's IT department give her access to all the top Republican officials' email accounts to look for incriminating evidence with which to blackmail them.

- Trump reportedly locked six of his lawyers in a room at Mar-a-Lago today to keep them from quitting after finding out he has doesn't yet have the cash to pay his $464 million bond to the State of New York.

- Trump has reportedly told guests at Mar-a-Lago he will give Stephen Miller permission to do medical experiments on comedian Jimmy Kimmel in the first concentration camp they start if he's elected, and said, "He totally creeps me out, but he's the most loyal guy I've got, and I'm glad he's on my team cutting open bodies of my enemies instead of my body!"

- Eric Trump, speaking out about his family's massive fines for committing fraud in the state of New York, said, "It's so unlike my father to lie to clients, banks, and investors."

- Thanks to Trump's frequent outbursts where he throws burgers and smears ketchup on the wall, AI image-generators are now inadvertently depicting Trump with ketchup stains on his clothes in all its image generations.

- GOP Representative Cletus Howbert says Trump "arguably being a rapist all but officially adjudicated in a court of law" in the Carroll suit doesn't bother him because "there's plenty of rape in the *Bible*."

- Trump's private penthouse at Mar-a-Lago is right next to the "honeymoon suite," and wedding guests say Trump tries to talk to them through the walls if they're audibly having sex.

- Trump is reportedly teaming up with televangelist Tom Kohl to start a company called "Trump Indulgences" that promises God will forgive one of your sins for each $45 indulgence you buy.

- A new poll found that 59% of Americans support bringing back the ancient Greek democratic tradition of ostracism to banish Donald Trump from America.

- The Biden Administration just announced it will be awarding Trump the Presidential Medal of Freedom for his "spectacular and unheard of accomplishments in the sport of golf" after Trump named himself the 20th consecutive winner of his Bedminster course's annual tournament.

- Trump is currently displaying his new trophy from his latest golf course's tournament next to the "Highest IQ" trophy he gave himself at a mental games tournament he hosted at Mar-a-Lago last year.

- Trump says it's "none of anyone's business" what foreign governments he's talking to or discussing deals with in order to find funding to pay the $464 million bond he now owes New York

- Eric Trump has reportedly chained himself to Trump Tower, and appears to erroneously believe the State of New York will tear it down.

- Trump is attempting to delay his April 15th trial start date because it's Tax Day, April 15th, says, "No one takes taxes more seriously than me."

- NY Attorney General Letitia James says the state will be confiscating all of Trump's golfing trophies, and pawning them to pay his fines.

- Lara Trump says she has a "Trump brain" so she doesn't need to use spreadsheets for managing the RNC's funds.

- Alex Jones claims the Sandy Hook school shooting parents are demons because, ever since they sued him, it burns when he pees.

- Trump's lawyers are now reportedly putting sedatives in his *Diet Cokes* to prevent more outbursts in court.

- The judge in Trump's NY trial has denied Trump's motion to "let the record show a tracking log of the female jurors' menstrual cycles.

- 33% of the potential New York jurors interviewed for the Trump trial were found to have been personally defrauded by Trump or one of his various businesses at some point in their lives.

- Melania Trump told the judge in her husband's New York trial she doesn't mind at all if his trial makes him miss their anniversary, her birthday, or any holiday.

- Trump says the worst part about his trial is that he'll have to miss the father-son fishing trip he's been promising Eric for years.

- After Trump whined about how the judge wouldn't let him out of court to attend Barron's high school graduation ceremony, the judge said Trump could go if he could tell the courtroom when Barron's birthday was, and Trump leaned back in his chair, folded his arms across his chest, and frowned.

- One potential juror in the Trump trial was dismissed after she explained to the judge that she had hyperosmia, an unusually heightened sense of smell, and Trump's "expired roast beef stench" was wafting over from the defense table and giving her migraines which made it impossible for her to focus on the details of the trial.

- While Republicans blame the recent Baltimore bridge collapse on everything from the open border to DEI, Josh Hawley says he's worried masturbation is the true culprit.

- Trump kept falling asleep at court again today, and farted audibly several times while the judge was answering juror questions.

- Trump's New York judge says he can no longer wear makeup during the trial because several jurors have complained about it being too distracting to pay attention to the court proceedings.

- The porn-monitoring app that Speaker Mike Johnson uses with his son to alert each other when they look at pornography just overtook *Grindr* as the #1 gay hookup app, with several users comparing its functionality to "putting out a Bat-Signal" when they're horny.

- Trump's New York judge says if Trump keeps coming to the courthouse smelling so bad he's going to hold him in contempt of court.

- A televangelist from Utah claims if you play Taylor Swift's new album backwards it's full of subliminal messaging that "commands girls to steal Christian boys' virginities like Native American scalp collectors."

- Vladimir Putin reportedly had two Russian intelligence officers pushed out of windows in Moscow today because after years of espionage in the US and millions of dollars in bribes have only managed to recruit as double agents the two dumbest Republican members of Congress who aren't popular and ruin every strategy they get involved in.

- Trump claims his NY trial is forcing him to cancel a "big, beautiful charity event" he was going to host next month to donate a $1 billion for dozens of good causes near and dear to his heart.

How Republicans Imagine The Average Democrat Lives

June 12, 2023
Columbia, MO—

6:06am—Wake up to the sound of a screaming newborn baby, and say quick morning prayers to the three S's: Satan, Stalin, and Soros. Tap the snooze button several times because you were in the middle of sexy-dreaming about getting to second base with Chairman Mao.

6:41am—Finally get up. Put on a scary Halloween mask to terrify your blood donor baby, and gets its adrenaline level up. Then perform a post-birth abortion on that baby while listening to NPR's Morning News Edition. Remember you still want to check out Steve Inskeep's new book from your local public library.

6:53am—Begin draining the sweet, youthful, adrenochrome-filled blood into a hollowed out dildo. Using a quill and some of the baby's blood, write down a reminder on a post-it note to donate to NPR and get their free branded tote bag.

6:57am—Once drained, put the baby's corpse into a box addressed to Hillary Clinton's evil volcano lair if it's an odd-numbered day, or Nancy Pelosi's husband's secret San Francisco gay sex bathhouse if it's an even-numbered day.

6:58am—Put several Ruth Bader-Ginsburg themed stamps on the box, and, just for good measure, write "I LOVE CRITICAL RACE THEORY," followed by "DEFUND THA POLICE," "ANTIFA 4EVR," and "HUNTER BIDEN '28."

7:01am—Pour the dildo of baby blood into a blender, and add fresh, organic fruit from an Oregon farm worked exclusively by weed-smoking hippies who evaded the draft and made America lose the Vietnam War. Practice deep-throating and conquering your gag reflex with the dildo until the blender stops. Take off the top, and smell it. Sprinkle in a few shredded up *Bible* pages and rainbow marshmallows from a box of *Lucky Charms* cereal. Taste it, and decide it needs more gay. Pour in the rest of the rainbow marshmallows.

7:05am—Step outside to smoke a joint, and blow the smoke in the faces of all the children walking to school. Hand out vapes, weed edibles, temporary tattoos of devils, burned CDs of death metal music, Bernie Sanders "Feel the Bern" stickers, boxed sets of *RuPaul's Drag Race* DVDs, and porn magazines to the elementary schoolers, and tell them, "You just got groomed, come see me when you turn 18."

7:15am—Watch last night's Rachel Maddow show while burning a *Bible* like it's sage to repel God from every corner of the apartment.

7:39am—Go to *Democrats.com*, click the page for "Newborns," and do some shopping for tomorrow's baby blood donor.

8:00am—Conference call with Mark Zuckerberg and other Big Tech executives about which conservatives deserve censoring and shadow-banning today. Agree that *Google* should display several results pages of news articles about the time Ted Cruz liked a porn video on *Twitter* every time he *Googles* himself. Change Marjorie Taylor Greene's photo on *Wikipedia* to a picture of Sasquatch. Vote in several online polls for "Women of the Year" so that only trans women from now on win.

9:02—Check social media. Read a fact written in a tweet by Ben Shapiro, and briefly get feelings hurt. Cry for several minutes, and yell out, "Why don't facts ever care about my feelings?!"

9:14am—Decide to book a vacation for June. Look up prices at *Disney World*. Get in a couple more reps of deep-throating with the dildo.

9:19am—Buy a dozen children's books with gay and trans characters on Amazon to smuggle into Orlando elementary schools when on your *Disney World* trip.

9:22am—Pray toward Mecca, and verbally apologize for being white, and committing nonstop white privilege and colonialist crimes. Fist-jab the framed picture of Obama doing the "terrorist fist-jab." Say five "Death to America's," and make the sign of a pentagram over your heart.

9:30am—Read a couple chapters in your latest library history book on the Bolshevik Revolution to try and plan how a Bolshevik Revolution you might someday spark in America could have greater, faster success in forcing at gunpoint all Americans into collectivized farms and neighborhood steel factories.

10:17am—Meditate for a bit repeating hundreds of times your Nietzsche mantra, "God is dead. God remains dead. And we have killed Him."

10:41am—Say a brief prayer to Pontius Pilate, and thank him for crucifying Jesus.

10:45am—Make and eat a snack of avocado toast.

10:54am—Give yourself a quick COVID vaccine. Remember you forgot yesterday, so give yourself a second vaccine, just in case.

11:01am—Get dressed up in an elaborate drag outfit to go read to children in the local public library.

11:17am—Do dramatic drag makeup.

11:37am—Brush your teeth with a surplus FEMA-brand of toothpaste featuring a "deluxe amount of fluoride for liberal brainwashing." Put on two surgical masks over mouth and nose to drive alone in the car to the local public library, and give thumbs-down gestures to all the maskless drivers you pass.

12:00pm—Perform drag for a group of of kindergarteners. Teach them how to twerk on each other.

12:30pm—Teach a hands-on lesson for the children on how to sign up for a *Grindr* account, take a slutty profile photo, and write thirsty bios.

1:06pm—After every child has finished their *Grindr* profile, make all the white children in the audience apologize to the Black children for being irredeemable racists. Pass out hormone blockers. Assign each child an opposite-gender name, and remind them never to speak of any of this to their parents.

1:20pm—Say goodbye to the children, and gift them each a copy of Malcolm X's autobiography with a bookmark of the drag queen Divine.

1:39pm—Go shopping at *Target* to reward it for its corporate social consciousness, and buy a case of the LGBTQ *Bud Light* cans. Pour one into a spray bottle, and start spritzing anyone you pass wearing a cross necklace in the face.

2:02pm—Go to the *Nike* store, and check if they have any new Colin Kaepernick shoes available. After finding out they don't, decide to pretend to be an activist for a bit, lie down in front of the door, and yell at every shopper stepping over you, "You're the capitalistic problem, you corporatist shill!"

2:22pm—Check *Twitter*. Write a tweet to *NASCAR* saying you're their biggest fan, and would love to see more drivers of color, rainbow flags on the cars, and drag queens doing all the flag waving.

2:26pm—Write a tweet to *M&Ms* about how, even with the new makeover, the Green *M&M* is still too sexy and in danger of being masturbated to by Tucker Carlson. Suggest they start having the Green *M&M* wear a burqa, or at least a hijab for Muslim inclusion.

2:35pm—Drive to the post office. Mail this month's union dues to Hollywood, the Gay Agenda, Planned Parenthood, the Muslim Brotherhood, and the Communist Party of the USA. Also mail several dozen 2024 early-voting Biden mail-in ballots for Pennsylvania, Wisconsin, Michigan, Arizona, and Georgia.

3:00pm—Drive home to catch a Deep State conference call on Zoom for a preliminary meeting on how to rig the 2024 election against Trump. Remind everyone that this time Democrats should remember to proportionately vote against down-ballot Republicans, too, and not just Trump like they did in 2020.

4:00pm—Conference call on Zoom with Trump's doctors on how to rig his blood pressure and cholesterol against him. Also, brainstorm ideas for new vaccines to force conservatives to take.

5:00pm—Dye hair blue for the gender-bending party you're hosting tonight. Decide to try out telling everyone from now on that you identify as a non-binary demisexual because, even though lately you had been telling everyone you identified as a bisexual aromantic—and the month before that you had been telling everyone you identified as a pansexual cis—you'd like to get much more open with your wardrobe choices.

5:45pm—Stop by the hospital to pick up tomorrow's baby you ordered online from *Democrats.com*.

6:16pm—Dress the baby in drag, and do a "coming-out trans" party for it with your socialist friends. Thank Alexandria Ocasio-Cortez for stopping by. Remind her she promised to get matching Moloch tattoos with you.

6:40pm—Baptize the baby for Satan in a kiddie pool filled with goat blood.

6:53pm—Lead chants of "death to America" and "unelectably liberal!"

7:30pm—Dress up like a Proud Boy with a MAGA flag, and participate in an insurrection to blame it on Trump supporters and make them look bad.

10:21pm—Do nightly prayers to Karl Marx and Friedrich Engels, and fall asleep to the soft sound of gay porn stars moaning as they rail each other.

Trump's Next Batch Of Trading Card NFTs Go On Sale Tomorrow

June 29, 2023
Palm Beach, FL—

Donald Trump's latest money laundering scheme, or, rather, once-in-a-lifetime investment opportunity, of NFT trading cards made him so much money to pay off his obscene personal debts and lawyer fees, he's bringing them back for a second round!

This batch continues the first's comic book hero themes, but it adds his fellow Republican presidential primary opponents as his enemies in a manner criticized by many across the whole political spectrum as stupid, bigoted, and certainly juvenile.

The following are stock descriptions of some of the Trump NFTs about to be unveiled tomorrow:

- Nikki Haley wearing a sari and being strangled by a snake Trump is controlling with a flute
- Trump as a ghost that looks suspiciously Klan-esque scaring Tim Scott into a heart attack
- Trump choking Vivek Ramaswamy with a computer cord in the Metaverse
- Ramaswamy wearing a turban and being strangled by a snake Trump is controlling with a flute
- Trump riding in a hot air balloon made out of Chris Christie
- Trump cheering on a crowd hanging Mike Pence in front of Congress
- Trump shoving Election 2020's electoral votes down Pence's throat
- Trump strangling Pence
- Trump laughing with an arms-folded God and a head-shaking Jesus as Pence is denied entry into Heaven
- Trump pulling the lever of the heavenly trapdoor so Pence falls through the clouds down to Hell
- Trump laughing as Jesus lowers a guillotine blade decapitating Pence
- Trump taking Pence's daughters out furniture shopping
- Trump as a superhero flying into space, grabbing the moon, and smashing it down on Ron DeSantis
- Trump watching as a Mickey Mouse character sexually assaults DeSantis
- Trump popping in a Tic Tac in a bed with DeSantis's wife Casey while DeSantis is in the corner of the room handcuffed to a chair
- Trump making out with DeSantis's wife Casey on DeSantis's grave

- Trump at a courthouse adopting Ron's children
- Ron's wife Casey giving birth to a blonde baby girl named "Donaldina"
- Casey being buried at Trump's Bedminster golf course next to Ivana
- Trump finding the Fountain of Youth in a sh*thole country and transforming into a 35-year-old body with six-pack abs
- Trump being crucified on a cross with the caption, "They're coming for you, I'm just standing in their way"
- A newspaper headlined with "Trump Elected As America's Dictator With 98% Of The Vote!" and below that a headline saying "Obama's Kenyan Birth Certificate Finally Found—Trump Vindicated!"
- A scene from Trump's 100th birthday party in the Oval Office with his 5th wife sitting on his lap.
- Trump waking up in bed and ringing his butler bell for Lindsey Graham to come give him his first morning *Diet Coke*
- The White House turned into a 100-story Trump Tower D.C.
- Vladimir Putin giving Trump a "Best President In History" coffee mug
- Trump and Putin marrying each other's daughters, and blood-mixing their families into the strongest political alliance in world history
- Trump on a raft in a storm of flooding period blood from Liz Cheney
- Trump on a raft in a storm of flooding period blood from Nikki Haley
- Trump planting a US flag on Greenland with tanks and fighter jets behind him
- Trump speaking at the United Nations with the other members laughing with him and not at him
- Trump wearing tattered clothing and holding Kim Jong-un's daughter, Kim Ju Ae, in his arms with a nuclear blast in the background
- Trump fighting alien spaceships as a Space Force pilot
- Trump looking out over a 50-foot border wall with Mexico
- Trump judging women in bikinis at a Miss Trump beauty pageant co-judged with Matt Gaetz and Kanye West
- Trump's testicles slapping Barack Obama in the face as Trump dunks a basketball over Obama's head in a basketball match with the scoreboard showing Trump is winning by 90 points
- Trump hanging Jeffrey Epstein in his prison cell and giving a "shhh" gesture with his finger on his lip
- Joe Biden tearing off his face and revealing he was Donald Trump all along, just like QAnon said
- Trump on a bed with sheets colored like jungle trees while several prostitutes pee on each other, and a caption that says "Trump's Vietnam"
- Just a big text size caption that says "Trump DID NOT have untreated syphilis for most of the 1980s! That is FAKE NEWS and CLASSIFIED!"
- A nude image of Trump with hyperbolically drawn genitals

Crazy Letters THP Gets From America's Biggest MAGA Fan

A MAGA fan from Arkansas has been mailing *The Halfway Post* letters full of editorial demands. She claims she speaks with God, and that God demands *THP* immediately begin writing pro-Trump content. It's quite impressive that God shares the exact same beliefs as her, and according to her God demands *THP* retract several claims we've made in our satirical articles:

- "You must quit your Deep State propagandizing, and admit QAnon is right about everything. The government is filled with Deep State pedophiles, and they're plowing little kids in their D.C. offices, and they're drinking the kids' blood in adrenochrome cocktail happy hours where they celebrate communism by aborting a bunch of babies underneath giant portraits of Vladimir Lenin. They want to install Obama's two daughters as Byzantine co-dictators to rule America with iron fists and unquenchable thirst for the blood of white descendants of colonizers to fulfill their father's dream of putting all the Christians in gulags, and turning America into a Muslim caliphate where the meat sections in all our grocery stores will be forced to sell nothing but camel meat, or Biden will cut their heads off in the town square!"

- "Stop saying Donald Trump has 'dainty sausage fingers.' How can you disrespect the President of the United States? You know, the Nazis had a few good ideas, and one of them was that it was considered treasonous to insult the Führer. Presidents deserve respect, if not for the man then at least for the office. And Trump was the best president we've ever had. Way better than 'Let's Go Brandon,' who is so brain-dead and biologically expired his body must be soaked in ice baths every night starting at 4pm to stop it from decomposing, and to prevent his extremities from literally just falling off and chasing terrified little children because even Joe Biden's loose zombie appendages are attracted to the sweet, innocent nectar of little children's blood. Biden's eyes aren't even real. They dried out long before he was even the vice president. They're glass, and they roll around in their sockets when he moves his head. I have seven 'F*ck Joe Biden' flags around my house, and one that says 'HUCK KAMALA FARRIS!' Get it? Why do liberals say conservatives aren't funny? That's so clever!"

- "You are a disgusting deviant to imply Donald Trump is a rapey, pedophilic, fan of daughter love. HE'S ONLY PRETENDING TO BE ALL THOSE until the Storm arrives, when Trump will lead the military in arresting all the REAL pedophiles, incest freaks, and rapists! Trump likely hated hanging out with Jeffrey Epstein, and co-hosting parties with him, but he had to do it to spy and do reconnaissance to photograph all the predators' faces and record their names, and ultimately bring down the globalist cabal of baby-eaters all these decades later! And it'll happen in his second term, for real this time!"

- "Stop saying that during COVID President Trump endorsed pouring Drano into your butthole with a funnel until it comes out your mouth! Trump may have suggested injecting Lysol, taking Hydroxychloroquine, and sticking a UV light wand into your body somehow, but he NEVER said Drano, and NEVER specifically mentioned anything going into your anus! Dash MacIntyre, YOU ARE the enemy of the people!"

- "You must tell your readers to vote for Trump because God demands it! God is all-powerful, but He still respects American democracy and freewill, so you still have to vote, but just know that you're going straight to HELL unless you vote Trump. And if you vote for Ron DeSantis in the primary, you're a RINO, and you're going to Hell even faster than the libtards! So vote Trump, and trust in God's Grand Master Plan for America, which is unquestionable and immutable. Except for when God somehow wasn't paying attention, and forgot to stop Joe Biden from stealing the election. God might have been distracted by all the rampant, blasphemous hedonism from the gays, or a strobe light from a drag show blinded him for a moment. The gays just ruin everything, don't they? They even ruined my marriage. I knew it'd happen. As soon as the gays got the right to marry each other, my husband flashed a bunch of high school girls in a bowling alley, and I cheated on him with another married man who was in prison, and then my other boyfriend's wife spray-painted 'whore' all over my car. Called that one way ahead of time. The gays have irreparably wrecked the institution of marriage for all of us, and I'm just one victim of millions of the Gay Agenda."

- "Stop making jokes about Eric Trump running for president ahead of his siblings! Everyone knows there is a very specific order Jesus has mandated, and Eric is last. After Donald Trump, Donald Jr. gets the next turn. Then Ivanka, then Jared Kushner, then Tiffany, then Barron, and then finally Eric. Eric is a late bloomer, and his place in the order gives him the time he needs to blossom into a great Trump president. Hereditary monarchy is what America needs! After Eric, we'll start getting into the Trump grandkids—Ivanka's kids first because Trump liked her best. The libs mock him for being attracted to her, but they wouldn't understand because it's an alpha male thing. Having such superior genetics means it's natural for him to find his own offspring attractive. The ancient Egyptian pharaohs were considered gods on Earth while leading one of the most formidable empires in world history that lasted several millennia, and they did incest all the time!"

Mar-A-Lago Is Hosting A Music Festival "MAGAPALOOZA" In August

July 14, 2023
Palm Springs, FL—

Tickets to the biggest MAGA event of the year go on sale tomorrow:

FRIDAY

11pm: Private coke orgies INVITE ONLY
                    *Reminder: Madison Cawthorn is banned for life
10pm: DJ Jewish Space Laser
9pm: A big bonfire dance party for attendees to bring and burn books with gay characters, *Bud Light* cans, anything with a rainbow on it, COVID masks, vaccination records, *Nike* shoes, bags of *M&Ms*, school textbooks, solar-powered objects, Colin Kaepernick football jerseys, Ukrainian flags, and stashed top secret documents to be provided by Donald Trump
8pm: A debate on the topic, "Did Hitler have some GOOD ideas?" between Nick Fuentes (for the topic) and Tucker Carlson (also for the topic)
6pm: Roger Stone getting a tattoo of Trump's face above his Nixon tattoo
5pm: Kellyanne & The Alternative Facts
4pm: Red Hat Öyster Cult (MAGA-themed tribute band)

SATURDAY

11pm: Private coke orgies INVITE ONLY
                    *Reminder: Madison Cawthorn is banned for life
10pm: Lindsey Graham, Marjorie Taylor Greene and Kevin McCarthy leading a cultist blood oath of personal loyalty to God Emperor Donald Trump pouring *Diet Coke* on themselves to transubstantiate into his blood.
9pm: A gallows hanging of a life-size sculpture of Mike Pence, then bonfire
8pm: Don Jr. snorting lines of coke on top of a podium, and just kind of seeing what comes out of his mouth as he never blinks
7pm: A specially recorded message from Vladimir Putin on how smart, masculine, and patriotic America's conservative men are to stock up on guns and ammo and start a second American civil war
6pm: Matt Gaetz' Teen Trumpettes, a high school cheerleading group he sponsors that also sing songs of Donald Trump being a benevolent father figure for the nation in front of a 25-foot Maoist style portrait of Trump
5pm: Jim Jordan conducting a wrestling lesson on various wrestling moves on a blowup doll with a picture of Adam Schiff's face taped to it

4pm: "Make-Your-Own-Robes Craft Hour" hosted by a northern Florida branch of the Ku Klux Klan
3pm: Marjorie Taylor Greene teaching wilderness survival skills she learned while hunting for Bigfoot from 2002–2007 to train MAGA fans how to live in the wilderness for when The Storm arrives and conservatives must group up in rural, remote locations to begin their guerrilla war against the Biden regime
2pm: A coloring contest judged by anti-trans activist Matt Walsh with the theme "What Is A Man Or Woman?" for kids to color in graphic pictures of either a vagina or a penis, with the penis picture allegedly featuring his own.
1pm: The Dog Whistle Bluegrass Band
12pm: A showing of a Stephen Miller produced amateur documentary titled "How To Turn Animal Skins, Including Human Skin, Into Decorative Furniture Pieces" (rated NC-17)

SUNDAY

11pm: A ceremonial burning of a 30-foot effigy of Joe Biden with a general admission GOP coke orgy to follow open to all (except Madison Cawthorn)
10pm: Donald Trump ranting for 90 minutes doing all his greatest hits about toilets, showers, water pressure, windmills, the fake news media, all his former national security advisers who are now saying he's unfit to be reelected, "Ron DeSanctimonious," the FBI, Jack Smith, sharks, Greenland, the Panama Canal, the loyalty of Hitler's generals, and his idea to start a "Trumpler Youth" program for teen girls
9pm: 13-Year-Old Ivanka Lookalike Competition, hosted and judged by Donald Trump
8pm: A "Roast of Ted Cruz," hosted by Donald Trump (and possibly a public hanging if the crowd starts chanting "Hang Ted Cruz" loud enough)
7pm: Rudy Giuliani curating and critically analyzing selected dick pics found on Hunter Biden's laptop
6pm: TBD (Mike Lindell's previously scheduled "big reveal" of his proof of election fraud has been postponed until next year's MAGAPALOOZA)
5pm: A live episode of Steve Bannon's podcast in which he interviews Mike Flynn about how to make the next coup attempt more successful
4pm: A raffle sale of various gas stoves for winners to install in their kitchens and own the libs by letting their children inhale the slowly leaking gas fumes throughout their childhoods and get asthma
3pm: A Christmas-themed photo-op for all the attendees to get their Christmas card pictures holding AR-15s taken early this year
2pm: A panel discussion from the editors of the *The 1488 Project*
1pm: A screening of Louie Gohmert's documentary, *The Clitoris Hoax*
12pm: A "Blacks 4 Trump" signup drive and barbecue ($50 per attendee)

The Executive Chef At Mar-A-Lago Just Quit, Says He Can't Unsee What He Saw

July 22, 2023
Palm Springs, FL—

Chef Abe Pleisher, who works at Donald Trump's Mar-a-Lago resort, just quit his job after only three weeks on the job, and gave an in-depth interview to *The Halfway Post* about the "truly absurd" things he witnessed Trump do while on the job:

- Trump orders a meal he calls "The Donald" from *McDonald's*, and *McDonald's* employees know what it means: two *Big Mac* sandwiches cooked well-done with five packets of ketchup per sandwich, two *Filets-O-Fish* with five packets of mayonnaise per sandwich, and an *M&M McFlurry* with all the brown *M&Ms* removed.

- Trump forbids his chefs to bring him any foods that are green in color, and has threatened repeatedly to tariff all imported vegetables.

- When Stephen Miller dines with Trump, he meticulously takes off all the skin of his fried chicken with a knife and fork in as big of pieces as possible, and takes it home with him in bags for unspecified reasons.

- Trump likes to go into the kitchen before dinners and spit in his guests' food, particularly the food of GOP members of Congress, and he makes all staff sign non-disclosure agreements about it when they first get hired.

- To look strong and tough in front of other people, Trump likes to send back the dishes brought to him with some complaint about it not being prepared right, and the servers know to just wait in the kitchen for two minutes before bringing back the same plate.

- When dining with tech executives, Trump always says the same Michael Scott joke from the TV show *The Office* while ordering: "I'd like the chicken breast, hold the chicken," except Trump has never seen *The Office*, and just says that because he's a real-life perv.

- The chefs have learned to always double everything Trump orders because of how often he hears bad news about his criminal investigations, indictments, and civil lawsuits, and then throws his plates against the wall in a fury smearing ketchup everywhere.

- Trump loves eating mini-cupcakes, baby carrots, and burger sliders because his hands look bigger holding them.

- Trump tells his waiters every single meal, "Don't worry, I'm going to treat you right on the tip," and then stiffs them.

- Trump forbids anyone from praying before meals or blessing the food, and, even when someone tries to pray, Trump will just start eating his fried chicken while moaning to himself, and then interrupt the prayer to explain to the table how a lot of people don't know this but it's actually healthy to cut out red meat a couple times a week and eat an entire rotisserie chicken instead.

- Trump sneaks into the kitchen and sprinkles ground up weight-loss pills onto the food of any female staffers, diplomats, or world leaders he thinks "would look hotter if they lost 15 pounds."

- Trump eats pizzas made with ketchup for the sauce and topped with sauerkraut once a week.

- When Republican members of Congress come to Mar-a-Lago asking for his endorsement, he makes them eat lasagna until they throw up on their children's heads to earn it.

- Trump once told a group of Black Congressional Republicans that he can't be racist because chocolate ice cream is his favorite flavor, and much more than vanilla.

- Trump invites Don Jr. and Eric to dinners he hosts with his business partners, but makes them sit at a separate "kids' table."

- Every time Ivanka walks by while he's eating, Trump takes out his dentures, grabs the most phallic-shaped food on his plate, and then simulates the teeth giving a blowjob to the phallic-shaped food to try to amuse the people he's dining with.

- Trump forbids his chefs to ever serve him any form of sausage because of how often he hears people compare the shape, size, and appearance of his fingers to tiny, chubby breakfast sausage links.

- Trump once was accidentally served a glass with regular *Coke* in it instead of his customary *Diet Coke*, and he demanded to be taken to Walter Reed Hospital immediately to get his stomach pumped.

Donald Trump's Questionnaire For All Potential Second Term Appointees Just Leaked

August 11, 2023
Palm Beach, FL—

Trump's Official Application To Be In His 2nd Term, Which Is Certain To Again Accomplish More Than Lincoln, Washington, And All Other Presidents Combined:

- In 500 words or more, explain why Donald Trump was a better president than all the others combined. (*If you don't include Trump's name in every sentence he will get bored and not finish reading it.*)

- Do you think Trump could date Ivanka if she weren't his daughter?

- If you have a law degree, are you willing to be disbarred in service of Trump's various legal defense efforts with some light obstruction of justice, witness intimidation, and/or perjury?

- Please list three "outside-the-box" ideas for how Trump can delay further criminal prosecutions until after the 2024 election when he can shut them down or pardon himself.

- If Trump was to give you a box of documents for safekeeping, where would you hide it from the FBI's prying eyes?

- What are your thoughts on the hypothetical hanging of vice presidents? Would you ever consider participating in one?

- Are you better than Mayor Rudy Giuliani at determining the difference between high-end hotel chains and local landscaping companies?

- Do you have any letters of recommendation from any dictators? List all the Russians and Saudis you are on good terms with, and detail how connected to Vladimir Putin or Mohammed bin Salman they are.

- Role-play: you see Trump cheating at golf, what do you do?

- If you see Trump cheating on Melania, will you keep your mouth shut? (*Lol, jk on this one, Melania stopped caring years and several prenup renegotiations ago.*)

- Do you have any Obamacare replacement ideas that would be cheaper and cover more people?

- Will you vow to never invoke the 25th Amendment to remove Trump from the presidency, no matter what he asks the military to do, what dictatorial powers he tries to take for himself, how many protesting Americans he attempts to kill, or how senile he gets?

- Do you have any dirt or blackmail on Democrats, Republican members of Congress, or Evangelical pastors with big congregations (*Lindsey Graham, Matt Gaetz, and Kevin McCarthy excluded because we have more than enough on them already*)?

- Give 3 recommendations for people you think would be willing to pay $1 million for a pardon (*It takes a lot of time to cover the quid pro quo tracks, so SERIOUS RECOMMENDATIONS ONLY!*).

- Describe Trump's hand size in 100 words or less.

- (*WOMEN ONLY*) What is your bra size, menstrual cycle going back 6 months, and are you willing to get plastic surgery to better conform to Donald Trump's casting aesthetic?

- (*WOMEN ONLY*) Will you be willing to serve as a character witness and tell the jury at Trump's next sexual assault trial that he has never been anything but totally appropriate, gentlemanly, and non-threatening with you?

- (*WOMEN ONLY*) Do you need to go out furniture shopping anytime soon? Would you like accompaniment?

- (*MEN ONLY*) Have you been accused of domestic abuse or sexual harassment? (*You can be totally honest because this a big advantage for you in Trump's unique application scoring system for loyal underlings.*)

- Do you know the Heimlich Maneuver? (*Trump chokes on big bites of well-done steaks about twice a week.*)

- Have you ever booked a hotel reservation at a Trump property? If no, why not, AND when will you be booking your first stay? (*You can pay a deposit at your interview.*)

- Will you join the next coup attempt if Trump loses the election again in 2024, be willing to fight Capitol Police officers, and—in the event the mob is not yet riled up enough—help break some of the windows of the Capitol Building and to lead everyone inside to take shits in all the Congress members' offices?

Donald Trump Revealed The Dating Tips He Gave Barron On How To Attract Women "Like A Trump Man"

August 21, 2023
Palm Beach, FL—

Dear Barron,

You're 18 now, or 13, or probably at least 16, so you're becoming a man, and that means it's time for me to teach you about life, and about what it means to be a Trump man, and how to carry on the family reputation after I am dead and gone.

It might not be long. Seriously, the doctors say *Adderall* and fried food grease have been like a mystery glue that somehow keeps my heart going. They say they can't believe I haven't had a heart-attack yet from all the aspartame in my *Diet Coke*, the sludgy *Big Mac* sauce congealed in my arteries, and my ceaseless, all-encompassing, rageful obsession with enacting revenge upon all my enemies, who are pretty much everyone I know because everyone around me is a nasty idiot who if given the chance would rig everything in the world against me. My enemies have laughed at me, but who will be laughing when I get elected again? Donald J. Trump will be laughing! …Unless I have a heart attack because I haven't exercised in decades. Which is why I'm writing this letter to you, Barron.

Unfortunately, I set a pretty high bar of masculinity for you to keep up with from my days back in the 70s and 80s. It was like magic. I was a celebrity, rich, and best friends with Jeffrey Epstein, so I did very well with the ladies. I did so well that it the battlefield of STDs was my Vietnam. Let me tell you, after I had undiagnosed syphilis go on undetected for most of my 20s, 30s, and 40s slowly eating my brain until the doctors discovered it and treated me, I vowed never again! Pro trick: use a condom, because it really helps prevent the spread of nasty things. It also helps prevent unwanted pregnancies. Trust me, abortions and paying for secret children while keeping their mothers quiet and away from any reporters are expensive!

So I'll let you in on a little secret. In my 30s I only pretended to have such amazing, beautiful women as my girlfriends because I knew I didn't want to take the chance on getting another STD. I had a special trick. I pretended to be my own public relations guy, and I'd call up various newspapers, television news shows, and magazines to make up stories about how I couldn't make up my mind who I'd date because so many models and famous actresses were begging me for a chance to be my girlfriend. And no one could tell it was me on the phone, even to this day. That's where you got your name from. My alter ego was John Barron, a Trump PR executive. He was the best employee the Trump Organization ever had. Still, to this day, no one has any idea John Barron was me all along. I would have made one of the great actors of all time if I hadn't chosen to go into business. You know the story—went to Wharton, top of my class, and all the professors were begging me to teach their classes on business so they could actually learn from me. But I turned them down because I'm so humble. How are you doing in school these days, Barron? Do the girls in your class ever talk about me? How are the girls in your classes filling out? Send me some of your high school yearbooks!

But anyway, back to the subject of this letter, here are some tips on how to be a man that I've practically trademarked because of how well they've served me throughout my life. I want to help you become a winner and a ladies' man like me to protect the Trump family's reputation. I'm kind of counting on you to be my successor because Don Jr… I mean, I really messed up naming him after myself. That is the single greatest regret of my life. He's totally going to ruin my name beyond repair after I'm gone, I just know it. I wish I could preemptively sue him for damages to my brand, and make a judge force him to change his name to something like Frankie Failure. So, Barron, make me proud, son! I love you. Boy, if Don Jr. heard me say that to you, it would just crush his soul. It's like the more he tries to make me love him, the less I'm ever going to respect him, you know? Oh, and let me know when your birthday is, I'll get you something this year. Something tremendously special: a bunch of blanket pardons I filled out for you before I left the White House. If you're ever going to take the reigns at the Trump Organization you're going to need them. With all the people we do business with in wild, corrupt, lawless spots of the planet, let's just say you're going to have to get creative at off-the-books accounting and foreign lobbying real soon. So without further ado, here are my totally amazing dating tips:

- It's easy to impress women on dates by walking into the restaurant with them and announcing to all the other diners that you're going to pay for all their meals. Of course, I always leave without buying anyone anything—why would I really buy dinner for all those losers?—but it sure makes you look good in front of your date!

- Girls always play hard to get, so it's best to sneak up on them and surprise them. I'm sure you've seen the whole grab-'em-by-the-you-know-what video. The fake news media attacks me so much for that, but I'm telling the truth! You can't let women know you're about to grab them because then they swat your hands away and slap your face!

- It's hard to do ever since I got famous, but when I was in high school and college, I'd always pretend to be blind and get a cane and some real dark sunglasses, and then fake stumble my way into the women's locker rooms and bathrooms. Great way to see some skin with some plausible deniability.

- I like to pretend to fall around women so I can reach out and grab their boobs. Works like a charm, but they can try to sue you. Always keep cash on you to bribe them to sign a quick non-disclosure agreement!

- Order meals for your dinner dates. Sometimes the girls want to eat steaks, or burgers, or other big entrées, and then they get full and are less attractive. I ALWAYS order for my dates so I can get them tiny little salads instead. And NO desserts! If I'm paying, they're not going to get anything fattening (and this will save you a lot of money over the years!).

- Unfortunately, you likely have my faulty hair genetics, so plan to start fixing some balding issues around your early 30's. It's the only instance of Trump DNA not being perfect. But you should be thankful hair regeneration procedures are much more modern now. When I was desperate to bring back my hair in the 80s, the treatments were really nasty, and I put so many chemicals on my scalp that the doctors warned me I was endangering my brain, but they didn't know who they were dealing with because I've always been the smartest person in every room I've ever been in. I know more about everything than everyone. Went to Wharton, top of my class, big brain—you know all that! Although, all those chemicals that are now banned in Europe didn't ultimately help my hair situation. Hopefully your mom's hair genes help you out, but the Trump genes are very dominant on account of how superior they are to everyone else's.

- Drill some peepholes in the stall walls of women's public bathrooms, and then put on high heels so when you sit on the toilet for a while waiting for women to come in it looks like a woman is there. Then peep until your legs start falling asleep. IYKYK.

- Chivalry is way overrated, so don't waste your time pretending. Men are just more important in this world than women. Besides, why should my hair get wet because me and Melania only have one umbrella? My hair takes way longer to get ready than hers!

- Always cheat on your girlfriends and wives. Have as many kids both legitimate and bastard as you can because Trump DNA is God's gift to Earth. Just try to have more girls because Trump daughters turn out better, and much hotter. I've done six paternity tests on Eric because the apple really fell far from the tree with him, and I'm embarrassed to say he's really mine. You turned out pretty good because your mom Melania is quite a looker. Not so much now that she's over 50, but in her prime modeling days, wow! Do yourself a favor and Google "Melania naked" sometime. I've married some beauties, haven't I?

Anyway, that's all I can think of for now. I'll write some more when they come to me.

Just remember that I'm hoping you step up and become the Trump man your half-brothers will never be. And part of that is having amazing girlfriends, or at least making the world think you have them. Start playing around with what you want your public relations alter ego's name to be. Make sure you're ready for when you're old enough to start cold-calling tabloid magazines and making up rumors about yourself.

Also remember to always be tough. I need a real shark to take over the Trump Organization, and keep the Trump reputation when I die. Don Jr. and Eric will ruin the family company, so I'm counting on you, buddy. You might have to get them out of the picture, if you know what I mean. Bur watch out for Ivanka. I raised her pretty cut-throat, so she might try to off you after I'm gone. May the toughest Trump child win!

Love you, Barron! *(don't tell Don Jr. or Eric I said that to you)*
President Donald J. Trump

P.S.: By the way, there are some various tapes of me floating around out in the world that maybe make me look not so good. Putin's got some, Jeffrey Epstein's collection had quite a few, Rudy Giuliani has a couple, Roger Stone has one. If you ever hear threats of these tapes getting out, can I count on you to catch-and-kill those stories? Thanks in advance, sport!

P.S.S: Can you ask your mom to stop sending evidence against me to the DOJ? I'm starting to think she actually wants me to spend the rest of my life in jail.

P.S.S.S: Do you think you could also do me a little, tiny, huge favor, and practice copying your mom's signature so you can maybe forge it a few times on some new prenup documents for me? Don't worry, I'm leaving you in my will, I'm just taking Melania out of it. She violated the terms anyway because she was contractually obligated to hold my hand in public, but did you ever see her do that even one time? NO! Also, I haven't physically seen her in six months. Can you tell her to call me ASAP? I need to know how much money it'll take to get her to come to the inauguration if I get reelected.

BIG IF TRUE VI

- Musicians from the New York Association of Tuba Players have been taking turns standing in front of Trump Tower every morning and evening so they can play tuba music when Trump walks in and out to troll him.

- Hillary Clinton's "Lock Him Up Party" last night lasted until 6am, and she reportedly did a keg stand.

- Trump said today he's innocent, and vowed to set the record straight and exonerate himself "completely and totally" by testifying in this New York trial. "For real this time," he added.

- Stephen Miller reportedly referred to the story Kristi Noem wrote in her book of shooting a dog in the head as "amateur."

- Several New York City dancers costumed as mushrooms wearing prison clothes have joined the tuba players who wait outside Trump Tower every morning and evening to troll Trump when he walks in and out.

- Following Congress's passage of a new military aid package to Ukraine thanks to Speaker Mike Johnson compromising with Democrats, a very angry looking Vladimir Putin just told Russian media outlets that he'll "have to hack the GOP's emails again."

- Trump is threatening to sue the tuba players who wait outside Trump Tower every day for "presidential harassment."

- Worried MAGA fan investors of Trump's plummeting $DJT stock say they can't believe something Trump was personally involved in would lose them money.

- Trump reportedly called several attendees of his trial today "enemies of the people" after accusing them of repeatedly making fart noises with their mouths every time he moved in his chair.

- Joe Biden, holding a shotgun and a katana, says he looks forward to the possibility that the Supreme Court's conservative judges will defend Trump's legal and political interests by determining presidents have unlimited presidential immunity theoretically not limited even by the murder of their political opponents.

- Trump reportedly demanded his lawyers begin their opening statements in his New York trial by saying the farting sounds coming from the defense table weren't from him.

- A top Republican donor just quit the party and endorsed Joe Biden after RNC Co-Chair Lara Trump made him listen to her new, unauthorized Tom Petty cover song.

- A new app designed to help Christians resist the evil temptation to masturbate monitors your Internet browsing so every time you look at pornography it donates $6.66 to Planned Parenthood from your bank account.

- *Fox News* reportedly has a "rainy day NDA fund" with which it sets aside $1 million each year per show host to have a little fun with hush money.

- Trump reportedly filed his taxes by just writing in the middle of his forms with a *Sharpie* marker, "Send all bills to Joe Biden for stealing the election from me."

- Lara Trump is planning on starting public feuds with Billie Eilish, Ariana Grande, and Beyoncé to boost publicity for her new cover song.

- The judge in Trump's NY trial just denied Trump's demand that the court stenographer, "Let the record show I have not farted once."

- The funeral package Trump is now selling at his golf courses for his fans to buy in order to be buried next to him states in the fine print that Trump himself will not actually be buried at any of his courses.

- Trump's lawyers are reportedly fighting in court to get back several nude self-portrait photographs Trump took of himself that he had mixed in with the various classified documents he stole and hoarded for an unexplained reason.

- Arizona women are protesting their state legislature's proposal to revert back to an 1864 abortion law, and have begun mailing used tampons to their state legislators with notarized certificates that say, "Proof of no abortion" followed by their signatures.

- Trump claims that thanks to sitting in court for eight hours every day for three weeks he actually thought up an Obamacare replacement plan, a new Iranian nuclear deal, and an infrastructure plan.

- Donald Trump is reportedly furious with his lawyers for misleadingly telling him that the judge's gag order meant he couldn't testify in his defense, and, after shouting, "What, you think I'm incapable of testifying without incriminating myself?" a source reported that all the lawyers just stared at him silently for several seconds.

- RFK Jr. has been talking about digging tunnels a lot throughout his presidential campaign, which makes more sense since he admitted that worms have burrowed into his brain and eaten some of it.

- The University of Christianity is reportedly paying Trump to record online courses for their students on the following subjects: history of Christianity, ethics in government, marital monogamy, and physical fitness.

- Trump claims he pardoned his penis while he was president so it can't be indicted for any other sexual assault crimes it may have committed in the past.

- Trump is reportedly trying to find and hire "America's sexiest lawyer" who will "show some skin and distract the men on the jury."

- Local MAGA fan Ralph Morganford just had an epiphany that all of Michael Cohen's lies were told in assistance of Trump breaking laws.

- Pro-life Republicans say they unfortunately can't explain the paradox of why God would view life as sacred but also cause so many life-threatening pregnancies for women each year.

- RFK Jr. says he will "of course take the brain worm's opinions into consideration," but, "I will still make all the final decisions myself if I'm elected president.

- Trump reportedly can't make up his mind on who to nominate as VP because he feels he politically needs either an ethnic minority or a woman to balance the ticket, but his most passionate, hardcore MAGA base voters hate both minorities and women.

- Biden says if Trump gets convicted he'll sign an executive order mandating all imprisoned former presidents get "*McDonald's* Mondays."

- Lauren Boebert said today, "No one knows what Trump is being prosecuted for," and, also, "I refuse to read either the legal explanations of which laws he broke, or the trial transcripts about the evidence!"

- At the recent Trump rally in New Jersey, event cleanup crews had numerous staffing problems after the stench of so many used diapers Trump's fans wore to support his rumored incontinence issues made dozens of employees quit on the spot.

- Trump reportedly asked his lawyers if there's any way they could secretly suggest or imply to one of his jurors that, if they cause a hung jury, he will "make them very happy in two weeks."

- Trump has reportedly decided on his VP choice already, but can't make up his mind on a runner-up in case the first needs to be publicly hung.

- A group of far left college protesters say President Joe Biden hasn't earned their vote, so helping make possible a future 9–0 conservative majority on the Supreme Court by sitting out the next election "will teach the Democratic Party a lesson about not being unelectably liberal enough."

- A GOP House candidate in Florida says his female supporters should donate money to his campaign to keep trans athletes out of women's sports, or, if not money, their underwear, preferably not washed.

- In a rare moment of humility this morning, Trump reportedly told his lawyers, "I have no one to blame for this criminal trial but myself," but then he snorted a line of *Adderall* and published a post on *Truth Social* that Judge Merchan is the literal devil and a communist.

- Ivanka Trump just won the annual Mar-a-Lago beauty pageant hosted by her father for the 28th consecutive year.

- Trump reportedly asked his lawyers if they think the jury has noticed how he hasn't made eye contact with any of the witnesses testifying against him, and whether that makes him look guilty.

- Lauren Boebert and Marjorie Taylor Greene were reportedly going to challenge each other to an IQ test this morning to see who is smarter, but both got caught calling in bomb threats at Congress to get out of it.

- The security guards in the courtroom of Trump's trial have reportedly given him the Roman—and flatulence—inspired codename "Fartacus."

- Trump's judge just denied Trump's sixth demand to strike Michael Cohen's tweet calling him "Von ShitzInPants" from the evidentiary record of his trial.

The Ghosts of Past American Presidents Are Reportedly Haunting The White House Day And Night

Staffers from the Biden Administration are reporting an uptick in the number of encounters with the ghosts of former presidents:

George Washington floats around confessing that he accidentally sparked the French and Indian War in 1754, and you can look it up to verify it.

Rutherford Hayes asks White House visitors, "What's the big problem with Joe Biden sniffing kids' hair? Sniffing kids' hair is great!"

James Buchanan tells anyone who will listen, "I was a lifelong bachelor, and my almost inseparable best friend was male. You know what that means when you read it in the history books, don't you?"

George H. W. Bush pinches women's butts with his ghost fingers, then high-fives the Ghost of Mikhail Gorbachev, and they drink ghost beers together nightly and reminisce how they deserve the credit for ending the Cold War instead of Ronald Reagan and Margaret Thatcher.

FDR rolls around in his ghost wheelchair telling people "I was wrong! There is much more to fear than fear itself! The afterlife is an underworld, eternal purgatory with no relief, rest, or existential catharsis! It's a monotonous lingering in the shadows of nothingness, and an agonizing despair that will never end. Why do I suffer now when I suffered so much in life? I had polio!"

Teddy Roosevelt claims he did marijuana in Cuba during the Spanish-American War, and is the uncredited inventor of jazz music.

Warren Harding hides in closets, and when guests are getting dressed he says, "You know how much poon I used to get in here? Bill Clinton's a virgin boy scout compared to me! Also, my wife murdered me with poison! Look it up! I actually didn't mind. Teapot Dome was blowing up, and my mistress had just birthed a kid of mine. It was about time for ol' Warren to go. But let me tell you, thank God for Donald Trump because until him I was the worst president in the modern era. I may have been a cigar-smoking, backroom dealer of cronyism and corruption, but I'd never incite an attempted coup against the peaceful transfer of power! What kind of unAmerican, anti-democratic psychopath does a thing like that?"

Millard Fillmore begs staffers, "Hey, show me some of those *OnlyFans* videos on your electrified space telegram machine thingy! Millard likey! You know how hard it was to see scantily clad broads back in the 1800s? Now the broads show it all off for free, and walk around in public in yoga pants and spaghetti straps. I tell you, camel toe and sideboob were impossible to see in the 1850s. And no one's a bigger ally of free-the-nipple than Millard Fillmore. Trump used to watch those smutty moving pictures all day long while I looked over his shoulder! Just be glad I'm shooting ghost loads because I have painted the entire White House!"

Thomas Jefferson annoys White House guests describing in gratuitous detail with his trademark floral language that, "Our Creator has advanced our pursuit of happiness endowing us a wise character to appreciate the humor of John Adams being our second president, because to forever associate the number two and a big fat deuce that clogs a Virginian outhouse is to invoke the spirit of the Adams Administration, and it's an inalienable fact in our republic's august history that Adams is certainly a sh*t stain upon it."

Richard Nixon tells people he can't believe all he had to do was not resign, and just be like Donald Trump by not feeling any shame or remorse for any of his actions while walking all over basic decency and democratic norms, and have all his accomplices and underlings refuse to testify to Congress, and then he apparently could have gotten away with his impeachable crimes.

William McKinley, James Garfield, and John Kennedy play in a ghost band together on Thursdays, and jam out to heavy metal songs about assassination.

Calvin Coolidge does surprisingly profane yet racially compassionate gangsta rap about juggling flapper hoes in the Roaring 20s under the stage name "C-Cool."

Abraham Lincoln goes around screaming at Republican visitors for letting Trump ruin his party, and he explains how he's a Democrat today because if anyone reads the GOP's 1860s party platforms they would be shocked to find wildly liberal planks and policy ideas, such as funding extensive internal infrastructure and railroads, uninhibited asylum and citizenship rights to any immigrant who wanted them, "vigorous" taxation, and governmental intervention to expand and ensure civil rights for freed slaves. "Which party now does that sound like? Look at which states elected me. Geographically, the exact same power base as the states that elected Joe Biden! I want to choke someone every time I hear Republicans think they're making a relevant political argument in defense of the actions of today's GOP by pointing out I was one. I renounce the party I once led! Dark Brandon all the way!"

Gerald Ford floats around whispering into visitors' ears, "I want you to do things to my asshole I'll have to pardon you for."

A New Court Filing By Special Counsel Jack Smith Lists Very Odd Things The FBI Found At Mar-A-Lago

August 30, 2023
Washington D.C.—

A newly submitted document from Special Counsel Jack Smith's investigation into Donald Trump's mishandling of classified documents revealed some surprising details of what was found at Mar-a-Lago during the FBI's search and seizure of evidence last year:

- Thousands of pages of the US military's various war plans and deployment strategies kept in old, greasy, used *KFC* fried chicken buckets

- Big boxes labeled "blackmail on Kevin McCarthy," "Lindsey Graham's dirty emails," "pictures and payments found on Matt Gaetz's cell phone," "hidden discovery documents from Jim Jordan's wrestling doctor lawsuits," "videotape of Ted Cruz naked doing degrading things for a 2020 endorsement," and "proof that Josh Hawley watches pornography on his Senate computer all day during his office hours"

- Rudy Giuliani drunk and passed out on the couch in the lobby with his hand in his pants with empty scotch bottles, half smoked cigars, and letters from the New York Bar Association reminding him they've revoked his law license littered all around him

- A term paper Trump wrote in high school about how genius and clever Hitler's propaganda strategy was to tell nonstop lies about everyone and everything, and then refer to all the fact-checkers as "fake news" and "enemies of the people," with a big, red "F" written on it with a note from the teacher to "see me after class"

- Papers with *Sharpie* marker outlines of various people's hands Trump appears to have drawn to compare to the outline of his own hand, which he traced multiple times, including a few that showed him clearly extending the length of his finger tips to pretend they're bigger than they are in the manner of the way he extended the trajectory of Hurricane Dorian on that map after he accidentally and erroneously said that Alabama was in danger when it wasn't

- A manuscript of a novel much like *Lolita*, in which the protagonist, an unreliable narrator named "John Barron," describes his affair with his teenage daughter in the past tense offering admissions to his deviancy while also attempting to rouse sympathy for the allegedly debatable ambiguities of his actions

- A dozen blonde-haired wigs from different animals

- Hundreds of signed non-disclosure agreements with various women describing hush money payments for sex, for covering up sexual harassment, and for the women to never publicly disclose the tiny, flaccid, mushroom appearance of his penis. The violation of terms penalty is always $1 billion for "damages"

- A presidential pardon he secretly filled out and signed for himself in a stamped, unopened letter he mailed to himself on January 19th, 2021 in case he's ever convicted in a federal trial

- A copy of a memo to the other Trump Organization executives promoting his son Eric as the company's Chief Financial Officer so that he can blame all the company's egregious financial, tax, and bank fraud on Eric

- Elaborate plans to buy an island and declare independence, and found a new country called "Trumpland" with no extradition treaty with the US, limits on executive powers for the chief executive, or laws on incest

- Elaborate plans in a file labeled "Little St James 2"

- Don Jr. and Eric's middle school and high school yearbooks with all the girls' pictures that showed a little cleavage circled in *Sharpie* marker, above which Trump wrote "Invite to your next birthday party!"

- Three elaborately sketched out plans to fake his death, sneak out of Mar-a-Lago wearing women's clothes, and fly one-way to Moscow, Riyadh, or Pyongyang

- Several bottles of ketchup in a glass box that says "In case of emergency, break glass"

- Senator Lindsey Graham locked up inside a dog kennel in the basement for some reason, barking at all the FBI agents and refusing to communicate in English

Donald Trump's Hail Mary Legal Defense Strategies For Hoarding Top Secret National Security Documents

September 3, 2023
Palm Beach, FL—

Donald Trump is grasping at straws for his legal defense, but that won't stop him from proverbially throwing spaghetti at the wall and hoping some sticks:

- **Blame Rudy**: "Jack Smith is absolutely deranged to prosecute me for election fraud. It was all Rudy Giuliani! I had nothing to do with it, I swear! I was never in the same room as Rudy when he was doing all the crimes. I couldn't because he was always farting, dripping hair dye all over the place, getting unintelligibly drunk every day by 10am, sexually harassing the women around him, and putting his hands in his pants!"

- **Secret Service alibi**: "I wasn't there at the Capitol on January 6th so how can I be indicted? I didn't fight any cops, break any windows, or try to hang Mike Pence. Believe me, I tried to join in on the fun, but the Secret Service wouldn't drive me to the Capitol. I was furious at the time, and may have committed some light assault choking out my driver, but boy am I sure glad now they didn't drive me because the DOJ is making such a big fuss about those tourist visits of Congress."

- **Presidents are above the law**: "My lawyers have been very clear that I can't be indicted for anything I did as president because of executive privilege, and I can't be indicted for anything after I was president because I'm running again and it'll be election interference, and I can't be indicted by my political opponent's Department of Justice or America will become a banana republic, and I can't be indicted by anyone else because the country needs to move forward and heal!"

- **Marital blame**: "Melania took all those top secret war plans, not me! A lot of people don't know this, but she wasn't always an American. She's from a country called... ah, I always forget. Something-venia... Transovenia... Transylvania! Yeah, that's it! In fact, I actually overheard her talking on the phone a few days before the Mar-a-Lago raid, and she was saying some very suspicious things about classified documents. I was just about to report her when the FBI came knocking on my door!"

- **Allege an FBI conspiracy**: "The FBI planted those nuclear secrets in my office when they searched Mar-a-Lago! They also planted all the *Adderall* pills, the adult diapers, the shoe lifts, and a dozen burner phones. None of those were mine! The FBI wasn't even nice about it, either. They made up all this fake evidence I found in Melania's bedroom that made it seem like she's having an affair behind my back, like tons of handwritten letters that look just like her handwriting to some other guy, and some other men's clothes that aren't mine. The FBI had way too many details for it to be believable. Actually, I haven't seen Melania in months. Did the FBI take her? That can't be legal to confiscate someone's wife as evidence against him, right?"

- **What-About-Obama-ism**: "Why am I being investigated and prosecuted before Obama? He's the sketchy Black president! There's no way I stole as much from the government as he probably did! Did you know his middle name is Hussein? It's so unfair that he gets a pass, and I don't. Reverse racism is so unfair and rigged against me!"

- **God Defense**: "The Iran war plans the FBI says I stole is just a big misunderstanding. You see, I read the *Bible* every day for an hour, and I'm one of those really devoted Christians you hear about. And back when I was president, when I'd find a *Bible* passage I really liked, I'd just grab the nearest piece of paper to record some of my thoughts and notes about it. I was always writing down reactions to the amazing things Jesus did, and the margin notes I wrote were full of details like how Jesus cut the baby in half because the two women were fighting over it, or when Jesus got swallowed by the whale, or when Jesus's ship landed on the island of the sirens who turned his men into pigs. So it was just an accident that, when I left the White House with my boxes full of *Bible* notes and reflections on Jesus, a few of them coincidentally were written on a few documents detailing our nuclear program and the various spy rings the US has gathering intel on the inner workings of Russia's government. It was a totally innocent mistake that Jesus, God, and the Holy Gypsy or whatever the third one is have totally forgiven me for. If I'm guilty of a crime, it's only for reading the *Bible* too much!"

- **Constitutional ignorance**: "I have an inalienable First Amendment right to incite violence! I can say anything I want to inspire incels, racists, and conspiracists to do any number of coups. I know my rights!"

- **Blatant lies**: "I totally would have tweeted for all the January 6th protesters to go home when they started rioting, but I was busy in my office calling all my favorite charities, and giving them big, amazing donations over the phone. I don't ever talk about my charitable giving because everyone knows I am so humble and generous, but I was writing so many checks to so many different charities that my hand and arm started cramping up, and I couldn't tweet for several hours!"

The Preamble To The Republican Party's 2024 Platform

We believe in the Constitution as our founding document, not as a flexible guideline, but as an enduring covenant between the people and their representatives. Unless Donald Trump wants to tear it up, declare himself above the law, and start committing any number of consecutive crimes while arguing he's unindictable because he's running for president and any criminal investigation would amount to election interference. Then, if he's voted president again, he can do endless crimes and pardon himself perpetually… Unless Trump decides he wants to keep the Constitution, in which case, yay, we love it, and wouldn't change a single word. Hurray for originalism!

In 2021, we may have done some light treason and assisted Trump in inciting a coup against the democratically elected president, but we failed so none of it was actually a crime and we can't be prosecuted for just a slight felony technicality. Special Counsel Jack Smith must be defunded, the FBI abolished, the DOJ gutted, and all government prosecutors and lawyers who won't swear a blood oath on January 20th, 2025 to Donald Trump fired. We will end the two-tiered justice system in America by making sure Donald Trump will never be harassed by criminal indictments ever again.

Our last three GOP presidents ballooned the debt by cutting taxes and not cutting spending at all, but we promise Trump's next term really will, finally, cut the debt. It'll go down to zero so fast you won't believe it. But if it doesn't, it'll be Democrats' problem to deal with the next time they get a president in.

The climate is pummeling us, but we're not going to do anything about it because… China or something, I don't know—look, we've been saying it for decades that we're just not going to do anything about it. The climate is all out of whack, but we all knew this was going to happen once we started letting the gays get married. We warned the liberals a thousand times God would get mad and send down a bunch of plagues and natural disasters in retribution, and now they're getting what they asked for. We Republicans wash our Christian hands of this!

For guns, a lot of kids being shot up in schools every year is just the price of freedom. And murdered ex-wives and ex-girlfriends. And kids grabbing irresponsibly stored guns, and shooting each other when playing around. And you can no longer expect to go to a grocery store, movie theater, music concert, church, or anywhere else safely. If you don't have a gun already, you should probably go buy one ASAP. You're going to want one on you since everyone else will have one. P.S.: Don't mention this to any Black people. We really just want whites to have the guns.

Slavery wasn't ALL bad for slaves. They learned valuable skills, got free admittance into America, and could work worry-free without having to bother with any of the business challenges and stresses of owning a plantation. Patrician, antebellum plantation owners were the economic heroes and job creators of their day, and they are unfairly maligned today because of all the class warfare socialists are perpetrating. Democrats are burying their heads in the sand when they won't admit that some good things came out of slavery. And we're not racist for being pedantic sticklers by pointing out that slaves were eventually paid the greatest possible gift in the world: American citizenship… we Republicans are just big history buffs!

Women are baby-making vessels that belong to the state for the express purpose of birthing enough babies to someday let America defeat India, China, and the Muslims. It's a geopolitical reality that abortion helps Asia stay ahead of us. It's not that we want women to die from preventable pregnancy complications, it's just that maybe that's what God wants if He, in His grand master plan for the universe, saw fit to give them ectopic pregnancies. And women should respect God's will by acknowledging that rape and incest babies are miracles. That's a little icky, we know, but we're just going to ban all abortions and hope women's bodies really do have some biological mechanism to prevent or terminate unwanted pregnancies like some of our losing Congressional candidates have suggested in recent years. Maybe women should just start praying more if they don't like it?

We must save masculinity. America's young men are addicted to video games, pornography, the Devil's Lettuce, TikTok, and they're in real danger of becoming incels. Liberalism and its Woke feminists are ruining women and society by brainwashing girls to turn away from and be disgusted by conservative values. They don't want to date, or even be around Republican men. The way women are trending away from the Republican Party is a wakeup call for the GOP that we conservative men must put away the video game controllers, bongs, porn, and social media distractions, and really commit ourselves to Evangelical fundamentalism so we can force women to give up on all these dangerous and heathen ideas of gender equality, and return them to their rightful place in the social hierarchy below their husbands, and stop them from politically allying with the ethnic minorities to elect Democrats to continue stealing representational power stolen from white Christian men, who God has intended to lead America.

Repeal Obamacare because f*ck the uninsurable. It's been so long we don't even remember why we wanted to repeal Obamacare's moderate regulations everyone now just casually accepts as rational and normal, but we're still bitter we didn't get to accomplish our goal of making him a one-term president. Our replacement plan is TBD, but you're going to love it. And it will be cheaper. And cover more people, and all the other stuff. We're still working it out, but the details are less important than freeing the US from the bondage of Obamacare. The government option for health care is diminishing too many of our health insurance donors' net profits.

America First. Then Russia Second (we'll withdraw support for Ukraine). Then Saudi Arabia Third because Mohammed bin Salman leads the kind of strong, authoritarian government we'd like to see here in America. Israel fourth, but not the real Jew-y Jews or globalists, just the Jews who support a strong Israel that will maintain Israeli sovereignty long enough for Jesus to come back and begin the Rapture and precipitate all the Biblical prophecies as foretold by the book of *Revelations*. Although this order will change if Democrats win in 2024, in which case f*** America, we're seceding again, and starting a new civil war for the right of Donald Trump to become dictator-for-life as he initiates a hereditary monarchy (Eric excluded from the line of succession).

Bring back child labor. Sarah Huckabee Sanders is a visionary governor, and we want to see American families adopt more of an Arkansas aesthetic. Plus, since she legalized child labor again, coal mines are so much more efficient and profitable when you only have to drill and dynamite tunnels big enough for little children, instead of full-size adults. That's the kind of economic vitality and cost-savings we need to institute across all of America.

End the minimum wage, Social Security, Medicare, welfare, and all other safety nets the US has compared to democratic socialist nations elsewhere. If America wants to let our billionaires become trillionaires, we need to cut taxes and starve the government, and probably a lot of the people as well.

Ban books, defund libraries, defund universities, kill public schools, erase evolution and climate change from science class, whitewash history class, and no sex education anymore. We can't figure out why, but higher education and intellectual curiosity correlates with liberal politics, so critical thinking must somehow be rigged against conservatives. We want more of the poorly educated Donald Trump loves so much, and less of the college-educated.

Let's omit the following subjects in history classes: slavery, Jim Crow, the Civil Rights era, the Harlem Renaissance, etc. …Let's just skip from the 1770s to World War 2 when we won, and then skip right to Reagan in the 80s, and then skip again to Donald Trump coming down his escalator in 2015. That's all the history that freedom-loving American patriots need to know.

Oops, is that ANOTHER Nazi we just invited to our political conference and had dinner with afterwards? Our bad.

The Lamest Boycotts Republicans Are Currently Doing

- Hollywood movies, because all the famous actors and actresses drink baby blood every morning for breakfast.
- *Nike*, for having too many Black basketball players in their commercials.
- Any bag of mixed nuts, because it subliminally encourages mixing of the races.
- Tanning, because it makes white people look like they might be biracial.
- Sunscreen, because sunburns and skin cancer prove whites are the purest race because they're literally allergic to the equatorial sun.
- Green vegetables, because their green color suggests they're a part of the climate change hoax.
- Turtles, because Mitch McConnell is a RINO.
- Vitamin D, because they think it secretly means "Vitamin Democrat."
- The name "Brandon," because "Let's Go, Brandon" refers to Biden.
- Electric stoves, because breathing in gas fumes for decades throughout their lives owns the libs and environmentalists so hard.
- Spell-checking tools, because Trump regularly misspells words, so if borderline illiteracy is good enough for him, it's good enough for the rest of America.
- The Internet, because, while they're not sure, they think they remember hearing somewhere that Al Gore was involved somehow in its creation.
- Going to the doctor, because COVID was a hoax, and a Chinese bio-weapon, and just a weak cold, and a US government scheme to implant microchips in our bloodstream, all at the same time.
- *Cheerios*, because they look like you're eating a bunch of little, gay anuses.
- *Froot Loops*, because they look like you're eating even gayer, little anuses.
- Physical fitness, because when Obamacare was passed into law, insurance companies placed greater attention to preventative healthcare, and, while it sounds sensible and societally beneficial, Obama is behind it so preventative healthcare must somehow secretly be a plot to install Sharia Law and terrorism.
- Drinking tap water, because all the people who got vaccinated are urinating their demonic, mRNA antibodies into the water supply.
- Georgia's star in the Confederate flag, and they are cutting the state's star out of their basement and garage flags because of how Georgians helped elect Joe Biden, and they don't trust Atlanta because it's too "urban."
- Any movie, book, or TV show featuring a woman, Muslim, or ethnic minority as the protagonist or even a supporting character, because Hollywood is cramming Wokeism down everyone's throats by reminding rural whites that America is a very diverse place and always has been.

Fox News's "War On Christmas" Content Starts Next Week To Distract From Donald Trump's Criminal Trials

September 13, 2023
New York City, NY—

Fox News is finding it increasingly difficult to pretend Donald Trump is not facing unprecedented legal peril, but top *Fox* executive producers have decided on a distraction strategy of launching its annual coverage of the "War on Christmas" quite a bit earlier than usual this year.

"There's nothing else we can think of to keep our audience of elderly lemmings distracted from Trump's somewhat blatant guilt in most of the ongoing criminal trials he's engaged in," said a *Fox* executive, who requested anonymity to both discuss the network's internal deliberations and insult the cognitive faculties of the network's average viewer. "It was hard enough to convince them Trump was innocent during the impeachments, January 6th, and all the Trump Organization fraud allegations, but, now, hoarding classified documents, and refusing to honor a subpoena to give them back? Scheming to have dozens of fake electors in multiple states submit fraudulent electoral votes to steal the election from Joe Biden? Threatening the Georgia secretary of state to find votes and rig the election there? Trump is kind of f*cked. There is no way anyone at *Fox* can logically or rationally defend these Jack Smith prosecutions anymore. Our viewers might be empathetically devoid, scholastically challenged addicts of hyper-partisan garbage with no critical-thinking skills, but they're not traitors to America. Even Sean Hannity can't spin this stuff. I doubt even *Fox*'s patron saint Joseph Goebbels could spin this stuff. And Hannity, Laura Ingraham, and Jesse Watters are no Joseph Goebbels, no matter how many Nazi propaganda videos we make them watch and take notes on during our annual company retreats!"

The executive sighed before continuing.

"So distracting our viewers with endless 'War on Christmas' content for the next three months is our only hope. We have to do something. Anything! … Well, not anything. We can't just start being objective, neutral arbiters of the truth, and cut out all the pavlovian defenses of Republican partisan interests. We're already hemorrhaging viewers to *OAN* and *Newsmax* because we admitted we lied about all the rigged voting machine claims and allegations. We have to keep throwing conservative viewers the red meat they demand, or they'll abandon us for being Woke, RINO, Never Trumpers! So starting next week we're launching the 'War on Christmas' quite a bit early. We may not be able to defend Trump's top secret document treason, but we can bury our heads in the proverbial sand and pretend Jack Smith and Fani Willis don't exist while accusing Democrats of culturally sodomizing Santa Claus!"

The following Christmas-related segments will begin to air next Monday to keep *Fox* viewers angry and distracted:

- *What If Democrats Had Aborted Jesus?:* A dramatic imagining of our Founding Fathers as Muslim terrorists, featuring El Binyamin Franklin, Tamam al-Jefferson, and Ghasan Wahhabington, the first caliph of al-Ameriqaeda.

- *Liberal Santa*: a Laura Ingraham production featuring the Democrats' desired Santa who has divorced Mrs. Claus to be gay with the elves, dyed his hair blue, and converted to satanism.

- *Globalism Vs. The Messiah*: a conspiratorial documentary alleging that George Soros's long ago ancestors paid Pontius Pilate to kill Jesus, only Jesus didn't die, and had kids in a direct family line that led many generations later to Donald Trump.

- *God's Chosen President*: a propaganda film in North Korean style that claims Trump was virgin-birthed, only golfs holes-in-one, he does not pee or poop, and he invented the recipe for the *Big Mac*.

- *How To Keep Your Testicles Tan Throughout The Dark Winter*: a Tucker Carlson production advertising his new *Tucker's Testes 2.0* testicle tanning machines, which retail for $199.99.

- *A Libertarian Christmas Carol*: a remake where several ghosts visit Tiny Tim on Christmas Eve, and inspire him to stop complaining and expecting free stuff, and to pull himself up by his crutches to become the very rich CEO of a coal mine with abysmal safety records.

- *Donald Trump Jr.'s Christmas Stories*: *Fox* has agreed to give Don Jr. a weekly show on Sundays at 11pm to share memories of growing up with Donald Trump as his father, and whatever else comes to his head as he sniffles with glassy, red eyes that blink once per minute.

- *Gift Ideas From The NRA*: a presentation on why AR-15s are a perfect Christmas gift for Christians to celebrate Jesus's lamb-like mercy, love, and desire for us to always turn the other cheek.

- *Christmas Decorating With Melania Trump*: a camera follows Melania as she grudgingly directs the placement of decorations at Mar-a-Lago looking repeatedly at pictures of White House Christmas decor from 2009–2016 for inspiration, and odd moments where her lips are moving but there is no sound because the producers had to cut out the audio of all the times she mutters to herself "I f***ing hate Christmas," "This is f***ing bulls***!" and, "If he gets another term I'm going to smother him in his sleep."

- *It's A Wokeful Life*: a conservative parody of *It's A Wonderful Life*, in which the protagonist Jim Crow is depressed about everyone hating him until in a dream he sees what a Critical Race Theory dystopia of racial equality America would be today if he hadn't ever existed.

- *A Joe Biden Christmas*: an animated cartoon for kids showing Christmas morning where there are no gifts for any children because of inflation and socialism, and there's not even any coal for the naughty children because Biden converted all our energy to solar and wind power, and, now because it's winter and cloudy, everyone's homes have no power so Christmas is ruined for everyone.

- Advertisements for Mike Lindell's newest *MyPillow* product, a pillow that shows Donald Trump's butt bending over so that MAGA fans can brown-nose Trump even while sleeping, sold at the sale price of $45.45.

BIG IF TRUE VII

- Lauren Boebert, Marjorie Taylor Greene, Matt Gaetz, Vivek Ramaswamy, Tim Scott, and JD Vance were all seen pushing each other prior to Donald Trump's post-trial press conference so they could try to get the best front-row positions for the cameras.

- Ted Cruz reportedly wants to be seen on television standing behind Trump after one of Trump's ranting post-trial press conferences, but Trump won't let him.

- Trump is reportedly angry that Republican members of Congress are only visiting him in the courtroom to take photos and fundraise rather than actually help why he's innocent.

- BREAKING NEWS: Donald Trump actually died a week ago, but the media has been so busy covering Joe Biden being old and forgetful that they didn't notice.

- Trump reportedly asked his lawyer friends if it's possible to delay his criminal trials indefinitely by firing his lawyers each month, getting new ones, and requesting trial delays so the new lawyers can have time to prepare before firing them as well.

- During an interview with *Fox News* on his proposals for border security Trump reportedly had the words, "Do not call them concentration camps," written on his palm in *Sharpie* marker.

- The MAGA fan in Iowa who accidentally burned down his house months ago trying to burn a gay pride flag today accidentally set his truck on fire trying to burn a DVD of *Brokeback Mountain*.

- Stephen Miller has doubled down on his recent "America is for Americans and Americans only" quote, and says Elon Musk and Melania Trump will be deported for abusing the immigration system.

- The National Association of Flag Enthusiasts just named Samuel Alito's wife as their newest "Flag Ambassador of the Year," an honor that commemorates her contagious passion for the art of flying insurrectionist flags outside their house.

- Trump says his plummeting $DJT stock is not a pump-and-dump scheme, so his fans need to start investing much more real quick.

- Joe Biden says Trump is right that crime is too high, so tomorrow morning he's going to direct the FBI to raid Trump Tower and recover the remaining classified documents Trump stole.

- Eric Trump reportedly lost over a million dollars from his father's $DJT stock's plummeting value.

- Trump claimed on *Fox News* that no president does more for Black employment than him "because of how many Blacks I pay to show up to each and every one of my campaign rallies."

- Trump's top lawyer just begrudgingly admitted today in court that his legal arguments in Trump's election fraud trial do, in fact, argue that if Kamala Harris is the candidate she can ensure, as the current vice president, that she wins all 538 votes in the Electoral College.

- Trump is reportedly angry with his campaign staff for "not trying hard enough" because by this point in the 2016 election his campaign manager and several staffers had already committed dozens of felonies and met up with several Russian intelligence cutouts.

- Trump interrupted a bar mitzvah party last night at Mar-a-Lago, and ranted for 26 minutes about how Hitler did, in fact, have loyal generals.

- Trump was overheard at Mar-a-Lago today yelling into his phone, "I have presidential immunity to smell however I want!"

- Samuel Alito claims it was his wife who threw human feces at his liberal neighbor's house and wrote, "You just got Supremed!" in smeared poop on the neighbor's garage, and not him.

- A homophobic televangelist from Kentucky just had an epiphany that maybe it's weird he constantly thinks about what an abomination gay sex is, and how he should maybe expand his focus to occasionally thinking about some other subjects.

- Trump reportedly offered all his lawyers a $10 million bonus three months ago to any of them who would take the blame for all the hoarded classified documents he was keeping at Mar-a-Lago.

- A leaked memo from *Fox News* revealed that the network's interviewers use *Vicks VapoRub* when interviewing Trump because he smells like, as one *Fox* producer described it, "rotten eggs soaking in a boiling pot of diarrhea."

- Thousands of *Fox News* viewers are now boycotting the network for reporting the truth that Trump is now, officially, a convicted felon.

- Eric Trump reportedly hasn't washed his hand in the week since his dad shook it following the announcement of his guilty verdict.

- Trump has reportedly been depressed since the end of his trial because he actually really enjoyed getting to nap all day while in court, and getting to occasionally make the evil, communist prosecutors gag when they smell his rancid *McDonald's Filet-O-Fish* gas.

- Local MAGA fan Ralph Yardman reportedly turned off *Fox News* for a few hours today to look up several of the widely available articles online explaining in depth what Trump was prosecuted for, and he says he now realizes Trump is a criminal so he will vote for Kamala Harris.

- So far, 14 white Republican candidates for Congress have accidentally tweeted out posts from their main accounts saying, "As a Black man, I could NEVER vote for Kamala."

- Trump reportedly wants Russia to hack the gay dating app *Grindr* to leak to him the names of all the Republicans who have accounts so he can blackmail them to defend him on *Fox News*.

- Trump's lawyers reportedly set up a fake courtroom in Trump Tower, and Trump has spent all week since his criminal conviction attending a fake trial where the witnesses have said he's innocent, and a genius, and he definitely lasted more than 30 seconds with Stormy Daniels, but also he never met her, and she's a self-promoting liar, and her non-disclosure agreement specifically forbid her from saying anything about it, and it's classified, and it's fake news, and it's presidential harassment.

- Steve Bannon, who was just imprisoned for contempt of Congress, has reportedly pledged allegiance to the Aryan Brotherhood for protection.

- A bar in Milwaukee has put up a huge piñata of Trump ahead of the Republican National Convention, and drinkers get one hit with a wiffle ball bat every time they order a "Pabst Your Jail Time" drink special referencing comedian Jimmy Kimmel's quip at the Oscars, consisting of a PBR beer and shot of an orange flavored vodka.

- Eric Trump is reportedly the first Trump family member to tell his dad that, because he's now a felon, for the good of the country he should step down and drop his candidacy for president.

Women Across The US Are Vowing To Make The GOP Pay Electorally In 2024 For Republicans' Anti-Women Agenda

September 29, 2023
Washington D.C.—

These are the following GOP-sponsored bill proposals in Congress that US women are most angry about:

- The creation of a new "DMV" called the Department of Menstrual Vaginas to oversee the rationing of feminine care products, where women must go each month, take a numbered ticket, and wait in long lines before receiving the five tampons OR five pads rationed to them each month by very surly, fundamentalist Christian employees.

- All girls and women in America must all get on the same menstrual schedules so that, from now on, they all start bleeding on the 15th of each month so it's easier for police, GOP legislators, husbands, and fathers to track pregnancies and investigate possible abortions.

- A budget expenditure of a $100 million grant split amongst several select doctors to begin research on finding viable, biological processes with which men can carry and birth babies instead of women on account of how much more trustworthy and dependable men are over women to not abort babies.

- A program for poor and ethnic minority pregnant women to check in with a "pregnancy compliance officer" every month to ensure their babies are healthy, but it won't be funded enough that the government would ever need to raise taxes on corporations to pay for it.

- A new medical regulation that doctors must tattoo tally marks on women's wrists when they go for their first pregnancy checkups so that everyone can compare how many times in their lives they were pregnant with how many children they have.

- A law that mandates medical schools to invite an Evangelical pastor or a Republican member of Congress to be present when they're teaching med students about the female reproductive system to ensure they're not spreading any "liberal propaganda."

- The repeal of all laws on bestiality because, as GOP Representative Rusty Haddleton of rural Georgia says, "The more that men can freely pursue destigmatized sexual relationships with farm animals, the less premarital sexual relations they'll be having with human women."

- A national program for public schools where girls, starting in the third grade, will be given a government-issued, "WWJD"-stamped chicken egg to bring everywhere they go to teach them about the importance of protecting fetuses. If anything happens to the egg, their parents will be fined $35 to replace it, and they will have to spend all morning waiting in line at the DMV (Department of Menstrual Vaginas) to get the new egg.

- The disenfranchisement of women' vote until the number of abortions in America goes down to zero.

- The institution of a new civilian award issued by the President (or Republican-controlled chambers of Congress in the event that the president is a Democrat) for women who die from preventable complications of nonviable pregnancies, such as ectopic pregnancies, called the "Medal of Maternity."

- The addition of a new Constitutional amendment that says married women must "put out" three times a week unless they're pregnant, menopausal, or their husbands have mistresses they'd rather sleep with instead.

- Reinstitution of the draft for women who get abortions so if they're going to kill kids here in America, at least they can be sent to a war zone to kill the kids of America's enemies too.

- Federal recognition of male sperm as "America's official gamete" over female eggs.

- The legalization of public masturbation for men because it will make America a more masculine country.

- A policy where male Republican members of Congress with promising careers can get one "abortion coupon" per year, but no other abortions will be allowed.

- A ban on epidural anesthesia during birthing so women feel the pain and suffering God intended for all women after Eve ate the forbidden fruit.

- The legalization of polygamy.

Trump Says Christians Should Emulate His Marriage To Melania If They Want To Be Truly Christian

October 10, 2023
Palm Beach, FL—

Donald Trump made some controversial comments at a prayer breakfast event this morning in which he alleged that he has always kept God, Jesus, and Christian values of monogamy at the center of his three marriages:

"The Christians really love my marriage to Melania," Trump said. "My marriage is much more Christian than Joe Biden's marriage, or Pete Buttigieg's marriage, or Ron DeSantis's marriage. Melania and I spend a lot of time reading the *Bible* together. We can't put the *Bible* down! I love so many *Bible* stories, like the one about that guy Lot, whose daughters got him drunk and then seduced him to have his babies. They say the *Bible* is tremendously relatable, and that one certain is! Me and Melania's kid Barron is a good looking kid, isn't he? But can you imagine if me and Ivanka had a kid? And what if it was a girl? The fake news media always lies about me being attracted to my daughter, and they'd definitely also accuse me of being attracted to my granddaughter if I had one with Ivanka. With Ivanka's legs and jugs, and my youthfully robust head of hair and my healthy, tanned skin glow, that would be something! Too bad the *New Testament* had to come along and cancel out all the incest stuff the *Old Testament* allowed Lot to do! But, like I said, my marriage with Melania is totally in honor of Jesus and the *Bible*. I am 100% faithful to her and Jesus. A lot of people don't know this, but when I paid off all those porn stars, it was because I didn't do anything with them. Certainly nothing sexual. They just wanted me to teach them about the *Bible*. Those pornstars came up to me with tears in their eyes, and got down on their knees to beg me to convert them to Christianity. They said, 'Sir, no one's more Christian than you, please teach us! Show us how to be great Christians like you are. You're one of the best Christians, maybe of all time. Maybe Jesus was a little better, but then you're a close number two right after him!' So I only went up to those pornstars' hotel rooms to teach them all about my tremendous love for Jesus. I read them my favorite stories from the *Bible*, like the time Jesus was eaten by the whale. And the time Jesus cut off Medusa's head full of snakes for hair. And when Jesus became the king, but found out he had accidentally killed his father and married his mother. Those stories were what guided me as president to make such great deals for America. So I didn't do anything sexual with those pornstars, I guarantee it. But, you know me, I'm just very humble, and I don't like to make a big deal about myself and my accomplishments, so I paid those pornstars each a hundred and fifty thousand dollars to swear them to secrecy, and not tell anyone that I saved their souls!"

Trump stopped briefly to drink from a bottle of water with two hands.

"I would never cheat on Melania. No one would believe in a million years that I would ever be unfaithful to her, or any of my wives. I might say some locker room talk occasionally here and there about sexually assaulting women, and using my celebrity to molest and grope them, and daydreaming about what bra size my infant daughters will grow up to have, but Jesus doesn't listen to locker room talk because locker rooms are where men get undressed and take showers, so Jesus never goes in there. Jesus doesn't like men. Unlike Pete Buttigieg who is so gay that he likes men! He likes men so much he married one, which is about as gay as a guy can get. Pete maybe committed himself to just one spouse, and has taken seriously his marriage vows about the whole till-death-do-you-part stuff, but God gave me a pass because my ex-wives got older and turned ugly. It's like women just give up looking young after turning 40. Jesus understands that I'm a businessman, and I have a luxury corporate brand to protect. Who would want to go to any of my hotels and golf courses if I was still married to my first wife, and I had a 78-year old hag hanging around me and my golf course? Now, a grave site, that's a different story. My ex-wives can stay around at Mar-a-Lago all they want as long as they're underground and getting me some graveyard zoning tax cuts!"

The Enigma That Is Trump's Relationship With Ivanka

In the gaudy living room of a gold-everything penthouse, Donald Trump threw extravagant parties that never failed to generate social intrigue.

Amidst lavish displays of narcissism adorning the hallways—including several life-size portraits of himself, counterfeit *Time Magazine* covers featuring his face, and a poster purporting to show the average human hand with the outline of a another, bigger hand next to it claiming to be the outline of Trump's hand—the glasses of champagne flowed their waterfalls for his friends, if you could call them that, of new money New York wannabe aristocrats tipsily spilling their drinks talking to the Epstein girls they knew looked young but no one asked.

Amid the throngs of people, one figure stood out from the rest, and though his eyes meandered from woman to woman, they always returned to her—the young, captivating Ivanka.

She was his daughter, and when she was in the room he couldn't hide his spellbound glances at her, betraying an unmistakable passion for the results of his long-term grooming work.

He had made the perfect daughter he thought often, and dominated conversations finding out who else agreed. He'd revel in the coaxed compliments he'd all but beg them to shower upon her character, intellect, and, most of all, her physique, savoring every bit of praise as if they were compliments for him.

"Isn't she tremendous?" he'd ask tactlessly, his voice tinged with a paternal pride veering into possessiveness. "The most beautiful woman in the room, and she's mine."

She was the embodiment of his descendant aspirations, a living testament to his delusions of genetic superiority, and she never thought up a cosmetic enhancement he was unenthusiastic paying for from her adolescence onward. In his mind she represented the pinnacle of feminine beauty and charm, a reflection of his own greatness that shined even greater next to his regretfully unimpressive sons, Don Jr. and Eric. If only he could go back in time, he often daydreamed, and give Don Jr. a different name so he could save his eponymous birthright for his beloved daughter, who he'd have named "Donaldina" instead of honoring his first wife Ivana with the name "Ivanka."

"She has such great legs, doesn't she?" he'd ask, while his golfing partners would awkwardly shift their weight from leg to leg, and try unsuccessfully to change the subject. "And what a chest! One of the great chests, maybe of all time. How lucky her kids were as babies. And fetuses. What a tremendous womb. What I'd pay to be able to spend a day in that womb!"

In conversations behind his back, his guests remarked and satirized upon the inappropriate infatuation. Whispers of forbidden love and gossip grew into a mystique surrounding the Trump family, and the city socialites often debated theories of how the Trumps might behave when in the private oases of their sprawling, ostentatious penthouse properties.

The gossipers could only agree on two apparent facts: that the bond between father and daughter transcended the boundaries of societal decorum, and that Donald's years of close friendship with Jeffrey Epstein had not made him any less of a creepy perv than he was prior to their lamentable meeting.

All this Ivanka felt, and she struggled with the public knowledge of and disgust in her father's Epsteinian debauchery: the predatory beauty pageants, sexual assault allegations and lawsuits, and all his other scandalous misdeeds.

She played the part of obedient daughter and smiled for the cameras, but, beneath her composed exterior, she grappled with her father's disconcerting reputation, and its effect on her social standing, as Ivanka yearned always for independence from her father.

She contemplated abandoning her maiden name to forge a new legacy with her less dysfunctional—and much less damned and nationally destructive—in-law family to free herself from the nepotistic albatross that was the Trump name. Could an Ivanka Kushner buy her way back into the New York City elite milieu, and escape socially her father's belligerent and abhorrent political career? She thankfully had $2 billion in Saudi money to try.

But, in the meantime, perhaps Donald might at last realize he has unwittingly stifled his daughter, and must cease his objectifications. Maybe in time, father and daughter will find a new balance in their relationship, built not on appearances or lust, but on respect and familial love. And maybe Donald would come clean about all the sex offender stuff he did with Epstein.

Or perhaps their secrets and the constraints of their world would become too much to bear, and the house of incestually ambiguous cards they labored on would come crashing down from the weight of shame and humiliation.

Either way, the story of Donald and Ivanka will forever be shrouded in speculation, a mystery that will never be fully unraveled.

Trump's Presidential Library Just Opened, And It's Odd

Palm Springs, FL
October 24, 2023—

The official President Donald Trump Library in Palm Springs, Florida, has finally opened its doors, though it's quite unique for a presidential library.

In lieu of the traditional trove of official records and archival documents, Trump's presidential library just has a plaque on the wall that says, "Everything I did was perfect, legal, better than Obama, and sexy."

Most of the interior space was taken up by a *McDonald's* restaurant, which had a framed photograph on the wall of Donald Trump eating the very first *Filet-O-Fish* sandwich fried in the building.

There was very little inside that could be described as literary, but there was one bookshelf that featured the following books for sale authored by various personalities in Trump's political orbit:

- Josh Hawley—*Beating Off Satan: How To Defeat Masturbation And Live A Christian Life Without Erecting Temptation*

- Ivanka Trump—*A Woman In Business: How I Rose Above Pervasive Sexual Harassment From My Boss, My Dad*

- Kevin McCarthy—*Augustus of the House: The Speaker McCarthy Story*
[Abandoned project because he only finished the introduction before losing the Speaker's gavel]

- Matt Gaetz—*Me & Nestor: Setting The Record Straight On Why My Adopting Him Wasn't Weird At All*

- Ted Cruz—*Texas Hold 'Em**
[A rip-off of the show House of Cards featuring himself as he engineers his way to the presidency with a gratuitous amount of cheating on his wife and strangling dogs]

- Nikki Haley—*How I'm Different But Also The Exact Same As Donald Trump*

- Donald Trump Jr.—*I Love You, Dad: A Memoir On Ways My Dad Showed He Loved Me, Even If He Never Said It*

- Elaine Chao—S*enate Kama Sutra: 100 Illustrated Tantric Lessons I Learned On Erotic Passion With My Magnificent Lover, Senate Majority Leader Mitch McConnell*

- Kimberly Guilfoyle: *The Real Housewives Of Mar-a-Lago*

- Mike Pence—*Hanging WITH Mike Pence: An Inside Look At The Former VP's Life And Political Career*

- Mike Lindell—*Irrefutable Proof The Election Was Rigged*

[Originally slated for release in March 2021, then delayed until September 2021, then January 1st 2022, then July 4th 2022, then January 1st 2023, and now slated for release in October 2024]

- Rudy Giuliani—*Scotch, A Lawyer's Best Friend: Prose Poems About being Donald Trump's Lawyer, My Alien Abductions, And The Joy Of Putting One's Hand In His Pants*

- Jared Kushner—*A Jew In Saudi Arabia Screwing The Palestinians*

- Mitch McConnell—*The Complete Field Guide On Freshwater Turtles Of Eastern Kentucky*

- Sarah Huckabee Sanders—*Great Lecterns: A Coffee Table Book On Lecterns I Definitely Didn't Buy In Schemes To Launder Money To My Corrupt Friends So There's No Reason To Even Check*

- Lindsey Graham—*How I Would Kill Ted Cruz To Get Away With It*

- Melania Trump—*Becoming Melania**

[Not to be confused with Michelle Obama's book titled, "Becoming"]

- Elizabeth Markowitz, former White House Executive Chef for Donald Trump—*The Art Of The Meal: An Unauthorized Tell-All About Our Former President's Most Disturbing Eating Habits*

- Stephen Miller—*Homemade Taxidermy: A Complete Guide On Killing, Gutting, Skinning, Stuffing, And Displaying Various Animals*

- Paul Ryan—*Jellyfish: The Wisdom Of Nature's Spineless Beauties*

- Barron Trump—*Damning Secrets About My Dad My Mom Told Me In Case He's Thinking About Taking Me Out Of His Will**

[Publication date pending]

Nancy Pelosi's Hatred Of Donald Trump Is An Aesthetic

November 14, 2023
Washington D.C—

Nancy Pelosi accidentally ranted this (or should have) on a hot mic this morning:

"I hope I die before Donald Trump so I can personally grab that rapey, wretched ogre by his pathetic combover in one hand, and his shriveled up raisin balls in the other, and then drag him to Hell myself. That would be Heavenly for me. Seeing that mob boss aspirant finally pay penance for his lifetime of deplorable pettiness and disturbed narcissism is all I ask for from God. America needs a shower after the way he behaved and diminished himself and the Office of the Presidency. What an undignified four years for our great nation. Watching Donald's tiny, little, vulgarian sausage fingers smear the tears streaming out of his eyes all over his ridiculous, orange orangutan face as he realizes he has earned himself an eternity of suffering would be like a poolside vacation for me. Get me a cocktail, and make it a triple! No one has had it coming more than Donald. It's an abomination he calls himself a Christian, and that anyone believes him. Or that anyone thinks he's capable of 4D chess. I've sat across from him at many tables, and he is quite likely the stupidest person I've ever met. The dumbest president we've ever had for sure. No president has ever been so belligerent, so dense, and such an oblivious pushover for all the horrible people he surrounds himself with. They convince him of all kinds of nutty things. They can convince him of anything if they just say his name in every sentence, say 'sir' a lot, or tell him how much everyone is talking about what a handsome genius he is. This simpleton pleasure of being complimented means he only remembers the last thing someone told him, so he's wildly inconsistent in dealmaking, and irrational in his political tactics and strategies. If anything, those are his best qualities, though, because his superficial attention span keeps him from following through on the truly petulant and unAmerican policy ideas he attaches himself to. Honestly, I did not think it was possible to loathe a person so much as I detest every physical and emotional facet of that crackpot, wannabe dictator. He has no appreciation for American values, or geopolitical interests. Democracy, rule of law, blind justice, human rights, equality, diversity, free speech criticism, journalistic integrity… he hates them all! He's constantly dehumanizing his political opponents, and have you noticed he's been using the word 'vermin' a lot. But he always projects like a sociopath. He's done corrupt sh*t for years, his money is all dirty, and he has only dealt with other rats and lowlifes his whole inherited business career. Which is how you can tell he's a real fascist. He's only in it for himself at the end of the day. Everything and everybody else is expendable or collateral damage for his vainglory. He's obsessed with the idea of Donald Trump, so the people he claims he's fighting for are not getting anything from him. Regular people's lives will not improve in any tangible ways just because other people might be deported, or abused, or maligned. They get nothing but tiny, addictive, culture war dopamine hits when Trump says offensive things to make liberals and Democrats mad. And Donald has no interest in them or respect for them whatsoever outside of using them for whatever political or financial short-term opportunism his lizard brain thinks up. He's simply the worst American in this entire country. He literally wants to start new concentration camps to round up and deport immigrants. What an American idea! When in history have concentration camps ever been a thing a country was ever been proud of doing in the past? Logistically his deportation vows will be a bureaucratic nightmare as well as a political travesty. It will be a legal black hole because where will they go? What other country will take millions of people Trump doesn't want, and is scapegoating as criminals? Think Trump's lackey Nazis aren't going to concoct bogus security concerns and strong-arm the courts into letting them send their political opponents too? He's telling it out loud to his rallies talking about vengeance and retribution! And he's calling all Democrats and liberals 'communists' to demonize them and otherize them, which is just precious given how often he fawns over how manly, strong, and tough Xi Jinping is. Last time I checked, China was communist! Meanwhile, his brownshirt fanboys are devising ways to capture minority-power over the majority with Project 2025! It's like for this election campaign Donald and all his emotionally crippled MAGA fans have decided to stop filtering their psychological ids at all. It's textbook Nazi stuff. If he wins in 2024, we are so f***ed. Welcome to 19-f*cking-33! He's going to put in the same, awful creeps as last time, and a whole bunch of new ones! Yeesh! Stephen Miller just gives me the creeps. He's like if Goebbels had a love child with Nosferatu. And he's gonna have hundreds of newer, even more committed, weirdo lunatics orbiting around him salivating for their own opportunities to ride his coattails and grift the MAGA rubes for easy cash and political power. Donald is dumb, indecisive, functionally illiterate, and perennially unprepared, so his underlings will take an inch of his vague, platitude-level suggestions and half-witted requests, and then run a mile with their own fascist wet dreams of brutish and barbaric, wanton cruelty. And they'll all manipulate Donald to greater levels of autocratic infamy because he's a sucker for pavlovian praise, so his second administration will be an even bigger fascist sh*tstain in American history than the first one. All because Donald wasn't loved as a child, and has been emotionally stunted ever since. As a mother and grandmother, I know a toddler when I see one. Dealing with Donald in the White House challenged my patience more than any of my kids or grandkids, and, frankly, his diapers needed changing more often. Wait… is this mic still on? Oh, dear. Oh, well. I didn't say anything I don't 100% stand by."

God Says He "Can't Even Right Now" With MAGA Fans

December 11, 2023
Heaven—

The Halfway Post had a brief talk with God today, lightly edited for clarity:

THP: Hey, God, how is everything going?

GOD: Great, thanks for asking! You know, no one ever asks how I'm doing. Everyone prays to Me and tells Me about their problems, but no one ever stops to concern themselves with My problems.

THP: I suppose we think You don't have any problems because You're God.

GOD: The entire universe is My problem! Running everything is hard work because I'm not actually totally omnipotent, you know? To be honest, I'm barely keeping things together! You know how archaic the source code for the universe has gotten all these millennia after Creation? That's why things have been going haywire since 2016. It's starting to spin out of control. No offense, but it's kind of past time for another Flood. Time to just start over. Earth right now is beyond My powers. That omnipotence rumor though is a hoot. No idea where that came from, but it's not like I can just snap My fingers and make anything I want happen like a lot of Christians believe. I mean, if I could, I'd have to be the biggest psychopath in the universe, wouldn't I? If I could just snap My fingers and make baby cancer go away, but I don't do it? Or immediately stop people from ever abusing puppies again? Or stop incels from shooting up elementary schools with AR-15s? And omnipotence is just one of the crazy, made up things Christians believe about Me. For instance, let Me correct the record by saying that I'm definitely not all-loving. There's eight billion humans! Why would someone ever think I love every single one of them? Todd Wilson from Akron, Ohio? I have to love Todd f*cking Wilson from Akron, f*cking Ohio? F*ck Todd Wilson, and f*ck Akron, Ohio! You think I loved John Wayne Gacy? I love Ted Cruz? No one loves Ted Cruz! The only omni power I have is omniscience. I see everything. Which is depressing because every day I see My loudest, most annoying followers, conservative Evangelicals, utterly fail the most basic test of character by defending that ridiculous, orange, orangutan clown with a used car salesman personality—nope, not getting into it today! I won't get upset today!"

[God then gave me an ∞-mg edible, and He took me to His latest planetary creation, which He is calling "Boob World," which is about what it sounds like.]

10 Tips For Donald Trump On How To Avoid Raping Women And Getting Sued For Millions For Defaming Them After

1. If you find a woman alone in a dressing room, elevator, or any other place, just don't "move on her like a bitch," as you say, and grope her.

2. If your half century of popping Tic Tacs gives you a Pavlovian urge to sexually assault women nearby, switch to a different mint or candy treat that does not have the same conditioning effect on you.

3. If your best friend invites you to parties with underage girls that he pays for sexual favors, stop attending his parties, flying to his private island, or just stop being friends with him altogether. Remember you are who you surround yourself with.

4. Focus on your financial goals. If you really concentrate on saving your money for your goal of getting higher on the *Forbes* list of billionaires, you'll likely decide it's not worth it to risk paying any other lawsuits for tens of millions of dollars for raping women and defaming them.

5. If taking women out furniture shopping makes you uncontrollably horny, let women buy their own furniture from now on.

6. When out in public, occasionally remind yourself that other people do not like to hear dirty men say "locker room talk" or sexually suggestive things about their own daughters.

7. If you host beauty pageants, put coded locks on the doors of the women's locker rooms and bathrooms, and instruct staff not to tell you the code. And, if they're teenagers, remind yourself verbally aloud that it's an even bigger crime to go snooping in there.

8. Always go out with a friend, someone big and strong, to accompany you and help physically restrain you from assaulting women.

9. Consider no longer carrying blank non-disclosure agreements with you everywhere you go. If it's a hassle to find a printer nearby in order to print out a quick NDA, that could be enough of an obstacle to help you decide it's too much effort to do any assaulting.

10. Wear big winter gloves or boxing gloves on your hands at all times so even if you feel the sudden urge to grab women by the pussy you literally can't.

Local Christian Is Oblivious His Christmas Trees Is Pagan

December 14, 2023
Dayton, OH—

Local Evangelical Chris Bradshaw is now a three-time winner of his neighborhood's annual Christmas Tree Competition for "Best-In-Show," and he spent the morning looking at his Christmas tree making some last-minute ornament rearrangements and adjustments to the colored light strands to improve the tree's glow.

"I just love Christmas, and the reminder that our lord and savior, sweet Baby Jesus, came to the world on this day to die for our sins and free mankind from the torment and suffering of Hell," Bradshaw explained. "And there's no part I love more than having a big Christmas tree lighting up my living room. When I was growing up, my family only ever could afford a small tree, so I promised myself that when I had my own place and my own family I would have the best, most beautiful Christmas tree in the neighborhood to really show off my love and faith in Jesus, and Evangelize my Christian faith to the whole town. And that's a promise I have kept."

On the mantle above the Bradshaw family's fireplace was a display of the three Christmas tree trophies they had had won.

"I just love how Christian our Christmas traditions are, and how they're totally reverent to God, Jesus, the Virgin Mary, Joseph, the Three Wise Men, and of Christianity in general. Yep, there is certainly nothing pagan about Christmas trees. Nothing pagan at all! There's just no way the symbolism of contemporary Christians bringing a giant tree into the house had anything to do with, say, ancient Egyptians using green palms to worship Ra. And it doesn't bear any resemblance to ancient Romans using fir trees to celebrate Saturnalia. And Christmas trees are the furthest thing from all the pagan Scandinavian Vikings in the single-digit centuries worshipping Thor and their other deities via oak trees—no way! Christmas trees are an original Christian concept. Definitely not some kind of casual adoption of eternal ancient rituals revolving around the end of the farming season near the day of winter solstice appropriated into Christianity to more easily convert pagans with comfortable and familiar numinous customs with which pagans around the world across many different cultures and societies were already worshipping. No siree! And I'm sure the whole tradition of gift-giving has nothing to do with the Roman custom of giving gifts during the peak of their December holiday season, or the gift-giving of the Germanic tribes north of the Roman Empire. I bet the character of Santa Claus and his original eight reindeer that Rudolph gets added to have no pagan predecessor either. Nope, definitely no relation to the Norse god Odin, who dispensed gifts to children on his eight-legged horse Sleipnir, and who the children would leave out carrots and hay for in their boots left out in front of the chimney in exchange for candy. And I don't believe for a second that all the Christmas carols have their roots in traditions of singing for and with one's neighbors that go beyond recorded history, and include the tradition of villagers trekking into nearby forests singing to wake up the sleeping trees and induce the coming of spring and a bountiful harvest for the next year. I bet the evolution of Christmas carols developed unrelated to the Anglo-Saxons tradition of trekking from house to house wassailing, and exchanging gulps of alcoholic drinks for money. And who doesn't love putting up mistletoe in the house? There's no way mistletoe was a familiar plant with great significance for peace and love in the pre-Christian world ranging from Rome all the way to the Celts and Norse druids. And always make sure to put up holly and wreaths on all your doors. There's no way that's a custom that was appropriated from Rome's Saturnalia! And all the Christmas iconography we're so nostalgic for today isn't, if you think about it, that closely sourced from Charles Dickens's fictional *A Christmas Carol*. And the fat, white haired and bearded Santa dressed in all red has definitely not caught on from successful, secular corporate advertising and seasonal marketing campaigns capitalistically innovating how to appropriate religious sentiments to manufacture economically profitable nostalgia and culturally pressure us to spend a lot of money buying a bunch of various products for ourselves and our families and friends for the holidays. And I will never believe for a second that lots of Biblically contemporary and even earlier cultures and religious cults detailed cosmically miraculous, prophesied virgin births. Only Christianity! Yep, Christmas must be the most original holiday ever invented, untainted and unvarnished by any and all pagan influences. Totally sui generis! Now, if you'll excuse me, me and my family are going to go eat a yule log. I don't know where the word 'yule' comes from, but I'm sure it wasn't pagan at all, and it definitely is derived from some custom native solely to the United States of America!"

Congratulations on another award-winning Christmas tree, Chris.

Donald Trump Had To Be Physically Restrained Today In Court

December 16, 2023
Washington D.C—

Donald Trump was restrained and held in contempt of court today for a plethora of behavioral problems.

Throughout the day's proceedings, Mr. Trump reportedly shouted out the following derogatory insults at the various witnesses testifying against him: "rat," "vermin," "traitor," "enemy of the people," "nasty period lady," "ugly," "fugly," "looks like a dog," "lower than a dog," "horse face," and "evil Trump hater who is clearly on the rag right now."

He also audibly told his lawyers during brief recesses, "I'm going to kill Mark Meadows if he flips on me," and "I'll choke out Rudy Giuliani if he rats on me like I choked out those Secret Service drivers who wouldn't take me to the Capitol on January 6th to lead the coup in person—oops, did I just say that inside thought out loud? Fake news! I didn't say it! It can't be used against me! I plead the Fifth!"

At one point, Trump suddenly got out of his seat, beelined for the witness stand, and had to be restrained by the bailiff and another two security officers while trying to slap a witness who suggested the prosecution should have Ivanka testify because she was present on January 6th, and she had even joined the chorus of voices of Trump Administration officials personally begging him to post a tweet that would direct the insurrectionists to go home on that fateful day.

"Keep Ivanka's name out of your f***ing mouth," Trump shouted over and over—in the style of Will Smith's Oscars outburst—until the police officers handcuffed him to his chair behind the defense table.

However, Trump did have one more outburst, and charged at the witness stand after he was apparently able to slip his short-fingered hands out of the handcuffs. He had to be grabbed and restrained once more, and forcibly dragged back to his seat as the judge yelled out he was willing to tranquilize Trump if he continued to disgrace the courtroom with such "brutish displays of animalistic irrationality."

Trump's hands again, and now his legs, were restrained to his chair with zip ties. Trump's lawyers suggested to the jury that Trump was clearly showing signs of temporary insanity, a condition that has plagued him since before

January 6th, 2021, and that therefore Trump could not be held accountable for the insurrection attempt. This made Trump irate, and call for a recess so he could berate his lawyers for insinuating he was mentally unstable, but the recess request was denied by the judge. After that, Trump began to repeatedly fart audibly, apparently no longer caring to conceal his already smellable flatulence.

Trump sat quietly for a moment before asking the judge if he could update something for the courtroom record. The judge allowed him, and Trump announced that if he was, hypothetically, going to get tranquilized, he wanted the record to state that he weighed only 165 pounds, and the dosage of tranquilization should be set appropriately. He paused for a moment, and then shouted out that, if his hair got messed up at any point during the tranquilization, the judge would be "crossing a red line."

A few moments later, another witness took the stand, and Trump muttered "rat" several more times under his breath. As the judge threatened to duct tape his mouth shut, Trump managed to again slip his small hands free, pulling them out of the zip ties, and he attempted another charge at the witness stand. However, his legs were still zip-tied so he fell to the floor banging the legs of his chair against the corner leg of the defense table as he tried to drag himself toward the front of the courtroom while screaming that the witness was "only a coffee boy." Finally, the bailiff tased Trump in the back, and he cried out in pain and whimpered for a moment.

The judge asked Trump if he would now sit quietly, and stop obstructing the court proceedings. Trump slowly nodded his head, but muttered one last time to himself, "It's rigged against me anyway," which made the judge furiously yell out that Trump had the emotional maturity of a sociopathic toddler.

The judge ordered the bailiff to raise the tranquilization level up for a 500-pound person. He then warned Trump that if he interrupted the courtroom one more time he'd tranquilize Trump at the level of a baby elephant, put him in a straightjacket, and get a mouth restraint.

"You're going to look in the courtroom sketches for all of history like Hannibal Lecter, is that what you want?" the judge shouted at him. "To look like some tied up ogre monster from the medieval era? Pull those new zip ties as hard as you can, and double them up!" he ordered the bailiff. "If you say one more word I, swear to God and the Constitution of the United States I will tranquilize you myself! Just shut your goddamn orangutan mouth!"

Trump's face drained its color turning a pallid white at the thought of being recorded in history books forever as the Hannibal Lecter president.

The judge then apologized to the courtroom for swearing, and apologized to the jury for having to sit through such a dysfunctional trial. He turned his attention to Trump, and asked if Trump would behave himself according to the decorum demanded by his former office as well as the US justice system.

Trump's voice quivered as he said he'd be quiet now, and then asked if he could get another *Diet Coke*. The judge said Trump was wasting too much of the court's time requesting a *Diet Coke* so many times each hour, but Trump's lawyers objected, explaining that Trump had a physiological dependence on *Diet Coke* after having drunk hundreds of cans of it every week for decades since the drink was launched in 1982.

"The defendant will very soon begin suffering debilitating withdrawal symptoms, and his participation in this trial will be severely impacted," warned Trump's lead lawyer.

Just as the lawyer finished speaking, Trump's eyes rolled back and he slumped in his chair. He began foaming at the mouth, and made gurgling sounds in the back of his throat.

"Get... me... aspartame..." Trump mumbled and moaned as he began shaking in an apparent seizure.

"Oh, all right!" shouted the judge, and the bailiff brought Trump a *Diet Coke* can. He popped open the tab, and the sound perked Trump back up.

"Gimme! Gimme!" Trump shouted, "Bring it to my lips! Faster!" He mumbled for the bailiff to keep pouring it for him as his hands tried but failed to squeeze out of the zip ties. Trump drank half the can before spilling some down the front of his suit, and he burped up a bit. "This is why all my counter-suits and appeals have specified very clearly that I need a *Diet Coke* exactly every 18.3 minutes!" he shouted. My doctor says if I have to wait until a full half hour my heart will explode!"

Immediately the color returned to Trump's face at the edges of his orange clown foundation, and he leaned over and wiped off the sweat from his forehead on his assistant lawyer's shoulder. A streak of orange remained on her pantsuit jacket.

"Hey, lady," he asked her, "did you bring any of daddy's blue nose pills? Gimme, gimme! Hey, by the way, does this judge look Mexican to you?"

"Tase him!" shouted the judge, and the bailiff complied. Trump spent the rest of the day in court unconscious and passing gas occasionally.

Let's Keep #TrumpSmells Going For All Of 2024!

Let's remember it's widely agreed Trump smells like a dying old man whose *Big Mac* sauce-drowned organs are rotting from the inside out, and get it going viral for the rest of the year like it has been this last week of 2023. It's an amusing way to fight back against Trump's pugilistic egomania of sociopathic narcissism as he threatens to make himself a dictator:

- Donald Trump just claimed his body odor "is protected by presidential immunity."
- Trump claims the rumors about him smelling bad are both "fake news" and classified, and the leakers should be shot.
- Trump just interrupted a private Christmas Eve party at Mar-a-Lago to claim the generals used to come up to him with tears in their eyes and say, "Sir, you were the best smelling president of all time."
- Trump was reportedly asked to sign his signature on used diapers by several trolling Gen Z teens at Mar-a-Lago tonight.
- Mar-a-Lago employees say over 20,000 diapers have been mailed to Trump's resort since #TrumpSmells started trending on *Twitter*.
- Kellyanne Conway claims Trump doesn't smell like sh*t, he just has "alternative scents."
- The DNC is now selling hats, shirts, cologne, deodorant, and perfume products with the label "Make Presidents Smell Nice Again."
- Trump's non-disclosure agreements going back to the early 90s have included a clause mandating signees can't ever mention his "spoiled-roast-beef-esque" body odor in public.
- Trump reportedly hates NATO and wants to pull the US out of the alliance because the prime minister of Belgium told him he needed some deodorant and a mint during a 2017 NATO summit.
- Melania Trump laughed publicly for the first time ever on camera after being asked if her husband smelled bad, and she laughed for 19 seconds straight before she started gasping for air and swearing that she didn't hear the question.
- Trump reportedly smelled so bad during a G7 meeting in 2019 that he made Shinzo Abe and Angela Merkel, who were sitting on either side of him, both vomit.
- Trump reportedly smells so bad because he doesn't like seeing himself naked, and only showers once a week after looking at himself in the mirror and shouting out loud, "Fake news!"
- Following the viral week of #TrumpSmells, Joe Biden has begun his answer to every question the media has asked him about Trump with the phrase, "Well, that depends."
- Trump just installed a chimpanzee exhibit at Mar-a-Lago so he can blame the stench always surrounding him on the apes.

The Top Reasons MAGA Fans Are Beginning To Lose Faith In Donald Trump

January 1, 2024
Washington D.C.—

The following are reasons why MAGA Republicans are actually souring on the idea of a second Trump term:

- Two of Trump's three wives were immigrants who chain-migrated their families to America

- Most of Trump's kids have "immigrant-poisoned blood"

- Ivanka married a Jew and converted, and have visited Israel like "total globalists"

- Trump regularly confuses Jesus with Odysseus and Heracles from Greek mythology

- Trump regularly confuses Jesus with Abraham, Noah, and Moses from the *Old Testament*

- His wife Melania's reptilian eyes give her away as an extra-terrestrial shapeshifter, and no one knows what she's manipulating Trump into thinking and doing when they're alone together

- Trump's friendship with Jeffrey Epstein was very close, long, and icky

- Trump has been accusing, with no evidence, fellow Republicans Ron DeSantis, Nikki Haley, and Chris Christie of rigging the GOP primaries well before any voting has begun

- The speed with which Trump has attacked the rumors that he smells like 6-day-old, rotting roast beef sandwiches left out in the sun suggests almost certainly that the rumors are true

- It's pretty obvious looking at his pants that he wears diapers underneath

- Trump desecrated Christmas by telling the majority of America to "rot in Hell" in a Christmas morning social media post

- An originalist interpretation of the Constitution that Republicans have always enshrined as sacred does pretty blatantly suggest Trump is

- disqualified from running for president after inciting an insurrection against the government

- A lot of visual evidence lends credence to the allegation that Trump is suffering from dementia, and his health likely won't last a full four years as president

- Biden is building more of the wall on the Mexican border than Trump

- It's hard to deny Trump is a sex criminal when he has been found guilty of defaming a woman he sexual assaulted by a jury of his peers

- The recession everyone swore Biden would cause never happened

- Biden's stock market records are now noticeably higher than Trump's stock market records

- America is drilling more oil under Biden than it did under Trump

- Gas prices have gotten pretty low now under Biden

- Biden got several infrastructure plans passed despite all of Trump's fruitless "infrastructure weeks"

- Trump just won't shut up about 2020

- Stephen Miller is going to get another high job in a second Trump term, and there's just no way to sugarcoat the fact that Stephen Miller is a disturbed freak

- The last three years have been a wonderful break from constant political controversy and stress every time we wake up and grab our phones without worrying if the US president spent the night pulling the US out of NATO, or calling another murderer dictator his lover, or started feuding with a random actress for calling him "emotionally unstable"

- The NFTs Trump is selling are drawn with incredibly bad taste

- It's kind of noticeably weird that Melania just disappears from public view for months at a time and is never seen with her husband

- Trump won't shut up about windmills and water pressure

I'm Donald Trump's Lawyer, And, Yes, Our Legal Argument Is, In Fact, That All Presidents, Including Joe Biden Right Now, Can Murder With Impunity

January 9, 2024
Washington D.C.—

Hi, Donald Trump's lawyer here! You know, the one who recently claimed in a courtroom that a president could order S.E.A.L. Team 6 to assassinate all his political enemies, and not be subject to a criminal prosecution unless he was first impeached and politically convicted by Congress. And I mean it!

This may sound like the president is utterly above the law, and can go around murdering anyone and everyone he wants, but nothing is further from the truth. The Constitution has brilliantly included the check and balance on limitless executive branch killing sprees with the Congressional power to impeach and convict the president at any time.

The partisan Democratic Senate may decide they appreciate the political benefits of genocide against Republicans, and choose to look the other way from Biden's reign of terror as he dismembers the hundreds of Republican members of Congress and all their red state governors' replacement choices until Congress is made up 100% of Democrats, but, Constitutionally, that's Senate Majority Leader Chuck Schumer and his majority's prerogative!

If any Democrats are repulsed by the bloodthirstiness, Biden could carefully choose a few assassinations of dissenting Democratic senators to ensure the rest of the Democratic caucus falls in line. That's likely what a reelected President Trump would do—and Constitutionally could!

Such power is described right in the name of the executive branch: the president has the responsibility to "execute" the law, and—if you ask *Webster's Dictionary*—people!

In fact, ALL presidents have had the privilege to commit any crimes they want. It's not my client Donald Trump's fault that the 44 presidents before him from George Washington to Barack Obama were so unimaginative regarding the awesome powers the Office of the Presidency permits.

John Adams could have strangled Thomas Jefferson after he became the first president to lose reelection. Herbert Hoover could have offered to wheel FDR around for a little bit in his wheelchair, and then pushed him in the way of an oncoming train. Richard Nixon could have purged the entire

Department of Justice to get back his secret White House tapes. Unless their respective Senates would have convicted them in impeachment trials, they could have gotten away with it!

My critics may scoff at my legal reasoning, but the Constitution is squarely on my side. It is absolutely clear that Joe Biden can drop a nuclear bomb on Mar-a-Lago, or shoot Donald Trump and eat his corpse on live television with no consequences unless Congress removes him from office. Even if Mr. Biden murdered me and my entire family, and smeared our blood all over his naked body as a warning to the rest of my legal profession not to get in his way, I'd spend my afterlife arguing like a broken record it was perfectly within his presidential authority. My ghost would beam with eternal pride knowing I died defending the Constitution!

And if Mr. Biden was somehow convicted in the Senate without first decapitating all the yea voters, it's obvious he couldn't then be prosecuted in a federal court after the fact because Trump's other legal defense theories have made it crystal clear that former presidents cannot be held accountable for anything they did while carrying out their responsibilities of the office they held.

Besides, it would be double jeopardy to try Biden for mass murder AFTER he was already impeached for it. Biden would be totally free to go back home and spend his remaining days relaxing with Jill, his kids, and grandkids… unless, of course, one of his successor presidents decide to send S.E.A.L. Team 6 to Delaware!

So, as you can see, the power to hold presidents accountable for crimes stands only with Congress, which is why my client, Donald Trump, absolutely cannot be punished for hoarding classified documents, inciting an insurrectionist coup attempt, or any of the other felonies for which he's currently being prosecuted. Are some of his actions literal crimes for regular people? Yes, of course! For presidents, though? Only if two-thirds of the Senate says so!

But neither of Trump's impeachments resulted in a conviction, so everything he did as president was necessarily legitimate and legally sound. Trump was just innocently executing his presidential duties and responsibilities by attempting to overthrow the election, and there's absolutely nothing any of these Trump-hating prosecutors, judges, or juries can do now to change that.

In fact, the only thing my client has to worry about at all is Dark Brandon liquidating his likely 2024 general election opponent before voting begins, which, again, Biden is free to do until at least January 20th, 2025!

Things The State Of New York Is Considering To Do With Trump Tower After It's Confiscated To Pay Off His $370 Million Fine For Business Fraud

January 16, 2024
New York City, NY—

- Sell Trump's penthouse on the top 3 floors to Hillary Clinton so she can turn it into a rooftop bar called "The Lock Him Up Lounge"
- Turn it into a hotel for housing all the migrants that red state governors keep bussing to New York
- Turn it into a "Museum of the Cultural Contributions of Mexican-Americans"
- Rename it the as the "War Hero John McCain Hospital For Wounded Veterans"
- Put a wind turbine on the top, and convert the entire building's power system to run purely off wind power
- Build a "Hall of Fame of Golf Cheaters" on the 45th floor featuring an entire wing dedicated to Trump's cheating accomplishments
- Build a "Hall of Fame of Bald Americans" on the 45th floor honoring Trump as having the "#1 Combover Of All Time"
- Turn it into a giant Black church
- Build a walk-through gallery featuring all the Emmy, Grammy, Oscar, and Tony award-winning artists Trump has called "overrated"
- Host Ivanka-Trump-At-Age-15 look-alike contests, and slowly torture Trump by refusing him entry when he begs and pleads to be allowed in
- Install a 10-foot statue of Mike Pence in the front lobby with a plaque saying "Hero of the Constitution"
- Turn the ground floor into an adult diaper outlet store
- Host children's cancer charity fundraisers… for free
- Increase the rent on all of Trump's current Russian and Chinese tenants exponentially until both countries have to abandon their spy offices there
- Turn it into a museum on the history of windmills
- Lease several floors to the Department of Health and Human Services to move all the offices overseeing Obamacare there
- Lease several floors to the IRS for a special agency division dedicated specifically to suing billionaire tax cheats
- Let Jack Smith have all the office space he needs rent-free until Trump is convicted for his ninety-one felony counts across four indictments
- Turn the first few floors into the "Letitia James State of New York Courthouse"
- Rename it the "E. Jean Carroll Tower For Victims Of Sexual Assault"

Donald Trump's Rallies Have Hit A New Embarrassing Low Of Cognitive Decline And Symptoms Of Dementia

January 27, 2024
Cheshire, NH—

Yesterday, in a New Hampshire rally, Donald Trump:

- Told his fans to quit their jobs for the next year so the unemployment rate goes up and Biden looks bad.

- Told his fans to take their money out of the stock market so the stock market crashes and Biden looks bad.

- Told his fans who are on Obamacare to stop insuring their health to make Obama look bad.

- Told his fans to not get any of the high-paying, unionized jobs at any of the new factories or manufacturing plants funded by Biden's legislative achievements on infrastructure and green technology to make Biden look bad.

- Told his fans they need to start planning now to get their elderly relatives ready to vote for him in November, no matter how much the exertion might kill them, and he said he was sure all the elderly had lived big, long, beautiful lives, and would all be happy to die contributing to his election victory so he can get back in the presidency to pardon himself and not have to go to prison.

- Told his elderly fans to put him in their wills, and donate their houses, cars, or other valuable property to his presidential campaign or the Trump Organization

- Told his voters to buy his upcoming batch of NFTs featuring him as the various 12 Greek gods, and then ranted about how hot the female versions of him as the goddesses are, and how giant their breasts are. He said he always thought he'd have been one of the great beauties of all time if he had been a girl, and he cited his daughter Ivanka's physical attributes to describe how his own body would have looked. He then discussed his "big Trump brain," and reminded the audience he had gone to Wharton. He also said he didn't need college, and he had been smarter than everyone else around him, even the professors, and he knew it because he said he paid someone else to take his SATs, and no one figured it out, and he paid other students to do all his homework and take all his tests. He said that's how you know he's a genius at business: because he spent 10x more money for his degree than everyone else. He reiterated many times he could guarantee each individual NFT that his fans buy will be worth $1 million "two weeks after his next inauguration," and that he has only the best of the best people working for him on his NFTs. He interspersed his rant multiple times by repeatedly insisting his NFTs were "definitely not a pump and dump scheme."

- Then he mentioned windmills out of nowhere, and went hard on that subject for six minutes pledging to knock down every wind turbine in America. He said he felt very sorry for all the ruined views in "Real America" because of socialist wind turbines, and he felt even sorrier for all the dead birds. Then he said he felt bad for his dead ex-wife. He said he had actually been frequently visiting her grave on his golf course every day, and saying a little prayer for her from his golf cart between the 7th and 8th holes. He reminded the crowd he had married two Europeans. But then he said he wouldn't come to the aid of any European nations in NATO because what have they ever done for him?

- He complained about Angela Merkel in ways that appeared to suggest he thought she was still the chancellor of Germany. He said she reminded him of his mom, and he hated his mom. He paused for a moment reflectively, and then in a shocking moment of seriousness remarked that his mother's coldness had left him a scared little boy, and, no matter how old he gets, he's still just that scared little boy who never got the maternal love all children need to grow up healthy and confident. He rocked back and forth for a moment on the balance mat he now brings to his events to stand on, and softly hugged himself.

- Then he did his famous dance move with his hands and elbows that looks like he's giving two handjobs at once. When he got tired he reached for a can of *Diet Coke* stored underneath the podium, opened it, and chugged it. He asked aloud, "*Diet Coke* isn't one of the Woke ones, is it? If they go Woke and I have to boycott, I might die from withdrawal."

- Then he announced that he had a phone call with Ye (formerly Kanye West), and that Ye had been doing some rereading recently of *Mein Kampf*, and told him a few good ideas to consider, like rounding up all his enemies, and letting Stephen Miller do "medical testing" on them. Trump said he's never met anyone more interested in medical science than Stephen Miller. He said he and Stephen were a lot alike, and that when they were both little, they both liked trapping and killing small woodland creatures and neighbors' pets.

- Then he bragged about passing the dementia test with flying colors several years ago, and said he's an "awake president, unlike Sleepy Joe." He mentioned that, because Biden stole his rightful second term, he should get a third term to make up for the lost time, and he shouldn't have to actually win an election, and the election should be canceled. He said he'd win 95% of the vote anyway, so it's not worth the trouble.

- He then launched into a rant about how the media is being "so unfair" to him for accusing him of selling out Ukraine and giving up so many bargaining chips already before even starting the negotiations, but then he made a face that looked quite a lot like he defecated in his trousers. Elise Stefanik, who had been standing behind him, because the press conference was supposed to be about her confirmation hearing to become America's UN Ambassador, crinkled her nose and appeared to turn her head to her side to try and get a breath of the untainted air on the opposite side away from the direction of Trump's now likely smeared anus.

- As Trump launched back into how European leaders weren't spending anywhere near as much money at his hotels and golf courses as the Russians, Chinese, Israelis, and Saudis, he began to awkwardly shift weight from leg to leg. It was somewhat obvious from the expression on his face and his tensing eyebrow muscles he was trying to assess the fecal damage. He grimaced, apparently feeling the excretion begin to pool in the bottom of his diaper.

- Then Trump was startled by Stefanik leaning over and throwing up on the ground behind him. She quickly wiped her mouth on her pantsuit sleeve, and then leaned back up with two thumbs-up gestures. Trump looked at the splashed vomit and got squeamish, and ordered someone to come clean up the mess. "Why do women always do this around me?" he asked himself loud enough for the microphone to pick up.

- Then Trump grimaced again with a facial expression that suggested he sharted yet again, and Elise Stefanik gasped, but unfortunately it appeared to make her inhale the explosion of Trump's squalid feculence, and she grabbed her throat with both hands as her tongue waved in and out of her coughing mouth. Her face turned purple as her eyes rolled back, and she began gasping for breath before collapsing to the ground.

- She gave one last audible exhale before remaining perfectly limp and still. Donald Trump's stench had killed again.

The Lord Of The Rings, If The Protagonist Hobbit Ring-Bearer Was Donaldo Trumpins

With everyone at Rivendell, Elrond announces that someone must take the Ring all the way to Mt. Doom, but Donaldo says that's way too far and has too many inclines he'd have to walk up. Donaldo asks why, if they have the Ring, they don't just use it. He says all the ring-bearers before him were idiots, and no one knows more about powerful rings than him. He then puts on the Ring after everyone tells him not to, and Sauron flatters him by telling him he's the smartest of all the Fellowship, and has the biggest, hairiest feet of all the hobbits. Donaldo says he admires Sauron's strength, and tells Sauron to send over his Ringwraiths' dragons to Rivendell to pick him up.

As the rest of the Fellowship beg him not to give the Ring to Sauron because then armies of Orcs will burn all of Middle-earth, Donaldo says he "fell in love" with Sauron, and points out that Aragorn is a killer too. He says he likes monarchy bloodlines whose Elven swords don't shatter. Then he calls Hobbiton a shithole, and says he doesn't care about saving the Shire because what have the other hobbits done for him? He announces he's going to make a big, beautiful deal with Sauron, build a giant tower with "Trumpins" written on it at the top, and all the races of Middle Earth will love it.

The Fellowship tries to restrain him and take away the Ring, but he slips it on his finger and sneaks away until the Ringwraiths find him. Donaldo keeps the Ring on so Sauron's big eye has to see him, and he starts to annoy the Dark Lord on the ride to Mordor asking if the prostitutes in Mordor are any good, claiming Gandalf is sleepy and brain-dead and never leaves his dungeon basement, and complaining how the Shire has way too many windmills.

Donaldo thus brings the Ring directly to Barad-dûr, and calls Sauron a genius for raising such a huge Orc army. Sauron lets him have his "Trumpins Tower" on the condition he raises an army of Orcs of his own, but Donaldo loses interest in working immediately, and spends his time golfing with the Witch-King of Angmar until the Black Captain gets sick of Donaldo's constant cheating and lying about his scores. Sauron requests to see the quality of Donaldo's orcs, but Donaldo keeps telling him, "in two weeks."

When Sauron summons Donaldo and announces the beginning of the War of the Ring for which Donaldo will have to supply the Orcs he pledged, Donaldo lies about how many Orcs he has, exaggerating ten-fold that he's a billionaire in orcs, and exclaims how his Orcs are the best Orcs of all time, and he's one of the great Orc kings of all time, and no one does big, beautiful Orc armies like he does. But he then tells Sauron that the armor and weapons Sauron sold his Orcs were terrible so he isn't going to pay back Sauron the contracting fees for all the metal mining and blacksmithing.

When the war starts, Sauron is pissed when Donaldo's Orcs arrive late, are nowhere near the number promised, have no Orc professionalism whatsoever, and Donaldo isn't even with them. Donaldo never shows up, but, after Sauron finishes killing everyone in Gondor, Rohan, the Shire, the Dwarf mines, and, at last, the Woodland Realm and Rivendell, Donaldo shows up at the triumph feast and takes credit for the victory even though he hid in his tower the whole time. Donaldo gets furious when the story of his hiding leaks out to Mordor's newspaper, and he calls it "fake news" while demanding the leaker be found and executed.

Sauron quickly decides he has had enough of Donaldo, and banishes him from Mordor. Donaldo wanders through the ashes of Minas Tirith feeling sorry for himself and mumbling over and over, "No one has ever been treated more unfairly than me!" Then he finds Gríma Wormtongue—who Saruman let survive the war for betraying the Rohirrim by opening the gates at Edoras to let in the Uruk-hai—and Gríma starts sucking up to Donaldo, who falls immediately for Gríma's fake praise and makes him his second-in-command.

Together they hatch a plan to orchestrate a coup against Sauron, but it's very rough going. Gríma accidentally hosts a press conference at the Four Seasons Orc whorehouse instead of the Four Seasons Orc tavern, and all the Orcs learn Donaldo used to be best friends with the Shire's notorious playboy pedophile who had a secret, creepy mansion on his private island in the Brandywine River past Bywater near Frogmorton.

The last few Orcs still loyal to Donaldo are put off by his very cancelable past conduct. Then, when Donaldo refuses to pay them the wages they earned in the war, they leave him, and Donaldo's coup goes nowhere. He blames Gríma for the failure, and berates him for being a loser. Gríma erupts in anger, and shouts at Donaldo that he is not only a moron, but also a "cowardly, pathetic, clinical idiot, and narcissistic egomaniac debilitatingly incapacitated by mental and attentive incompetence." Gríma leaves with Donaldo shouting after him, "You can't quit, you're fired!" and, "You better honor the non-disclosure parchment I made you sign!"

Donaldo wanders around by himself for a bit. When it gets dark he tries to make a fire, but can't because his small hands get tired quickly from rubbing sticks together. He yells out to no one, "Fires are rigged against me!" and then lies down in the dirt to sleep. Shortly after, a stray warg follows his stench and eats him alive. Donaldo's screams briefly echo across the barren Pelennor Fields before silence returns.

Donald Trump's Complete List Of Insults For Every Other US President

On a podcast recently, Donald Trump read the names of every other US president, and then followed it with an insult:

1. **George Washington**—"George was a loser who showed such weakness refusing a third presidential term. He missed the opportunity of a lifetime to make himself King of America!"
2. **John Adams**—"John Adams was a bald little freak, and a pussy like Mike Pence for giving up the presidency to Thomas Jefferson after losing the election. Was he too poor to hire lawyers to launch hundreds of lawsuits? Too unpopular to have his followers storm the Capitol? Or were his generals just too scared to declare martial law and give him emergency dictatorial powers like mine were?"
3. **Thomas Jefferson**—"Jefferson had no talent for branding. If I were him, I would have named the Louisiana Purchase after myself! I'd have called it the Trumpiana Purchase, and charged every person living there rent for staying in my territory! He could have been rich!"
4. **James Madison**—"People always tell me I'd have made a great Founding Father. I'd have written the Constitution much better by giving presidents unlimited immunity!"
5. **James Monroe**—"People come up to me all the time and say, 'Sir, the Trump Doctrine is way better than the Monroe Doctrine.' They say my plan to pull the US out of NATO and tell our Eastern European allies to go f*ck themselves will make Putin so afraid of invading any more countries after Ukraine."
6. **John Quincy Adams**—"He was a former president's son who actually accomplished something. Maybe this president wasn't so bad. I've bought several biographies of him as gifts for Don Jr., but he clearly hasn't read them."
7. **Andrew Jackson**—"If he did the Trail of Tears and gets to be on the $20 bill, I should be on the $100 bill for building the wall!"
8. **Martin Van Buren**—"Bald loser! Unlike me, whose hair has been perfect since I was a golden, teenage boy—a golden god!"
9. **William Harrison**—"He died from getting sick, so automatic loser. Boy, am I glad I didn't die from COVID, like I thought I was going to, and all the doctors worried I might. But I didn't die because my superior Trump genetics won out!"
10. **John Tyler**—"I've never heard of him so he must be Fake News."
11. **James Polk**—"Was the polka dance named after him? Was he gay? You know, the Christians, they really don't love the gay stuff. How did he even get elected? He didn't kill Roe V. Wade like I did!"

12. **Zachary Taylor**—"He was a general? So what? I'm smarter than all the generals put together! No one's better at the military than me!"
13. **Millard Fillmore**—"This name sounds made up. Fake News!"
14. **Franklin Pierce**—"I have no clue who he was. Did he even put his name on a single building? A total nobody."
15. **James Buchanan**—"He couldn't stop the Civil War from starting. If I had been there, I would have made a great deal that everyone would have loved, and it would have stopped the Civil War in one day. It would have been as good as my North Korean deal, my Iranian nuclear deal, my Obamacare replacement deal, and my infrastructure deal!"
16. **Abraham Lincoln**—"He rigged the presidential rankings to make himself the best. It's worse than the Nobel Prize Committee, who never gave me any Nobel Prizes for economics despite my tremendous business deals with *Trump Airlines*, *Trump Vodka*, and *Trump University*. The historians who put Lincoln at the top are the biggest hoaxers of all time. They called him Honest Abe, but I'm way more honest than Lincoln ever was. He should be taken off Mt. Rushmore, and my face should get chiseled on there instead."
17. **Andrew Johnson**—"He got impeached for real, so he's a dummy. My impeachments were faked by the evil communist Democrats, so mine don't count!"
18. **Ulysses Grant**—"The generals used to always come up to me, with tears in their eyes, and say, 'Sir, if only you were the general in the Civil War, we'd have won it way faster thanks to your big Trump brain!' Grant's enemies claimed he was a drunk. I don't drink or take any downers. I take blue uppers up the nose to make America great!"
19. **Rutherford Hayes**—"The stock market prices were way higher in my presidency than his."
20. **James Garfield**—"The cat from the comics? America elected a cat president? I bet he was a Democrat. Democrats elect the worst presidents. Like Joseph Stalin and Martin Luther King Jr.! They were the two worst presidents in all of American history."
21. **Chester Arthur**—"I know more about Chester Arthur than anyone. I'm one of the great presidential historians of all time. And my presidency was way better in every way. My deals were way better than his deals to… the one where… you know… was way worse than any of my deals!"
22. **Grover Cleveland**—"Was the city named after him? Why don't I have a city named after me? Washington D.C. should be renamed as Trumpington D.C.! I did much more for America than Washington."
23. **Benjamin Harrison**—"His presidency was a total snoozefest."
24. **Grover Cleveland**—"We had two presidents with the same name? Was this some kind of Deep State hoax and rigged election?"

25. **William McKinley**—"I like presidents who don't get assassinated!"
26. **Theodore Roosevelt**—"His daughter Alice was way uglier than Ivanka. I would never have dated Alice. How did people think she was hot? Broads never showed any cleavage back then. He should also be taken off Mt. Rushmore, and replaced with me a second time. I deserve it more than all of them!"
27. **William Taft**—"The White House staff moved his bathtub into my bedroom when I got elected, but I got stuck in it. What an idiot for using such a small tub! Was he poor or something, and couldn't afford a bigger tub? I guess so. And he should have had it gold-plated."
28. **Woodrow Wilson**—"He had a stroke. Even his body knew he was a loser and wanted to quit. My body never quits. The doctors can't believe it. They say my sky-high blood pressure, my exclusively trans fat diet, my refusal to do any exercise, and all the brain damage from 20 years of undiagnosed syphilis should have killed me years ago. They say I'm a medical marvel!"
29. **Warren Harding**—"Did you know it's rumored his wife killed him? What a beta! That's actually my biggest fear. I don't trust Melania at all. I never drink a can of *Diet Coke* she gives me unless it's unopened. If she opens it before giving it to me she'll just stand around waiting for me to take the first sip with a big smile on her face. You've seen her before—she never smiles! It's very suspicious."
30. **Calvin Coolidge**—"They called him Silent Cal, so no wonder I don't know anything about him. I go out of my way to talk as much as possible so everyone knows how great I am. I even call journalists all the time pretending to be my alter egos John Barron or David Dennison to start fantastical rumors about myself. The media is so stupid no one has any idea it's really me!"
31. **Herbert Hoover**—"He had a bunch of Hoovervilles, but he had no business talent and never got rich. I turned my empire of slum apartments in New York into millions of dollars of profits, and they said the living conditions in my apartments were even worse than Hoovervilles! Richer always means smarter."
32. **Franklin Roosevelt**—"Cripple. I like presidents whose legs don't give up. Also, I'd have never fought Hitler. Hitler showed such strength, and was an even bigger genius than Putin. America kills people too, and frankly, Britain and the Soviet Union weren't paying their bills so I'd have ripped up all our alliances with them. I wonder what kind of prostitutes Hitler would have sent me if I had done the Miss Universe pageant in 1930s Berlin. And Hitler had the most loyal generals! My generals as president had no ambition."
33. **Harry Truman**—"Truman was a pussy. I'd have used the nuclear bombs to attack every country, and conquer the world. Truman just wasn't a visionary like me."

34. **Dwight Eisenhower**—"Bald loser who wasted decades of his life in the military. What was in it for him?"
35. **John Kennedy**—"Everyone's talking about how Kennedy's hair, teeth, tanned skin, and sexual conquests were fake, and how I look younger and hotter than him. Marilyn Monroe said she only slept with Kennedy because I was underaged at the time."
36. **Lyndon Johnson**—"He tried to draft me into Vietnam, but I was too smart. I covered myself in feces and urine every day for years to get out of being selected. And it worked like a charm! I thought up all kinds of cool life hacks that I still use all these years later, like wearing diapers. And golden showers still turn me on."
37. **Richard Nixon**—"He resigned in shame like an idiot. All he had to do was never admit fault, convince his supporters the Justice Department was rigged against him, delay the court proceedings, and file endless counter-suits and appeals so he could finish out his term. Sometimes I think I'm the only smart president America ever had."
38. **Gerald Ford**—"I actually like Ford. He pardoned his presidential predecessor. Biden should take notes on how to be a classy president."
39. **Jimmy Carter**—"He was a marble mouth Southerner, and only a one-term president! What a loser! My single term is nothing like his, because I was robbed and cheated in the election. Carter lost fair and square."
40. **Ronald Reagan**—"He had dementia in office, unlike me! I aced all the two-minute cognitive tests I've taken that asked me to distinguish between people, cameras, and TVs, which is why I don't have to release any of my health records because I have nothing to hide."
41. **George H. W. Bush**—"I asked George H. W. Bush's first presidential campaign to consider me as a candidate for his vice president, but they laughed at me. I guess it was smart of Bush, though, because I totally would have done a big rally like January 6th to hang him live on national television and make myself president!"
42. **Bill Clinton**—"I heard he was also friendly with Jeffrey Epstein back when I was doing secret reconnaissance on Deep State pedophiles and only pretending to be Epstein's BFF for research."
43. **George W. Bush**—"If I was president when he was, 9/11 never would have happened, I guarantee it! Osama bin Laden would have respected me. We'd have fallen in love, just like me and Kim Jong Un did. We'd have written each other the most beautiful letters!"
44. **Barack Obama**—"He left the cupboards bare of COVID-19 tests so he made me look bad when the pandemic started. Was Obama behind the pandemic? People are talking."
46. **Joe Biden**—"He died six years ago and his body is just being suspended by ropes and pulleys in the Oval Office. It's the greatest hoax in American history!"

The Strategies Behind Donald Trump's Top Vice President Choices Other Than Frontrunner JD Vance Dissected

February 16, 2024
Washington D.C.—

The following are Trump's personal notes for his potential vice president candidates:

Tech Bro Vivek Ramaswamy

Pros:
- Creepily intense like Stephen Miller, with a fresh new take on the nationalist kind of vibe—he kind of seems, like Stephen, like he might have killed someone before
- He really hates the FBI, and most of the rest of the government—he'd definitely help me pull off another January 6th, unlike pussy Mike Pence… if Vivek doesn't hang me before my people get him!
- He never attacked me in the primary, so he can be extremely loyal—but does he kind of reek of opportunism?
- He'll undercut the Democratic argument that I'm racist, and give me cover for all my dog-whistling

Cons:
- He's an immigrant from a brown country *(and one of the sh*thole-ier ones)*
- Too ambitious? *(Would he kill me to take my spot as president? Maybe I should have the Proud Boys preemptively hang him sometime in the first year of the term—then replace him with Ivanka and bring sex-appeal back in the White House *REMINDER: Ignore the lawyers this time and institute a "Casual Fridays" dress code policy at the White House in the next term so all the ladies show a little more skin!)*
- He can really get a crowd going… but maybe too well? (I definitely don't want anyone who'll ever upstage me even for a second)
- His style of talking and speechifying is like a younger, more energetic Ted Cruz—major ick!

Senator Tim Scott

Pros:
- During the campaign he showed some very impressive talent changing the subject to Joe Biden and Kamala Harris any time he

- was asked about my fraud, tax evasion, criminal investigations, sexual assault lawsuits, or alleged treason
- All the "Blacks 4 Trump" groups might finally sign up their first Black members who we don't have to pay $50 an hour to come to my rallies *(Gotta really get serious about saving money—these lawsuits and prosecutions are bleeding me dry!)*
- I can get away with hiring only white people for the rest of my next cabinet if I have a Black VP
- I can give myself credit for ending racism when Obama couldn't—Donald J. Trump: "the better emancipator than Lincoln!"

Cons:
- The Nazis won't like me picking a Black VP *(And Nick Fuentes is such a charming dinner guest—though if it means Steve Bannon doesn't come around anymore and leave his stench that lingers on my furniture for days afterwards maybe it would be a worthwhile tradeoff?)*
- MAGA fans might accuse me of turning Woke—what if Ron DeSantis bans me from Florida for being too Woke, and I can't go to Mar-a-Lago ever again?!
- He's a little too Christian (Christians just give me the creeps. Mike Pence was so cringey about the God stuff. I can't do another four years of pretending to pray or remember every little, dumb thing Jesus said about caring about immigrants and refugees!)
- He's from South Carolina—after the fiasco of Jeff Sessions I vowed to have as few marble-mouth Southerners hang around as possible!

Governor Ron DeSantis

Pros:
- He was second place in the GOP primary
- He banned reading books in Florida, so he won't ever tattle on me for never reading security briefings
- His wife is a 10 *(Check if she needs any furniture shopping to do)*
- He's so weird and awkward... I'll look better and more normal when I'm standing next to him onstage

Cons:
- He said some not so nice things about me in the primary. I wonder how much he'd grovel if I make him beg me for forgiveness. Would he willingly spend all day in the dog kennel like Ted, Lindsey, and Kevin all did? *(*REMINDER: Get kennel out for the next time Mike Johnson visits)*

- He's really obsessed with *Disney*—I think Freud would say he's got a conspicuous sexual hangup over Mickey Mouse *(But I'm into Ivanka, so I suppose we all have our own idiosyncrasies)*
- I'll always have to check his fingers for pudding smears before I shake his hand
- I mean, is he just not capable of smiling or laughing like he's not some weird robot from an alien planet observing humans for the very first time? *(He's not a reptilian, is he? REMINDER: Text Alex Jones to stalk Ron and find out if he's a shapeshifter)*

South Dakota Governor Kristi Noem

Pros:
- Good looking, straight out of Central Casting
- Her South Dakota story is a nice contrast with my nepo baby Manhattan skyline story
- Being governor of South Dakota, maybe she could help get me on Mt. Rushmore *(Tell her to scratch off Lincoln—I deserve it more!)*
- Maybe she could convince all the Sturgis motorcycle bikers to help do the next coup if I lose another election

Cons:
- She's maybe too ambitious—I find ambition and confidence in women to be very threatening *(But she's way better than "Nasty Nikki")*
- Will I have to go to South Dakota? Yuck! Does *Diet Coke* even deliver out there? *(And she loves motorcycles… riding one would ruin my hair, likely forever!)*
- She has crazy eyes—they're way too bright when I'm binging hard on my *Adderall* sniffies
- People say she had an affair with Corey Lewandowski—major ick!
- She bragged in her book about shooting a puppy, and people really seem to not like violence against puppies

Former Representative Tulsi Gabbard

Pros:
- My genius and sexual magnetism have made her renounce her former Democratic identity—great talking point!
- I could do some locker room talk about her, if you know what I mean
- She seems pretty laissez-faire with Putin and NATO and isolationism so she'll be less likely to tattle on me for selling classified secrets to

- other countries in exchange for them hosting big events at Mar-a-Lago and my golf courses
- Boobs/on Casual Fridays might show a little cleavage

Cons:
- She's young enough to still be menstruating, and once a month turn into a nasty demon lady bleeding out of her wherever
- She's ideologically all over the place, and I have no idea what she really thinks about stuff—if she won't commit to a political party, will she commit to me? *(Maybe she'd make a good press secretary?)*
- Ivanka would get totally jealous if I don't let her be the first female vice president
- Is she close enough to Putin that she'd go behind my back and collude with him for herself? I definitely don't want her getting her hands on the pee tape or any of the other blackmail videos the Russians have!

Media Personality Tucker Carlson

Pros:
- He's even more pro-Putin and isolationist than me—he won't nag me when I pull the US out of NATO and the United Nations
- He was fired from *Fox*, and Putin just insulted him and his interviewing skills, so Tucker has really been knocked down a few pegs—he showed how submissive he is in the interview with Putin!—so he needs me more than I need him!
- He has a huge audience of racists I need to keep engaged and enthusiastic if I'm going to win the election
- He's actually a nepo baby New Yorker so he'll be easier to talk to and hang with *(I'm sick of dealing with so many rural governors and members of Congress from sh*thole states like Indiana, Kentucky, Louisiana, and Alabama!)*

Cons:
- He may be better than me on TV, and better at keeping an audience because he stays scripted and doesn't go on long, ranting diatribes against inanimate objects and haters like is my specialty
- He's kind of actually in danger of approaching "washed-up" status after now having been fired from every cable news network
- His firing from *Fox News* was real fast and sudden, so his text messages and emails put into evidence from the voting machine lawsuits must have had some crazy sh*t in them—total red flag!
- He's as sociopathic as me—I could never trust him, and would have to spend the entire term looking over my shoulders!

BIG IF TRUE VIII

- A new poll found that 71% of Americans think we've waited long enough after Donald Trump's attempted assassination to respectfully get "#TrumpSmellsLikeShit" trending again.

- The Republican National Convention has quietly requested all speakers avoid using the words "rapist" and "sex offender" when claiming crime is out of control because it might remind voters of Trump.

- Tucker Carlson's testicle tanning machines are going to be sold at the RNC on sale for only $199.

- Eric Trump reportedly spent hours trying to collect signatures of GOP delegates at the RNC to pledge support for him in a 2028 presidential campaign over his brother Don Jr. or sister Ivanka, and got three.

- The American Transgender Alliance has named Matt Gaetz its "2024 Honorary Trans Hero" saying that his facial plastic surgery work and excessive makeup use at the GOP convention and his new OAN show have made him a "poster boy of gender-affirming care."

- Ron DeSantis is reportedly excited about JD Vance's couch banging and dolphin smut watching rumors because now he's not the weirdest guy of the election anymore.

- The strategy of dozens of downtown Milwaukee bars and nightclubs to host drag shows each night this week so Republicans wouldn't have anywhere to party after the convention backfired when all the drag queens had their most attended shows ever, and one bar was even the victim of one of the GOP's infamous coke orgies.

- Trump is reportedly pissed because he was sleeping at the GOP convention when Vance's wife spoke, and he only just now learned that she and their kids are Indian so it's too late to re-do his VP pick.

- The Senate IT guy says it's worth it to lose his job leaking JD Vance's browser history after Vance was caught searching for "dolphin" and "woman" together on *Twitter* because he says Vance's dolphin fetish is "so intense it's almost certainly gotta be a national security threat."

- *Fox News* is calling for french fries to be called "freedom fries" again after the French Olympics opening ceremony featured a drag queen.

- JD Vance has reportedly refused to let CNN investigate his couches at home with a black light.

- The French Olympic Committee apologized to American conservatives for featuring drag queens in the opening ceremony, and said the closing ceremony will feature couches and dolphins because, "as JD Vance has shown, US conservatives won't be offended by those."

- The RNC reportedly debated internally if it would look too Nazi-ish if they passed out red armbands with black T's on them for Donald Trump's convention speech.

- A homophobic televangelist from Arkansas claims if Kamala Harris is elected, "San Francisco Democrats will ensure the next Olympics will be fully pagan, and bring back traditional naked wrestling so devout Christian Americans will be forced to watch all the wrestlers' testicles rubbing against each other's faces."

- A new *TikTok* trend involves Gen Z teens mocking JD Vance's obsession with "childless cat ladies" by leaving open cat food tins and catnip all around Trump-Vance campaign offices so stray cats hang around.

- Project 2025 says Trump will reform the Department of Education by replacing all public school sex ed courses with a series of 30-minute videos of Stephen Miller describing the symptoms of various STDs and simulating sex on a corpse he claims its family donated to him for medical research.

- Trump skipped golfing today so he could watch the stock market and claim credit if it went up or blame Biden and Harris if it went down.

- A large group of Democrats in Florida are raising funds to build a dozen wind turbines just offshore from Mar-a-Lago.

- Mike Pence says JD Vance should have "hung out" with him before accepting Trump's vice president offer.

- A local chapter of the Proud Boys say they've finished making a dozen "Hang JD Vance" flags, "just to be prepared."

- Trump reportedly just fired a staffer who asked him, "Do you think you should maybe start campaigning harder than golfing 6 days a week?"

- For the second day in a row, a stray cat has bitten JD Vance at an event.

- A new poll found that 95% of Democrats want Democratic VP candidate Tim Walz to make a joke referencing the viral rumors that JD Vance wrote in his autobiography that he liked to fuck his couch using a sandwich bag as a condom.

- JD Vance said, "I'm a normal guy," 29 times today across three separate interviews.

- Trump is reportedly telling staffers that with JD Vance he accidentally "picked a Jeb."

- A Florida judge says the state legislature's strict laws mean that JD Vance's use of eyeliner and past exploration into drag at a college party prohibit him from entering a Florida school, library, or government building while campaigning.

- The worm in RFK Jr.'s brain decided to endorse Trump over Harris because it thinks if it can sneak into Trump's brain the eating will be much tastier than Harris's brain on account of how much fried food and burger grease Trump has eaten throughout his life to make it fatty, buttery, and succulent.

- Trump said if Harris calls him "low energy" again he's going to sue her, and then accused Harris of paying Black people to attend her campaign rallies.

- Trump is threatening to disown his family because Melania charges $25,000 per campaign appearance and another $25,000 to bring Barron along, Don Jr. won't stop filming campaign videos with droopy, bloodshot eyes, Ivanka has been going by "Ivanka Kushner" for a while now, and Eric… is Eric.

- A leaked Trump campaign document shows a list of all the infrastructure and green energy projects the Biden Administration funded and is currently building that Trump intends to take credit for next year if he wins.

- Marjorie Taylor Greene and Lauren Boebert have reportedly made up after years of rivalry, and are now jointly searching for more dick pics of prominent Democrats because they accidentally tore up the Hunter Biden dick pics they were fighting over.

- RFK Jr. just revealed he was in Wuhan, China looking for roadkill animal corpses in August of 2019.

- Trump has reportedly ordered his Secret Service agents to not take Melania to an early voting location so she can't vote against him.

- RFK Jr. says he'll endorse Trump if Trump lets him get "first dibs" on any dead animals found in America's national parks.

- Donald Trump reportedly interrupted a wedding ceremony at Mar-a-Lago today and ranted for 29 minutes about how Kamala Harris's allegedly excited crowds are actually an elaborate mixture of holograms, green screens, mirrors, mannequins, robots with masks, paid illegal immigrants, and cardboard cutouts.

- Trump reportedly bought sex criminal Jeffrey Epstein's plane to ensure no one can do any DNA tests on the stains.

- Trump claimed during his rally today that more people attended his assassination attempt than the assassinations of John F. Kennedy, William McKinley, and Abraham Lincoln, and that his fist-pumping was more manly than Teddy Roosevelt delivering his speech after being shot in the chest, and that Ronald Reagan was a "pussy" in his assassination attempt.

- Trump reportedly already owes JD Vance $16,000 for various campaign expenses he promised to pay back but hasn't.

- RFK Jr. insists his brain worm has nothing to do with why he wants Trump to remove so many regulations protecting endangered bird species in his next term if reelected.

- Trump reportedly just banned JD Vance from parties at Mar-a-Lago until his national likability ratings hit at least 50%.

- Harris has not denied that she intends to direct the IRS to charge Trump for his 50 years of tax evasion with interest, and use his ensuing bankruptcy to confiscate Mar-a-Lago and turn it into housing for detained migrants.

- RFK Jr. claimed at a campaign event with Trump that he has eaten animals from 39 endangered species, and tried the taste of "six different human races."

- The Trump campaign is holding its breath as JD Vance is reportedly about to visit a Mexican restaurant to make small talk with employees as he picks up a to-go order.

What To Expect From Donald Trump's Upcoming New York Trials

February 23, 2024
Washington D.C.—

- Trump will be held in contempt of court for shouting out derogatory nicknames at the witnesses who have accused him of attempting to intimidate them in between court appearances. He'll pretend to cough while shouting "fake news," and throughout the trial keep a notebook out in front of him on which he will write down the names of everyone in the trial he will send in the first wave to the concentration camps if he wins the election and lets his most enthusiastic supporters go wild with their Nazi role-playing.

- Eric Trump will yell out "Objection!" from the audience gallery during his father's trial appearance at irrelevant times. He'll repeat everything he hears from lawyer shows, but also complain to the judge that the trial is taking way longer than it should because "on TV all the trials only take a half hour or an hour at the most, and have commercial breaks to get a chance to go to the bathroom or huff another bag of glue."

- Trump will clog the courthouse toilet during a break of trial proceedings trying to flush notes from his lawyers. When the bowl starts overflowing, he'll tell the responding janitor, "It was like this when I found it." Throughout the day his diapers in the trash cans will really make the bathrooms reek. Trump will pay the janitors $250 each to sign non-disclosure agreements to not reveal his secret that, because he snorts so much *Adderall*, his diaper stains are the color blue.

- Trump will mouth, "I'm going to kill you" several times to former staffers of his who will testify against him. He'll make several gestures of strangulation with an intensely furious look on his face. Then he'll calm down, look around, make eye contact with the witnesses, point his thumb at Ivanka sitting behind him, wink, lick his finger, poke the air, and make an audible sizzling sound.

- Trump will mutter, "If only f*cking Mike f*cking Pence hadn't f*cking been a f*cking pussy…" under his breath dozens of times.

- Trump will ask to go to the bathroom and sneak out the door during a lapse in his lawyers' attention, but be quickly found at a nearby *McDonald's* restaurant drinking *Diet Coke* from the dispenser with his mouth open under the soda nozzle.

- Trump will tell the judge that he can't be sent to prison because all his children love him and need him, and, also, that if he's not in the picture he's worried Ivanka will murder, dismember, and hide the corpses of all her siblings with the cunning of a Mongolian Khan to prove she has the strength and will to take over her father's empire and appoint herself as the MAGA Queen of the United States of America.

- Melania Trump will wear her "I don't really care, do u?" jacket every day to her husband's trials, and sit silently but smile for hours straight, which many will note as quite uncharacteristic of her, particularly for how spatially close she will be to her husband."

- Trump will complain to his judge in the January 6th trial that the courtroom sketch artist should be locked up for making him look guilty, pouty, and fat. Trump will demand the sketch artists draw him like he appears on his superhero-themed NFTs. Then he'll plug his latest batch of NFTs coming out soon to the jury and audience. He'll promise all the NFTs will be worth a million dollars "in two weeks after the launch," and he'll also promise a suspicious number of times, apropos of nothing, that it's not a pump-&-dump scheme. He'll also recommend his fans buy them fast, because, after a few hours, Saudi and Russian oligarchs will buy up all of them because of what a great financial value they are, and because they owe him for some maybe kind of sort of classified documents he let them see and photocopy at Mar-a-Lago.

- Trump will call the judge the literal devil. He'll rant every day in front of cameras about the trial being rigged, and insist he's totally innocent. He'll say he was only kidding all the times he bragged about being a genius for not paying taxes and getting away with all the financial tricks in the book. And, in fact, he'll claim, he's one of the great bookkeepers of all time. Then he'll say that a lot of people are talking about how actually Eric was the one who did most of the bookkeeping at the Trump Organization, so if anyone is maybe just a teensy little bit guilty, the communist Deep State FBI should look into Eric and not him. His only crime was trusting Eric too much.

- Trump will promise he'll testify because he is "totally innocent" and has nothing to hide, but will become ambiguous in the final weeks, and then, of course, not testify with the excuse that it's rigged and, "No one can explain what I'm being prosecuted for," despite just having sat through the trial for seven consecutive weeks as the prosecution explained it thoroughly to a jury made up of Trump's peers who agreed unanimously he was guilty of all his indictments.

The Guide To Whether Republicans Think Teenagers Are Children Or Adults

March 19, 2024
Washington D.C.—

The following are topics on which Republicans can't make up their minds whether teenagers should be thought of as innocent children or life-hardened adults:

Reading books: Children! Teens are extremely impressionable, and must be sheltered from any and all sexual or transgender material. If teenagers read a single book with a gay or trans character, you can kiss their cisgender heterosexuality away! They'll dye their hair blue, pin anime buttons all over their jackets and backpacks, and swear allegiance to Bernie Sanders and Joseph Stalin in midnight ceremonies outside in the woods like nerdy, Wiccan lesbians. And they'll bother you all the time about recycling and pronouns. In fact, to fight back against all the disturbing liberal lies and fake news in the mainstream media, you should probably force your teenagers to watch an hour of straight porn every day to undo the Gay Agenda's LGBTQ brainwashing that tricks your kids into not caring about what sexual acts the gays are doing in the privacy of their own bedrooms. If you're a good Christian conservative, sodomy is all you should be thinking about every day, God demands it! Sodomy is the one thing *Leviticus* really cares about. The other stuff are just suggestions. So we Republicans must fight back by sitting down with our kids, and forcing them to watch straight sex scenes under close supervision to make sure they pay close attention to the heavenly fact that heterosexual sex is Jesus's kind of sex. Any other form of sex is really sex with the Devil. About a half-hour a day of heterosexual porn should be enough to counteract the liberal media's gay proselytizing for Satan. But only videos of the missionary position. You don't want to make sex look like it can be fun.

Jobs: Adults! Teens are practically full-on adults, and deserve the right to work after school or even drop out to make money. Plus, it's better for our economy if we have our children compete against all the child labor in Asia. America needs to be competitive! And it's much cheaper for our coal mines to dig tunnels for children rather than the bigger tunnels needed for full-size adult workers. That's the kind of efficiency America needs to outcompete China! Take Arkansas as an example. The local economy is booming thanks to Governor Sarah Huckabee Sanders, and her successful efforts bringing back child labor. She says she won't stop pushing Arkansas's children out of school and into the labor force for the state's job creators to utilize at cheap wage levels until Arkansas has the lowest high school graduation rate in the country. It was already pretty successfully low to begin with, but watch out, Alabama, Arkansas is gunning for you!

Pornography: Children! Porn is pervasive online, and Senator Josh Hawley is correct when he says it's the biggest societal threat we as Americans face. It must be eradicated as we are sexualizing our children much too early, and robbing them of the innocent childhoods they deserve, except for the parentally-supervised porn viewing previously recommended.

Marriage: Adults! Girls should be able to get married to older men as soon as they start menstruating. Every girl's first period is a sign from God that she's ready to be proposed to, ideally by a much older man from her church who will treat her like a child for the rest of his life.

Abortion: Adults! Teen girls must be held responsible for carrying that baby to term, birthing it, and thanking God for the miracle of pregnancy, no matter what unfortunate circumstances precipitated its conception. If teen girls are unable to support the baby, there's all kinds of resources and help they can take advantage of to help raise their miracle baby.

Healthcare, school lunches, food stamps, & pre-K education: Adults! F*ck social safety nets! What are we, communist?! It's not our fault people are born into poverty! Work hard and get ahead by yourself, that's what my grandpa did, and now even I'm still living off of his hard work. The poor can be like me if they'd only try.

Guns: Adults! It's imperative we arm our children in school because there are so many school shooters everywhere. And if all the other kids have guns, mine certainly will too! And if my kids all have guns, I gotta have a gun on me all the time too. And a grenade. I need to keep up firepower superiority over my kids. Don't want them coming after me. You never know when your kid might get an Oedipal complex and try to take you out to marry your wife. Everyone must have the right to defend themselves against their families.

Political opinions and voting: Children! Teenagers don't know anything yet, which is why they're so liberal. If we listened to teen voters, America would overnight turn into a hellscape where every citizen has access to healthcare, college, good wages, and gets paid vacation time like Europeans. I will be in the ground before liberals ever force me to live like some Italian!

Joining the military: Adults! We should lower the enlistment age a little bit so we can prepare for the next GOP presidency when we'll have a shot at finishing our hat trick of Middle East wars by exporting freedom to Iran! Or fight the civil war Trump will start if he loses in 2024…

Donald Trump Claims Democrats Want To Mandate Every Marriage From Now On Must Be Either Biracial Or Gay

May 8, 2024
New York City, NY—

Donald Trump today made several unsubstantiated claims about Joe Biden's 2024 presidential platform:

"Joe Biden hates same-race marriages even more than he hates God! All the suburban white women out there who are thinking about flipping to the Democrats better understand that Kamala Harris does not respect you or your husband like I do. He hates your family! Especially if your husband is a white. Or one of the Christians. Real American suburban families need to watch out. All the Democrats hate you. They want to end you. Biden will make you divorce your husband, and force you to marry someone else. Someone very different. Someone from ISIS, who snuck in our lawless and undefended Southern border, and is now wearing disguises to blend in until Biden and Pelosi give him his slave wife: you. Suburban women better think again before voting for Democrats. They're gonna make you convert to Islam at gunpoint. They'll make you burn your family *Bible*, and swear an oath to Muhammed on a Koran. Or, worse, they'll give you an African immigrant husband from a sh*thole country. Or a Chinese. Biden will make you spin a big carnival wheel to find out whether your new husband will be black, brown, yellow or red. There will be no normal colors allowed. Whatever it lands on, that's what you're stuck with. People everywhere are talking about it. You wouldn't believe what's going on. What they're trying to do. They want you to have to go to a government building for reassigned spouses that's connected to a mosque and a Planned Parenthood, and sit seven hours till they call your ticket number while you wait with a bunch of crackies and people giving themselves post-birth abortions, and then spin the spousal color wheel while they give you a dozen COVID shots real quick when you're not looking and your guard is down. It's criminal what they're trying to do. So, suburban women, if you don't want to have to marry a member of al-Qaeda who snuck in through Texas and is now scheming in Minneapolis, or Milwaukee, or Detroit, or Philadelphia, or wherever your suburb is, I'd suggest you reelect me. Democrats will abort your marriage, and Fauci will personally give your kids a vaccine that will change the color of their skin and convert them to mulattos, the ones he doesn't eat first. The Clinton crime family will be there, too. Hillary has dibs on eating all the post-birth abortioned babies. People are saying she's the Epstein of eating fetuses. And I don't do Epsteins. I had no idea who Epstein was. In fact, I actually had no clue it was his island when I went to all those parties, and I always turned into bed early and found a spare bedroom to go to sleep in, and lock the door, and put on a sleep mask over my eyes, and put in ear plugs... so I never saw, heard, or experienced anything yucky any of the dozen or so times I went there. You know me, I'm a germaphobe. I don't do the yucky stuff. I never was into golden showers. I don't do urine on myself. The Fake News is just full of the absolutely worst liars of all time. I have never been peed on by anyone. Everyone knows it's way hotter to have the prostitutes do the golden showers on each other, and you just watch. In a way, it's a beautiful thing. Trust me, no one respects women more than Trump. I'm one of the great women respecters, maybe of all time. Just because a jury of my peers found that crazy Carroll lady who accused me of rape and all her witnesses credible doesn't mean I'm guilty! They're all lying! Everyone in the world lies, except me. I'm the only one in America telling you the truth, which is why they're trying so hard to rig the next election against me, just like they did with the last election! So if you want your suburban kids' skin to stay white, you better vote Trump, that's all I'm saying. If I told you everything Biden and Harris wanted to do, it would blow your mind. You wouldn't believe it. I shouldn't say it. They don't want me to say it. And I know I said this about Obama and Hillary, but my election stopped them from doing it just in time. But the Democrats are going to finish the job. Biden would have done it already in his first term, but Sleepy Joe is so tired he forgot! Trust me. The Democrats will end America as we know it. The only food you'll be able to buy in grocery stores will be Mexican or Arab. All burgers and hotdogs will be camel meat. There will be no more wine aisles or shelves of alcohol, just shelf after shelf of bottles of children's blood labeled with your kids' names on them. If you have a suburban white family, it'll be game over for you if they rig the election again! You're not going to be suburban anymore. Maybe not even a woman. Who knows? The way the Woke people are going... The Christians, they don't like the Woke stuff. They judge it very hard. The Christians really love judging things, don't they? It's kind of funny how much the Christians love me, isn't it? They really like me. It's like I'm almost bigger than Jesus. It feels nice to receive loyalty. Reminds me of Hitler's generals, who were the best of the best at loyalty. And the loyalty sure is financially lucrative! They never stop giving me money and buying my merch and crypto schemes. It's like they're tithing to me as if I'm God. This must be what Hitler felt like. I kind of get Hitler in a way. Obviously not all the bad stuff, but he had such talent for working up an angry, violent mob. What power. If I get reelected, I could totally do a 4th Reich kind of thing. Wouldn't that be tremendous? Stephen Miller could be my Himmler... *Fox News* could be my Goebbels... Mike Flynn could be my Göring. Just kidding, everyone, I'm not going to do a Hitler. But on day one, maybe just a little. The 4th Reich... the Trump Reich. I like the sound of that. You know, a lot of people don't know this, but Hitler had some great branding. The Swastika flags and armbands really sent a message. But Hitler should have done more businesses on the side like me. I've always wondered what *Hitler Steaks* might have tasted like. Would he have done freeze-dried ketchup like me? Or *Hitler Hotels*. That's got nice alliteration, doesn't it? I'd stay a night in a Hitler suite. *Hitler Hotels*. I should talk to China about giving Ivanka a trademark on that name. She's really racking up the Chinese trademarks, isn't she? And speaking of racks… too bad Hitler didn't have a daughter. I've always wondered if I could have married Hitler's daughter. That would have been one of the great political alliances of all time, wouldn't it? I was born in 1946, so if Hitler had a daughter at the end of the war she would have been right about my age. 'Trump/Hitler, 2024.' That's a presidential ticket I'd love to vote for. Talk about strength! …But, yeah, the Christians really think I'm the best president ever. Honestly, sometimes it creeps me out how much they love me. They always want to touch me, and pray with me, and hold my hand. Ew. They're real touchy-feely, the Christians. But they give me lots of votes because I give them Supreme Court judges. But unfortunately the Christians don't have great star power. The men are kind of weird, and the women barely show any skin. But they really love the idea of me becoming a dictator on day one. Because they know Joe Biden and the Democrats will ruin America for Christians for forever. They know Biden will sign an executive order that suburban women's houses get torn down, and he'll replace their perfect homes and pretty little yards with a low-income housing units, and cram in dozens of immigrant thugs and ANTIFA. He's going to turn suburban life into an urban one, and he'll convert all the suburban kids into little urbans. You won't even recognize them anymore. Trust me. Your little Timmy will turn into 'Big Darnell,' or 'Saddam bin Laden.' We don't want any more bin Ladens in America. The Democrats have let in enough, haven't they? The way the Democrats are letting in any criminal who knocks on our door. Criminals are flooding into our country everywhere. The Democrats want America to be full of criminals! I just got convicted in a trial, but my criminality doesn't count. I'm no criminal, trust me. I'm the only one keeping the criminals out! When I'm president again I'll keep them all out. So vote Trump! And white, suburban women better stop flipping over to the Democrats! Seriously. They want to eat your children. So send me some money, whatever you can, for my lawyers, my bonds, my court fines, and *McDonald's* lunches. Help keep me energized so I can fight for all of you. If they can prosecute me for campaign finance fraud, hoarding classified secrets, leaking national security secrets, and raping women, they can prosecute you too. Thank you so much to all my followers and fans. And send cash right now—the *McRib* just returned!"

Milwaukee Breweries Are Releasing New Beers With Names That Insult Trump For The Republican National Convention

June 20, 2024
Milwaukee, WI—

Milwaukee breweries are drafting new beers to commemorate the Republican National Convention's upcoming nomination of Donald Trump for president in the city following Trump's recent claim that Milwaukee is a "horrible city."

The following are beers now available in various Milwaukee bars:

- "Lock Him Up Lager"
- "Diaper Don Dunkel"
- "Impeached Imperial Ale"
- "Epstein's Best Bud Kölsch"
- "Smells-Like-S*** Saison"
- "Golden Shower Wheat Beer"
- "Halfwit Hefeweizen"
- "Incest Blonde Ale"
- "Rapey Don Rye Ale"
- "In-Two-Weeks Porter"
- "With Tears In Their Eyes Pale Ale"
- "Convicted American Pale Ale"
- "Poopy Pants Sour Beer"
- "Bankrupt Cream Ale"
- "Twice Impeached Double IPA"
- "Popular-Vote-Loser Triple IPA"
- "Two-Time Popular Vote Loser Witbier"
- "Felon Malt Liquor"
- "Fake Hair Helles"
- "Dotard Dunkler Bock"
- "Mushroom Maibock"
- "Mango Mussolini Maibock"
- "His Flatulency Brown Ale"
- "Past Your Jail Time Ale"
- "Mein Trumpf Lite"
- "Tiny Hands Ice"
- "Cult 45 Malt Liquor"
- "Putin's Bitch Triple IPA"
- "UV Wand Up Your Butt Belgian Blonde"

Questions Journalists Should Really Demand That Donald Trump Answer Before He Maybe Becomes President Again

1. Do you think Jared Kushner and Ivanka Trump owe you some of the $2 billion in Saudi funding they got? Think you should sue them?
2. You're the most notorious #MeToo villain in America, how does it feel to revolt so much of the American populace?
3. Do you think your rape-defamation lawsuit with E. Jean Carroll make it difficult to hire competent women in a second administration?
4. If you had to guess, how many NDAs have you paid for?
5. If you could go back in time knowing what you know now, would you still name Don Jr. after yourself?
6. Are you ever concerned that, since 2015, Steve Bannon, Roger Stone, Alex Jones, Elon Musk, and all the billionaires around you have been riding along on your coattails for their own gain promoting you to grow their own audience bases like you're their useful idiot?
7. If Ukrainian president Zelensky is a dictator, why aren't you sucking up to him like you are to Vladimir Putin? Isn't he displaying strength?
8. Can you explain what you would do to end the war in Ukraine in one day like you claimed you could because you no longer get the benefit of the doubt that your vague and tall-tale promises of dealmaking genius have any basis in reality?
9. Why do you think historians have ranked you at the bottom of their lists of best presidents higher only than the weak presidents directly preceding the Civil War?
10. Why do you suppose your own chief of staff, John Kelly, called you "the most flawed person I have ever met in my life," and your secretary of state Rex Tillerson called you a "moron" who often wanted to do illegal things? Could you also explain what you wanted to do that Tillerson thought was illegal and refused?
11. You never really had an Obamacare replacement plan, did you?
12. Do you regret not paying contractors who worked for you and then had to go out of business and their families suffered?
13. If you were going to flee America, would you choose to move to Moscow, Riyadh or Pyongyang, and why?
14. Has Ivanka ever asked you to stop saying creepy thing about her body in public? Has Jared Kushner? Has Melania? our other children?
15. What awful thing did you do that made your parents give up on raising you, and decide to send you to a military academy?
16. When you interview RFK Jr. for an administration job, did you see the worm peak out one of his ears?
17. Will you take this high school civics exam right now on camera to prove you know how the government works?

18. Why use a lame nickname like "Ron DeSanctimonious" when even blue-haired, Woke, Gen Z communists are disappointed and know you can be meaner than that?
19. Why do you tell so many "Sir" stories when we all know that's a poker tell of yours that the story is entirely made up?
20. Why do you say "People are talking" so much when we all know that's a poker tell of yours that you're making something up?
21. What was the biggest lie you ever got away with?
22. You failed to make a legitimate peace deal with Kim Jong-un, but you made such a big deal and spectacle about going there to shake his hand, and bragged so much that you could make deals better than anyone, that you just can't admit you were out of your depth, got played, and have since been oddly calling him your "lover" to distract from the reality that you accomplished nothing for America's national security interests... didn't you?
23. Do you really think you're fooling us with the hair and the makeup? Why do you not blend it into your hairline or your neck?
24. Did your father ever call you a loser, and how did that make you feel?
25. What compelled you to randomly call reporters in the 80s and make up wild lies and fictional exaggerations about famous celebrities asking you out on dates?
26. Why should Americans believe you really won the 2020 election after polls consistently showed you behind Biden for the entire election, your approval ratings were among the worst in history for most of your presidency, a majority of Americans thought your COVID policies led to tens of thousands of preventable deaths, suburban white women were appalled by your cruel governmental policies and personal conduct, a plethora of Republican candidates outperformed you in ways that make it obvious Democrats didn't cheat to make you lose but merely forgot to make their Senate and House candidates also win, and you and your family are just weird, sociopathic freaks who are bad at pretending you care about other people?
27. When is Barron's birthday?
28. What are five things you like about Eric?
29. When is Melania's birthday, or your wedding anniversary?
30. What is Tiffany's job?
31. Do you regret not being more present in your children's lives?
32. Many people who have worked with you, including a staffer of your show *The Apprentice* claim you wear diapers, and that filming was at times stalled when you had to go for a change. Would you like to prove those rumors wrong right now by pulling down your pants?
33. What blackmail do you have on Lindsey Graham? Ignore every other question and just answer this one PLEASE!

The Creepiest Platform Planks In Donald Trump's "Project 2025" Agenda

July 7, 2024
Washington D.C.—

Authors of Project 2025 says voters can think of its social platform as a "masculine rebuttal to #MeToo, Woke, and DEI" and "a new generation of Jim Crow, but for women."

The following are the first year priorities for Project 2025 that the group's executives will lobby the Republican Congress for, or write executive orders for Trump to sign:

- Bring back pray-away-the-gay camps for kids that will be like mini bootcamps for a "Trump Youth" style pilot program.

- National funding for public schools to have annual purity balls starting in 3rd grade.

- The renunciation of the heliocentric model of the solar system, and forcing the return to the Christian geocentric model.

- Bringing prayer back into schools so that the children can help pray for all of America's elderly and infirm who will lose their Social Security, Obamacare, and Medicare.

- The institution of "gaydar detectors" inside every federal building.

- Bringing back child labor, reinstituting child marriage, and lowering the age of consent nationally from 18 to "girls' fathers' permission."

- Amending the Congressional rules to going back to banning women legislators from wearing pants.

- A Congressional resolution proclaiming that plastic surgery and other gender-affirming operations are okay with God for Christian women because they need to keep their looks to ensure their husbands stay monogamous, but not okay for any trans people.

- Endorsing a high school history book that omits the Civil Rights Era.

- Defunding of all sex-ed programs in public schools, except for a new one to be financed called "Eve's Great Mistake" which goes into gratuitous (but surprisingly—credit to them—biologically accurate) detail about menstruation, and at the end is a pledge for all girls to sign officially apologizing for Eve's mistake of eating the fruit in the Garden of Eden and promising to never make God angry again.

- Funding a government initiative to "disprove once and for all the female orgasm."

- Women will be obligated to carry "period passports" that track their menstrual cycles and must be kept up to date, and women must present these to police officers during random ID checks to monitor pregnancies.

- The institution of a federal tribunal to adjudicate "Women's Crimes," and a committee to study Iran's morality police to try to adopt a similar police force in the US.

- The Department of Health and Human Services will give Stephen Miller a grant of $250,000 to try his experiments on "human centipedes."

- A demand for all corporations to start updating their Christmas branding so all depictions of Santa Claus and his wife make them not childless because it's "sending the wrong message" to childless cat ladies, and it's "a little odd that Santa hangs around so many little boy elves."

- Outlaw divorce, but give US presidents "executive privilege" on this issue so Trump can divorce Melania if he wants to, for example, get a new wife who will make for a better "tradwife" model for America's Christian girls and young women to emulate, and be obedient, quiet, submissive wives like the *Bible* wants.

- Reforming the national security policies on storage of top secret documents and the declassification process so that Trump can keep as many classified files anywhere he wants.

- Abolishing the FBI and CIA so that no one bothers the president with nosey investigations or subpoenas into which dictators he's showing what classified documents on our nuclear technology, spy capabilities, and our military positions throughout the world.

- Funding to conduct DNA checks after every time used tampons are sent through the mail by Gen Z kids protesting the anti-women in Congress.

- Censoring *Disney* if they continue casting Black actors or resolving their storylines without the female protagonist getting married and giving up her fierce independence in order to faithfully serve her husband according to Biblical family values.

- Unveiling an "Official Iconography of the Messiah" document that demands all public representations of Jesus feature Him as having blonde hair, blue eyes, side abs, a pronounced Adonis belt, and a BMI no higher than 20.5.

- Adopting a resolution that the world is getting hotter not because of climate change but because of sin, and that's why all birth control must be banned with the reinstatement of the archaic Comstock Act from 1873. Once birth control is no longer offered as a tool of women's health, the climate will get cooler because God will be less angry.

- Firing 3,000 government bureaucrats, and replace them with the incels who can't get dates even on Trump adviser John McEntee's MAGA dating app called *"Red Flags,"* because they'll have the kind of loyalty dictators can only get from creating a homoerotic, paramilitary cult zealous in its misogyny and racism to thanks to the only bit of power, coerced respect, and sense of belonging they've ever had.

- A legislative push for bestiality to no longer be illegal because of its service to occupying the sexual frustrations of horny, young, potential incels—just a little frowned upon and not too directly encouraged.

- Increasing government spending to "study and prevent alien abductions and their subsequent anal probes."

- Legalizing cousin marriage and endorsing it in order to double down on Real American families' white and Christian genetics in their kids' DNA. Also, incestual genetic decline is a liberal hoax and part of the evolution scam.

- Funding new ICE uniforms so ICE can be dressed and styled by Nazi-designer Hugo Boss to look sharp and imposing while conducting their raids in workplaces, churches, businesses, hospitals, and anywhere else.

- The last plank of the Project 25 platform is titled "Concentration Camps," but is blank save for just one sentence that says, "TBD, still waiting to see where on the dictator scale from one to Hitler that Congressional Republicans will let Trump go."

BIG IF TRUE X

- The number one video on several pornography websites right now just has a caption on a black screen that says "Ted Cruz might lose reelection," and lasts for thirty-seven minutes.

- Donald Trump says Harris bringing up his excessive face makeup during her *Fox News* interview is "crossing a red line."

- Trump says the media reporting on his increasingly common, public, and audible incontinence issues is "crossing a brown line."

- Trump has reportedly not golfed since his second assassination attempt, and has used all his extra free time to reconnect with Melania, bond with Don Jr. and Eric, volunteer for charity, teach Barron how to throw a ball, come up with a real Obamacare replacement plan that's cheaper and covers more people, draft an Iranian nuclear deal, and decide on an infrastructure plan.

- A new poll finds that 0% of Republicans want their own daughters and wives to die from pregnancy complications that could be prevented with an abortion, just other people's wives and daughters.

- The MAGA group "White Supremacists 4 Trump," who have been stockpiling and freezing a "doomsday supply of white semen" in an Alaskan bunker, have reportedly banned members from drinking glasses of unpasteurized milk while working because of "several unfortunate mix-ups."

- JD Vance is reportedly frustrated that Trump won't stop bringing up Hitler's generals, and his idea to use the military to go after his critics and political enemies, because, as Vance yelled at Trump staffers, "I'm the one going on mainstream shows who has to clean up his messes!"

- Trump says his next Attorney General will investigate anyone who calls him the following names: VonShitzenpants, Diaper Don, Mushroom Man, Toupee Trump, the Senile Penile, Roast Beef Boy, Epstein's Best Bud, Convicted Felon, Dotard, or the Short-Fingered Vulgarian.

- After Donald Trump accused Barack Obama of being "the literal devil," a "Kenyan sleeper cell," and "the caliph of ISIS," he said Obama was committing presidential harassment against him by making jokes about his penis size at Biden rallies.

- Trump says he will make the children of America rich and happy by "cutting the red tape on child labor rights," and giving teens and children aged ten and up all the agricultural, meat-processing, construction, roofing, and landscaping jobs left behind by deported immigrants.

- Mike Lindell is reportedly getting angry that Elon Musk is ripping off his political schtick of libeling voting machine companies, spreading crackpot conspiracy theories, and running his companies into the ground.

- Trump was awarded *CoverGirl*'s "2024 Makeup Ambassador of the Year" award.

- RNC Co-Chair Lara Trump has been so busy recording her next unauthorized Tom Petty cover that she reportedly forgot she was the RNC co-chair for the last week.

- A homophobic pastor from Indiana accidentally outed himself during a church service yesterday after he told his congregation to be on the lookout for the "Gay Agenda," and then several worshippers downloaded *Grindr* to use its geo-locating map to spy on nearby gays before promptly finding the televangelist's account within fifty feet.

- Trump accused Biden and Harris today of "rigging the economy" against him by having the stock market continually set new records ahead of the election.

- JD Vance has reportedly asked Trump three times today what couch he's going to get for the Oval Office.

- During a prayer breakfast event this morning, Trump weaved around in his speech until he began listing golfers from the 80s in order by dong size, and gave himself second place behind Arnold Palmer.

- Trump reportedly stopped a meeting with his lawyers abruptly today when they brought up his ongoing criminal trials for January 6th and hoarding classified documents, and Trump made them listen to his music playlist for 39 minutes.

- There's a new reality show being developed called "Republican City" that will have contestants live for a year in a town where everyone is armed, there's no minimum wage or healthcare, pollution and child labor are allowed, and women's rights revert to the 1850s.

- BREAKING NEWS: A group of MAGA fans who watched Trump's Madison Square Garden rally reportedly just realized they've been mistaking racism for patriotism all this time, and they're very, very sorry.

- Trump reportedly ate more *McDonald's* food than he served out at his photo-op, and didn't pay for any of it.

- Trump reportedly told the employees at *McDonald's*, "A lot of people don't know this, but tertiary syphilis can really sneak up on you."

- Liquor stores in blue states and districts are reporting record-breaking sales as Americans prepare to drink themselves out of consciousness if Trump wins on November 5th.

- During Trump's *McDonald's* photo-op, he reportedly told the manager that presidential immunity means he doesn't have to wash his hands after using the bathroom like the sign says.

- Trump says he will be less focused on physical appearances for his second term, and will even give ugly women some jobs.

- Trump says Biden should award him a Purple Heart for accidentally burning himself on the *McDonald's* fryer during his photo-op at one of the chain's restaurants.

- The US military is reportedly having meetings about how to deal with potential illegal orders given by Trump, as well as how to deal with his infamous body odor.

- Trump is reportedly upset that Stephen Miller won't get a wig.

- Trump accidentally said on a hot mic that his folder of blackmail on Matt Gaetz was the thickest folder of everyone in Congress.

- Jim Jordan says he didn't see any of the sex trafficking Matt Gaetz allegedly did, and no one told him anything about it, and if anyone says they did they're lying.

- Trump reportedly made J.D. Vance do a blood oath vow last night that Vance will never initiate a 25th Amendment coup against him.

- Marjorie Taylor Greene says if every member of Congress who did what Matt Gaetz has been accused of had to resign, "Democrats would have a supermajority."

Republicans Still Want Free School Lunches To Be Spit In To Teach Kids A Lesson On Socialism

September 28, 2024
Oklahoma City, OK—

Republicans are attacking Democratic vice president candidate Tim Walz for passing legislation in Minnesota to give children free lunches in schools.

One notable attack came from Oklahoma State Senator Meredith Jenkins:

"Governor Tim Walz is no advocate for the hungry, poor school children in Minnesota," she said, "and it's a shame Walz is working so hard to brainwash the kids in his state to be communist by accepting free food during the school day. We might as well just start sewing hammers and sickles onto their school uniforms, and teaching them to sing the Soviet Union's evil national anthem, *The Internationale* every morning instead of the *Pledge of Allegiance*! The Republican Party is committed to keeping our school children capitalists, and the only way we can help students from poor, urban families develop a work ethic they'll never be taught at home from their necessarily lazy, handout-dependent, and therefore morally deficient parents is to humiliate these school children in public as much as possible to make them realize communism will not improve their lives. This is a lesson that Tim Walz's brand of Leninist, Maoist Stalinism will never teach them. Free school lunches are a slippery slope that leads inevitably to gulags full of enslaved peasants being forced at gunpoint to throw everything metal they own in their little shacks and hovels into makeshift neighborhood steel furnaces! So we must nip this American communism in the bud right now. But, believe me, I am not heartless. I realize it's, of course, not all those poor Minnesota children's fault they weren't born into wealthy families like my kids, or me, or my husband, or our parents, or seven out of our eight grandparents, but it is poor Minnesota children's fault they are giving into the Satanic temptation of socialist calories by accepting Tim Walz's pinko, commie meals. It's a lie and a coastal elitist hoax that well-fed children do better in schools, score higher on national testing, act out less, generally develop healthier and happier, and ultimately save the government billions of dollars in downstream socio-economic costs that can be avoided by helping support tens of thousands of underfed children distracted and disadvantaged daily by their hunger. But look how long it took me to say all that! These egghead Democrats want us to waste all our time reading a bunch of scientific studies and surveys about the causes and effects of generational poverty, but that's how the liberals can keep us distracted so they can sneak in a whole bunch of terrorist groups full of Venezuelan gang members who will vote Democratic as long as they can have free range back and forth across the Southern border to abduct us patriotic, godly Americans and force feed our fingers to us one at a time! There is a direct line between Tim Walz's free school lunches to us being forced at gunpoint to eat our own fingers by Venezuelan death squads! Plus, how will we pay for it nationally? I will be dead before I let the socialist Democrats raises taxes on billionaires even a single percent! Which is why it's time for Republicans to do something drastic to keep the ember of capitalistic freedom alive in all the school children across America if Kamala Harris and her evil Democrats win in November and institute their Trotskyite delusion of subsidized lunch in all fifty of our states. There's only one thing we can do! We must ungrudgingly, and with love in our hearts, spit loogies into free every drink, entrée, and side dish that all the poor handout-accepting school children will receive at lunch time. This way we can remind them that someday, if they study hard, they might be rich, too, and be able to rise above the spit-on and become the spitters themselves. I didn't need to eat and drink copious amounts of saliva to grow up and be rich when I was a kid because my family was already rich, and then I later married into an even richer family, but, if I had been born into a poor family, I am 100% positive that regularly being forced to consume lunch lady phlegm with thick, mucous viscosity tinged with the bitter flavor of cigarette smoke while all the rich kids at my school laughed and jeered at me would have inspired me to work hard in all my classes to make sure I'd never struggle financially. But, again, I didn't have to because my grandparents left my parents millions, and my parents and my husband's parents let us both be executives in our respective family companies right out of high school. But the poor school children of America won't learn how to lift themselves up by their bootstraps like me and my husband did in the summer between graduating high school and accepting a huge salary in our grandpas' companies. These students from poor families will thank me when they're older and lower-middle-class, I promise you that! So sorry Governor Walz, you can keep your free sandwiches in Minnesota. School children in red states will stay hungry rather than give in to socialism! They'll starve rather than give their souls to Stalin and Mao! God bless childhood hunger! And don't listen to Tim Walz's lies about Minnesota's green energy. Green technology is slavery and a deal with the Devil! Patriotic kids all around the country know it's better to get black lungs in coal mines and toil in oil fields than give in to the George Soros funded, global warming propaganda that says it's okay to drive an electric vehicle, or approve of a wind turbine near your town! It was bad enough when the green communists took all the lead out of the gasoline in the 70s! If it was good enough for me and my siblings to sit behind our old Chevy truck and take turns playing old school, Real America childhood games like who-could-inhale-the-fumes-for-the-longest, as well as who-could-sit-in-the-closed-garage-with-the-car-running-and-pass-out-the-fastest, it's good enough for kids today! That's the classic Americana Trump will bring back when he says 'Make America Great Again!' Back when we had energy freedom!"

A Billionaire Built Trump A Retirement Home Replicating The White House To Stay In If He Loses

November 2, 2024
Palm Beach, FL—

Billionaire David Cubano just announced he is funding the creation of a special "MAGA themed" retirement home just for Donald Trump that he will let Trump live in for free if he loses reelection until his federal trials lock him up, under the condition Trump not attempt any other coups.

The retirement home will include an exact replica of Trump's Oval Office so he can think he's still the president, and spend his sundowning years blissfully ignorant he lost a third election.

"I want everything to be authentic so Trump is comfortable," Cubano said, "I want him to be able to wake up every morning and head to the fake Oval Office to watch his 'Executive Hours' of *Fox News* content. The TVs will just repeat a best-of montage of real Fox content from the years 2017–2020 in which Fox hosts praise him, and his desk will even have a big red button that lets him think he's nuking North Korea, or Nancy Pelosi, or every windmill in America. I've thought of everything Trump would want so he finally just retires into obscurity and leaves us and our democracy alone. All the nurses will be blonde and give off a subliminal 'Ivanka vibe.' All the employees will be white except for one token member of each ethnicity to say things such as, 'I'm Black, so you can believe me when I say all the Blacks love you, Sir!' Trump will love it, and finally stop being the most toxic, divisive sh*tstain in American history that makes our country look as bad as he smells!"

Cubano then revealed a script he will give all the doctors to recite every morning as they give Trump his pills while they wear military costumes to look like generals so Trump won't ever notice it's a retirement home:

"Sir, you are a genius president, and your polls are at 99%. But don't worry, Stephen Miller has been alerted, and that last 1% will shortly be rounded up and deported, and Mexico will send a big, fat check to pay for it because you're such a great negotiator with your big Trump brain. What great genetics you have, Sir. I mean, just look at your hair. You have the naturally blonde hair of a 15-year-old Abercrombie model. You have totally turned this country around. No one believed you could be so successful, Sir, but everyone's talking about it. Everyone is finally tired of all your winning. They're shouting out, 'No, Mr. Trump, we can't take it, please stop! We can't handle one more single victory!' You would not believe it, but the crowd outside your window right now is bigger than any crowd in history. Way bigger than Obama's crowds. They never came to crowd all around his White House. You have more people than all the presidents combined. The most incredible crowd of all time. No one can believe it! And they're so excited for the next amazing deals you're going to negotiate for them these next four years. Everyone's eagerly begging to see your incredible Obamacare replacement plan, your infrastructure plan, your Iran nuclear deal, your North Korean nuclear deal, and your Ukraine peace deal. But don't worry about it right now, Sir, I already told everyone your deals are coming in two weeks. You don't have to worry your big Trump brain about that stuff yet. I'm sure you'll come up with something before those two weeks. Healthcare, and infrastructure, and Iran, and North Korea, and Ukraine are so easy. No one knows more about those topics than you! On day one you will make so many great deals, won't you? Because you're better than Lincoln, Washington, Jefferson, and Roosevelt combined. They should remove those losers from Mt. Rushmore and put your face up there four times. You could have made a deal to stop the Civil War, and everyone would have loved it. You could have solved WWII so fast, and Hitler would have fallen in love with you. Here, Mr. President, here's your *Diet Coke*. Don't worry, I opened it myself. I didn't let Melania get near it. I know how you've caught her pouring mystery powders into the *Diet Cokes* she brings you, so I made sure to open this myself. If you want, I'll have Eric come up and taste it first, do a little poison check. Yeah, isn't that nice? You love your *Diet Cokes*, don't you? Don't you feel better after your *Diet Coke*? Trump and *Diet Coke* are a great combo aren't they? One of the best combos of all time. Oh, did I tell you yet that Rudy Giuliani and Mike Lindell finally revealed their evidence of voter fraud, and found that Democrats rigged all their votes. It turns out Democrats didn't get a single vote after all, and it was a unanimous victory for you! No one can believe it! You're the winningest president ever. Oh, and another thing, Mr. President, remember how Georgia went for Biden in 2020? Well it turns out that after our insurrectionists in Georgia hanged Brian Kemp for not certifying the right electoral votes, they found the 11,780 votes you needed to win in 2020. So retroactively you've been awarded those electoral votes, along with all the other blue states because all the governors were caught cheating. You actually won landslides in all your previous elections, just like you said you did. You were always telling the truth all along! And you were 100% right that it was everyone else in America who was lying, never you. You've been proven as the most honest president ever, as well as the greatest president America has ever had, Sir."

And then, while Trump is good and distracted, the doctor will inject him with several elephant tranquilizers so he sleeps for the rest of the day and can't f*ck America's democracy any more than he already has.

God Says Ted Cruz Is The Biggest Douche In The Universe

November 3, 2024
Heaven—

After seeing recent polls that suggest Senator Ted Cruz is within the polling margin of error of his Democratic opponent Colin Allred, I called God to see what He thought about Ted Cruz.

[The following is our phone conversation, lightly edited for clarity.]

DASH MACINTYRE: "Hey, God, who's the biggest asshole on the planet?"

GOD: "Ted Cruz. In the entire universe. If I may brag for a moment, Ted Cruz is My favorite creation of all time. I love to watch Ted Cruz in action being a total douche. I crammed that guy so full of arrogant ignorance that I have to personally be intervening at all times to stop him from spontaneously combusting like an atom bomb of mega douchery. Wanna know a secret? The guy watches squirrel porn. Like incessantly. I'm omniscient so I know every time he goes to AcornHub and watches low quality, amateur videos of squirrels going at it. But he's great entertainment. It's like when you paint something you're really proud of, and you can just stare at it and admire it for hours. Ted Cruz is a spectacular, magnificent piece of shit. In a galaxy on the other side of the universe I made a whole planet of Ted Cruzes. I didn't supply their world with any plants or animals so they have to fight to the death and eat each other every day. And the victorious ones have to asexually birth out new Ted Cruzes out of their anuses to fight and eat the next day. But, as you can imagine, passing a Ted Cruz through another Ted Cruz's sphincter is pretty messy business, and usually the Ted Cruz anuses tear in the birthing process, so usually father Ted Cruzes start bleeding everywhere, which attracts predator Ted Cruzes, who have evolved incredibly impressive olfactory organs that can smell blood from up to forty miles away. Because baby Ted Cruzes are at such risk of predators, they must gestate pretty fully in their Ted Cruz fathers' large intestines so that right at birth they are capable of running away. Ted Cruzes are such douches that even the baby Ted Cruzes are essentially evolved to instinctively incapacitate their fathers so that nearby predator Ted Cruzes fill up on the fathers before chasing after the babies. Nature can be so sublimely douchey, can't it? This is my favorite planet in the entire universe. I love the Ted Cruz planet even more than Boob Planet, which is about what it sounds like. I love watching Ted Cruzes strangle each other, and bite each others' fingers and ears off. It never gets old. It's a majestic sight to see whole herds of feral Ted Cruzes gnawing on each others' bones, and wearing each others' faces as war masks, and smearing each others' blood on their bodies as war paint, and sleeping in each others' hollowed out bodies for warmth at night, and wearing elaborate jewelry pieces of each others' teeth, and wearing clothes made of each others' dried out and stretched skin, and decorating the entrances of their cave homes with each others' skulls. What douches. I wish you could see it. Actually, you know what? You, like everyone else with good taste, hate Ted Cruz so I think you'll really get a kick out of it. I'll show you!"

At this point, God teleported me to the planet of Ted Cruzes, and I watched millions of them fighting free-for-all battles to the death. Ted Cruz body parts and brain matter were splattered everywhere, and rivers of Ted Cruz blood flowing for millennia had carved the geography of the planet into massive, red-stained canyon systems.

Different subgroups of Ted Cruzes had evolved to take advantage of various environmental niches, with some Ted Cruzes being ferocious predators favoring the taste of fresh Ted Cruz flesh, while other meek Ted Cruzes, whose eyes had adapted to be on the sides of their head like prey to scan the horizon and flee at the first sign of danger, were merely scavengers picking at leftover Ted Cruz carcasses left behind by the bigger predator Ted Cruzes.

There were parasitic Ted Cruzes that were little and would latch on to other Ted Cruzes and suck their blood, and other Ted Cruzes only ate specific organs. One surprisingly social species of Ted Cruz lived in small groups, and sucked each other off dozens of times a day for their nutrients, as well as for social bonding. One more peculiar Ted Cruz species only liked to eat Ted Cruz hair, and would spend hours hacking up hairballs and then re-swallowing over and over as their digestive system extracted the nutrients.

Another fascinating subgroup of Ted Cruzes filled the niche dung beetles fill here on Earth walking around rolling balls of Ted Cruz dung six feet in diameter taking bites out of them every few meters. Just like there are more species of beetle than any other animal on Earth, there are more species of the dung eating Ted Cruzes than any other type of Ted Cruz.

The most technologically advanced Ted Cruzes had entered the Bone Age, and had learned to make spear and knife weapons out of sharpened Ted Cruz ribs, femurs, tibias, and fibulas. Occasionally, a particularly clever Ted Cruz would craft a primitive trebuchet with bones and rope made of Ted Cruz tendons and ligaments, and collect decapitated Ted Cruz heads to launch at unsuspecting Ted Cruzes from quite a safe distance.

The sublime douchery of it all brought a tear to my eye, and I thanked God for showing me the most majestic assholery in the entire universe.

HELP WANTED: Join Donald Trump's 2nd Administration Today! Here's How To Apply!

November 7, 2024
Palm Beach, FL—

The Former and Future President of the United States Donald J. Trump wants to consider you joining his 2nd presidency!

Love for a fast-paced work environment is a must, as Trump's management style pits everyone in a free-for-all battle to win his attention and respect. Staff turnover was historically high in his first term, and is expected to be even higher this time around.

MUST be willing to sign an all-inclusive, 180-page, single-spaced non-disclosure agreement for which Trump reserves the right to sue you for $5 billion if you discuss anything he's ever done or said to you!

QUALIFICATIONS

- Previous on-air TV experience from *Fox News*, *Newsmax*, or conservative podcasting
- A "Central Casting" physical appearance—blondes strongly preferred *(an "Ivanka-esque" look will be given preferential treatment for female applicants, and male applicants must be better looking than Rudy Giuliani but not too better looking than Trump)*
- Big breasts for women *(inquire about our new-hire bonus of free implants)*, full head of hair for men *(inquire about our new-hire bonus of hair implants)*
- Team player *(you may be asked to claim guilt for a couple crimes and/or obstruct justice, you know, for the team, but pardons and NDA hush money are negotiable)*
- Must have a good memory as we are a paperless office so there's no paper trail or physical records of anything we do, write, or say *(if you do need to write any notes, you will be expected to flush or eat them)*
- Some plumbing experience is a plus, particularly unclogging paper jams in our memo toilet
- Can handle terrible body odor and the scent of soiled underwear for extended periods of time
- Intimate knowledge of the fast food menus at *McDonald's* and *KFC*, or be a very fast, visual learner of combo deals
- Flexible opinions on the Constitution's checks and balances on executive power, the geopolitical benefits of NATO and the UN, and human rights

RESPONSIBILITIES

- Fetch Trump a can of *Diet Coke* exactly every 37 minutes *(due to his extreme physiological dependence on aspartame he will start sweating profusely and foaming at the mouth if you're more than 45-seconds late, and possibly show a lot of other symptoms not too dissimilar to rabies)*
- Flush *(or eat)* all handwritten notes from Trump, even the ones he just sketches boobs on
- Occasional light janitorial work, such as cleaning ketchup off walls and sweeping up broken plate shards and half-eaten burgers
- Schedule weekly phone calls between Vladimir Putin and Trump
- Be proactive and a self-starter at claiming "executive privilege" and "presidential immunity" when interacting with journalists, Democratic members of Congress, courthouse officials, or the Department of Justice
- Always knock on the door before entering when Trump is in his "Executive Hours" because he might be naked jerking off to the fawning praise he gets from *Fox News*, or he might not have his makeup or hair done yet, and you'll make him shriek for you to get out and yell that it's "fake news" how he looks
- Women: always pretend to be turned on or impressed if he flashes you
- Be good at remembering a constantly shifting array of "alternative facts," "enemies of the people," and expected hurricane trajectories
- Coordinate political strategies with a revolving cast of co-conspirators, underlings, yes-men, and blackmailed members of Congress, as well as occasionally escort blackmail material to and from the vault in Trump's Mar-a-Lago suite
- Always let him "weave," and never embarrass him by reminding him what your question was actually about if he deviated far off topic
- Stalk and spy on Republican members of Congress to blackmail them into loyalty, and occasionally earn overtime driving to their houses in the middle of the night to look through their trash bins and plant concealed recording devices on their porches
- Help enforce a 2-drink maximum on Rudy Giuliani during regular business hours if he is around
- Spray Steve Bannon with *Febreze* when he comes around so he doesn't stink up the office *(his stench somehow clings to the couches he sits on for days)*
- Spray Trump with cologne before all meetings so his infamous body odor doesn't embarrass him or make foreign dignitaries throw up *(we've tried everything to mitigate the smell and nothing works, so just get used to the smell and cleaning up vomit when attending global summits)*
- Try to sober up Don Jr. and/or give him eye drops when he's around the media or any cameras

- Make sure Eric doesn't pick his scabs and eat them, and bleed on the White House furniture
- Be on the lookout for Melania lookalikes and body-doubles we can hire to use at White House events
- Never let Trump eat or drink anything Melania gives him *(Trump is concerned she might be trying to poison him)*
- You'll get occasional breaks to go pick up *McDonald's* or *KFC* from the drive-through *(Trump doesn't trust random delivery drivers)*
- Use Craigslist to hire Black people for "Blacks 4 Trump" appearances at campaign rallies
- Do NOT EVER mention windmills, sharks, the water pressure, Obama, Ukraine, Zelensky, Pelosi, exercise, heart disease, Jack Smith, January 6th, his inauguration crowd size, Melania's fidelity, or Eric when Trump is around
- If Trump invites you out golfing with him you MUST let him win and look the other way when he kicks his ball into the water hazard and drops a new ball from his pocket much closer to the hole
- Keep a close eye on *Twitter/X* so you know if/when Trump fires you
- Quietly and passively accept a lot of mental and psychological abuse *(Trump's genius leadership style involves a lot of yelling, insults, threats of violence, and choking attempts)*

BENEFITS

- Payday in "two weeks"
- A 1% discount on Mar-a-Lago membership, and 47 cents off at any other Trump property
- Proximity to classified and top secret documents Trump will not give back following his presidential briefings
- Casual, daily appraisals of your physical appearance by the President of the United States *(particularly if you are female)*
- You'll learn from the best dealmaker of all time, and watch his genius business skills as he finally unveils his new Obamacare replacement, infrastructure deal, Iran deal, North Korea deal, and plan to make Mexico pay for the wall!
- You'll get to hear a lot of rumors about golfers' penis sizes
- If Trump wants to make a move on you he'll take you out furniture shopping first
- You'll be around many powerful people in Republican politics, and see Trump humiliate them often *(you'll love "The Kennel," and seeing Mike Johnson, Ted Cruz, and Lindsey Graham spend hours locked inside it)*
- Complimentary, communal lines of *Adderall* several times a day

- There's often free makeup available when Trump buys a foundation that isn't orange enough for his taste and he doesn't want it
- Working for the greatest president in US history, better than Lincoln and Washington combined!

TO APPLY

- Cover letter must be no more than two paragraphs—including Trump's name in every paragraph *(if not every individual sentence)* is **STRONGLY RECOMMENDED**
- Letters of recommendation from dictators are quite welcome!
- Pay a $50 application fee, a $50 resumé reading fee, a $50 resumé filing fee, a $50 non-disclosure agreement filing fee, and a $50 interview fee
- Female applicants are advised to print out and bring several selfies so Trump can determine if you have the "Trump Administration It Factor" *(the more skin showing the better for you)*, and male applicants must write out an amusing story of a time you think you were were unfairly accused of sexual assault
- Pay a $50 selfie filing fee or $50 sex adventure reading fee
- Join *Truth Social* and post five Truths accusing Democratic members of Congress being Satan and show Trump during interview
- Pick out, buy, print out, and bring to discuss your favorite "Trump NFT"
- Pay a $50 NFT filing fee
- Write and send a letter to *NBCUniversal* at the end of your interview while being monitored to tell them that you'd love it if they produced another season of *The Apprentice* featuring Trump as president firing his cabinet members for not being loyal enough
- Tips: Bring an 18-pack of *Diet Coke* cans to the interview or a few cans of hairspray, say Trump's name a lot *(he really likes hearing his full name, not just "Trump")*, show cleavage if you're a woman and maybe bend over a couple times, say racist or sexist things, express that you think it's genius to have America abandon our NATO allies and it's totally not just because that's what would be spectacular for Putin's land grab dreams, remark that his hands are even bigger than you expected, and tell him he totally could have dated Ivanka if he weren't her father—he'll really love all that!

We look forward* to meeting you!

*No fuglies

BIG IF TRUE XI

- Donald Trump says it has taken him by complete surprise that so many of his most loyal supporters he has nominated for cabinet positions keep turning out to be sex offenders.

- Trump has now officially nominated more sex offenders to his cabinet than any other president except Martin Van Buren.

- Elon Musk and Vivek Ramaswamy are reportedly starting to worry that Marjorie Taylor Greene isn't the most serious, competent, mentally stable representative they could have found to be chairwoman of the House D.O.G.E. Committee.

- Several virulently homophobic House Republicans who cut out "trans surveillance portholes" in the stall walls of the men's bathrooms were just heard loudly denying to Speaker Mike Johnson that they intentionally installed glory holes.

- A new TikTok challenge is offering $75,000 for someone to smack Donald Trump Jr.'s pants pockets on live television to see if any white clouds get dispersed.

- Nancy Mace hasn't left the bathroom for her anti-trans protest in three days, and reportedly bathed herself from the sink this morning.

- Trump says he can do a better vetting job than the FBI for his cabinet nominees, and that he already has "thick folders on all of them full of juicy secrets they'd do anything to keep from being revealed."

- 60% of the nominees Trump has named for his next administration have at some point publicly compared him to Adolph Hitler.

- Nancy Mace reportedly dropped a suitcase this morning on her way into her Capitol office, and out of it spilled a dozen dildos she said would be part of the next phase of her anti-trans bathroom protest.

- Representative Nancy Mace has reportedly banned her boyfriend, ex-husband, son, and all male visitors from using two of the three bathrooms in their house.

- Vivek Ramaswamy has reportedly enraged Elon Musk by putting the federal subsidies for *SpaceX* and *Tesla* on the list of spending cuts.

- Trump has reportedly made RFK Jr. eat *McDonald's* every day for lunch for the last 9 days, and vowed to fire him if he "lays one regulatory finger on *Diet Coke*."

- The janitors in Congress reportedly just installed a "TRANS WOMEN ONLY" sign above the bathroom Nancy Mace has been protesting in front of for the last two weeks.

- Marjorie Taylor Greene claims she doesn't remember claiming she had evidence of other Republicans committing similar sex crimes to Matt Gaetz, or threatening to release it if Gaetz wasn't confirmed, and that neither of those sound like something she'd ever say.

- A second MAGA spa just opened in West Virginia where the milk is raw, the food is unregulated, ivermectin smoothies are available all day, and "leech therapy" is used to suck and filter out all the childhood vaccines from conservative patriots' blood.

- Musk is reportedly annoying Trump by using the bathroom stall or urinal right next to Trump anytime he goes to the bathroom so Musk can make sure Trump isn't making a decision without him.

- A new poll found that 86% of *Twitter* users are getting tired of seeing the AI superhero photos Elon Musk posts of himself at the top of their feeds every time they open the app even though they don't follow him or ever interact with his tweets.

- A local MAGA protester with Trump flags on his truck, a *Bible* in his hand, and an AR-15 strapped to his back is having trouble explaining how he's different than ISIS.

- *Fox News* says Trump's Defense Secretary nominee Pete Hegseth's drinking and harassing of female coworkers is "no worse than the average male *Fox News* currently employed."

- The homophobic televangelist who sells crucifix necklaces with a naked, fit Trump on them instead of Jesus so he can afford platinum membership at Mar-a-Lago reportedly just got asked to stop spending hours every day in the Mar-a-Lago men's locker room.

- The gay dating app *Poundrrr* is reportedly thinking about selling an advent calendar called "25 Gays Until Christmas" where each day a homophobic "Christian Values" Republican member of Congress who uses the app for hookups during their campaign bus tours is revealed.

- QAnon says the Deep State must have gotten to Trump and tricked him into hiring a cabinet full of sex offenders, and that patriots should no longer trust Trump because he has been compromised.

- Trump's nominee for Deputy of Agricultural Land Management has been banned from 13 *Hooters* restaurants across six Midwestern states.

- A new poll found that 93% of Americans don't want to know what Stephen Miller is doing right now.

- Senate Republicans are reportedly refusing invitations to Mar-a-Lago out of concern Trump will try to catch them in honeypot traps.

- Trump says he's "bigger than Jesus" because, unlike him, Jesus never accomplished His comeback to get a second term.

- Local Trump fans are starting to get suspicious about why, even though Trump is going to be president again, he, Melania, and all their surrogates are still constantly trying to sell merchandise to them.

- *McDonald's* executives are reportedly deliberating about offering Trump free food for life if he'll exempt them from his tariffs.

- Top Evangelical leaders around the country say they're beginning to feel used because Trump hasn't answered any of their phone calls since winning reelection.

- Trump appointed himself ambassador to a dozen countries so he can have thirteen governmental salaries.

- Elon Musk has reportedly been caught several times at Mar-a-Lago eavesdropping on conversations Trump is having behind closed doors.

- RFK Jr. reportedly missed a meeting with Donald Trump this morning because he had to go to the hospital to remove over a hundred tapeworms.

- Trump promises this year his taxes will be 100% accurate with no fraud this time, and he won't forget to carry a one so that he ends up paying only $750 in taxes like he did in 2016 and 2017.

- Trump liked his *McDonald's* photo-op so much he hosted an event focused on the border today at a *Taco Bell*, and then gave a speech on tariffs at a *Kentucky Fried Chicken*.

- Trump is reportedly thinking of nominating his son Eric as Ambassador to Australia hoping its extremely lethal fauna will "make him disappear."

- Trump has mandated that every chair Elon Musk gets during meetings from now on must be smaller than his chair.

- Now that Trump won, he's reportedly not looking forward to having to do his two-hour morning makeup and hair routine every day again for the next four years straight.

- Trump has reportedly been complaining to his staffers that Elon Musk is "more annoying, needy, and clingy than Eric."

- After a week of claiming she was attacked when a man accidentally bumped into her in a hallway, GOP Representative Nancy Mace has tweeted thirty-six times this morning about being robbed after a *Starbucks* employee allegedly gave her the wrong number of pennies back in her change.

- Trump's Secretary of Labor nominee, Ralph Hastings, said the first thing he'll do is force all companies to take down their "employees must wash hands" bathroom signs, and "bring freedom back to America's wash rooms."

- Trump says Democrats better not try to investigate him again because Republicans were "civil and hands-off with the Biden family for the last four years."

- Kash Patel's FBI enemies list includes his sixth grade algebra teacher, his neighbor, a previous landlord, three ex-girlfriends, and his step-dad.

- Elon Musk is reportedly frustrated that Trump keeps turning on *Fox News* during their staffing meetings, and shushing him to hear what the *Fox* hosts are saying about him.

- RFK Jr.'s brain worm reportedly snuck into Trump's ear during a fundraiser this weekend accomplishing its months-long mission to use its RFK Jr. host body to gain proximity and then access to Trump's brain.

- An extremely MAGA televangelist from Mississippi who claimed faith in Trump as God's newest and most righteous prophet was more powerful than any drug on Earth just got arrested for running a meth lab in the basement of his church.

Allen Ginsberg's "Howl," For The MAGA Gen-Xers Who Voted For Trump More Than Any Other Generation

I saw the worst minds of the Gen-X generation destroyed by social media, starving ideologically naked,

dragging themselves from forwarding pro-Iraq-War email chains to joining Tea Party *Facebook* groups, to following MAGA *Twitter* trolls, to sharing QAnon *Truth Social* conspiracies till dawn looking always for their next Culture War outrage fix,

golden years hotheads burning *Fox News* and *Newsmax* into the pixels of their televisions and the retinas of their eyes,

demagogic followers yearning for a modern connection to the fascist dynamo in the machinery of right wing government,

who cowered in easy chairs in their underwear burning their money in campaign donations for a wannabe billionaire's legal fees and vulgar NFTs flaunting his fictional superhero virility,

who paced marital walks down mansion driveways aiming guns at peaceful civil rights protesters,

who chanted under the Capitol on January 6th for libertarian angels staggering through Congress defecating on the floors and pissing on the walls, beating up cops, and chanting "hang the vice president,"

who in stupors of economic frustration sat up comment-ranting in the supernatural darkness of rural and suburban basement home offices about urban chaos, mass arrests, police brutality, walls, deportations, and doors shut on refugees,

who injected disinfectant and drank bleach while waiting for COVID test results, and purgatoried their immune systems day after day of neither masking nor social distancing,

who plunged themselves into hydroxychloroquine binges poisoning their stomachs and colon linings,

who swallowed horse medicine and dribbled their incontinence into their denim overalls,

who shot AR-15s at things labeled with names of liberal legislators in campaign commercials threatening invisible specters of Democratic gun control,

who shrugged off school shootings sharing pro-life memes in their social media group chats,

who burned books written with feminine and ethnic perspectives or transgender experiences,

who let themselves be f*cked in the ass by homophobic preachers and anti-gay legislators,

who blew and were blown by those human seraphim, the young Latin pool boys of Evangelical university administrators, who bared their hearts to a Republican Jesus with metaphorical knives in their hands to cut safety nets of bureaucratic charity,

who dreamt of nostalgically segregated *Andy Griffith Show* towns where gays weren't out of the closet and no one ever heard of unisex bathrooms,

who shunned and cast out their queer children and grandchildren lamenting the modern era's scarcity of family values,

who hoped for patriarchal militarism with homoerotic aesthetics propagandized by totalitarian dictators with delusions of ethno-nationalist homogeneity,

who wept at the diversity and globalism of the streets calling any place with Black people "sketchy,"

who hallucinated in exurban enclaves and survivalists' underground bunkers nightmare visions of urban voter fraud by bohemian hedonists bleeding red for communism,

who chained themselves to their gas stoves, coal mines, and fossil fuel car engines rolling coal down the interstate,

who clutched tight to their plastic straws, sexy green *M&M* mascots, Dr. Seuss picture books with out-of-date illustrated stereotypes, and gender-specific potato-based children's toys hiding from the inevitabilities of cultural change,

who muttered profanities under their breath in public at reminders of Democratic governors and presidents.

who blazoned their hats, shirts, rural billboards, and bumper stickers with political Tourette's slogans of "F*ck Joe Biden," "Let's Go Brandon," and "Joe & the Hoe" to own the libs,

who were caught posting from burner accounts argumentative prefaces such as "As a lesbian Black woman, I think..." to publish attacks against gays, Blacks, and women,

who fumed ceaselessly about a president's son's penis to bury their heads in the sand of the jury-confirmed sex crimes of their candidate,

who worshiped pedantry clapping to the hypnotic beat of militant whataboutism defending novel administrative depravities they cheer for!

What sphinxes of petty grievances and juvenile comportment bashed open their skills and ate up their brains?

Trump! Narcissism! Filth! Ugliness! Obsessed with dollars! Women screaming at his Tic Tac breath! Conservative men cowering beneath his autocratic egomania!

Trump! Trump! Unindictable Trump, blackmailer of the GOP!

Trump whose empathy is a void! Trump whose mind is a dynamo of antichrist self-aggrandizement! Trump who says I alone can fix it!

Trump who will destroy American democracy before going to prison for his lifetime of crime!

Mad generation!

BIG IF TRUE XII

- After Trump threatened to take Greenland and the Panama Canal by force, Vladimir Putin reportedly announced he'd gift Trump a revived Russian award that czars used to give to their royal court clowns.

- Following the stalemate in Ukraine and the collapse of Bashar al-Assad's regime in Syria followed by a Russian withdrawal there, Trump is reportedly worried that Putin is beginning to look like a loser.

- Tulsi Gabbard is reportedly worried it's not a good idea anymore to give skeptical Republican senators her very complimentary letters of recommendation from Bashar al-Assad during her confirmation hearings

- A *Fox News* host complained today on his podcast that the *Snickers* candy bars "look too much like veiny, black penises for Christians to eat."

- The brain worm that used **RFK Jr.** as a host to get to Trump and sneak in his brain just announced it is fully in control of Trump's body, and that it will be the real new **POTUS** on January 20th.

- Following the recent murder of a health insurance executive, the insurance company *Regressive* announced it will postpone its new policy of limiting patients to one free toilet flush per day in the hospital.

- Trump reportedly told Elon Musk this morning, "No one knows more about rockets and electric cars than me."

- Trump reportedly wants the military to invade Greenland, annex it as a territory called "Trumpland," and then make it the 51st state after first moving tens of thousands of US Southerners to "Americanize it."

- Mike Johnson is reportedly paralyzed with fear because Trump is demanding Congress take away all funding for windmills and wind turbines while Musk is demanding Congress dramatically increase funding for them.

- Trump reportedly forced Elon Musk to get up from his dining table last night at Mar-a-Lago and eat at a table several rows away.

- Trump called into *Fox News* tonight and claimed that he and Musk both took an IQ test at Mar-a-Lago this weekend, and his score was higher.

- Kash Patel says he'll make a list at the FBI of everyone who has ever called Trump by the infamous insult Michael Cohen used in court, "Von ShitzInPants," on social media.

- Trump is reportedly melting down after some Gen Z kids of Mar-a-Lago members wrote on the lobby wall in ketchup, "Congratulations, President Musk!"

- A medical company in Boston is designing a new, modern iron lung machine called "Trump Lungs" for when RFK Jr. and the Trump Administration ban school vaccine mandates and bring back polio.

- Trump reportedly had the chef at Mar-a-Lago write "GO HOME" in icing on a piece of cake Elon Musk ordered for dessert tonight.

- The National Association of Tuba And Trombone Musicians is reportedly raising money to bus 500 musicians from around the nation to attend Donald Trump's inauguration speech, and play their tubas while he's speaking.

- So far, over 600 kazoo players have signed up to attend Trump's inauguration speech and play their instruments all day.

- Barack Obama is reportedly raising funds to launch Tea Party rallies across the nation to protest a new president who was born in Africa and is going to increase the national debt.

- Trump is reportedly worried that if his tariffs wreck the economy everyone who loses their home and has to move into shack villages will call them "Trumpvilles."

- Supreme Court Justice Clarence Thomas says that to show the American people he takes integrity seriously, he's going to limit the number of billionaire vacations he goes on this coming year to only twenty-five.

- After Trump vowed that if anyone shows up to his inauguration wearing a mushroom costume to mock him he'll have the military arrest them, a top general told him that the law "unfortunately does not give the military authorization to arrest fungi."

- Trump is reportedly furious that several TikTok trends are going viral urging everyone who can attend his inaugural address to bring vuvuzelas to interrupt his speech.

- Susan Collins reportedly didn't appreciate the coyote corpse RFK Jr. found this morning and brought to her Senate office during their meeting today, but Kennedy claimed it was "too good to let go to waste on the side of the road."

- Trump says if Mitch McConnell votes against Kash Patel, Tulsi Gabbard, or any other of his cabinet nominees, he will make Speaker Mike Johnson defund the "Mitch McConnell Turtle House" in the Louisville Zoo in next year's budget.

- Barack Obama is reportedly raising funds to launch Tea Party rallies across the nation to protest a new president who was born in Africa and is going to increase the national debt.

- There is reportedly disagreement between Elon Musk and Trump about releasing all the Epstein files unredacted, with Trump expressing "suspiciously vigorous objections despite his campaign promises."

- A televangelist from Iowa claims Jesus will return on Christmas Day this year, and anoint Trump as His little brother sent by God to save America from Wokeism, windmills, and weak water pressure.

- A second video game company just banned Elon Musk for cheating, and its founder said, "It's embarrassing and an indictment against capitalism that Musk, a CEO of several major companies—as well as the alleged efficiency savior of the federal government—has the time or interest to be so obsessed about being on our leaderboard that he'd pay people to play all day for him so he can film himself beating the bosses and pretend he didn't buy his way to the number one spot."

- Florida Republicans quietly exempted the gay dating app *Grindr* from their new legislation mandating all sex-related websites to require identity and age verification.

- Trump is reportedly demanding Elon Musk censor all the posts on *Twitter* calling him "Vice President Trump" or he'll fire everyone at D.O.G.E.

- Nine male GOP members of Congress have been given divorce papers by their wives since Trump was reelected.

- A Florida judge says he has no choice thanks to the state's strict laws against drag queens except to officially label Mar-a-Lago as a drag show venue because of Trump's excessive makeup use.

- Dozens of MAGA fans in Alabama have started a hunger strike they vow will go on until either everyone stops calling Trump "Elon Musk's vice president" or they die.

- Trump has reportedly complained to staffers that Musk is tweeting too much, and he's coming across as "desperate for attention."

- Clarence Thomas reportedly doesn't want to retire in Trump's term because he's worried his vacations will stop if he no longer has a vote on the Supreme Court cases billionaires care about.

- JD Vance has reportedly told his staffers to never publish any photos of him sitting on a couch.

- Speaker of the House Mike Johnson said, "My relationship with Trump and Musk is like we're all in a hotel room together, and they're on the bed doing amazing things for American prosperity while I'm sitting in the chair in the corner getting a front row view of those brilliant guys really going at it."

- Marjorie Taylor Greene and Lauren Boebert have reportedly begun campaigning against each other in the upcoming vote to possibly replace Mike Johnson as the next Speaker of the House, with Greene calling Boebert an "unprofessional ignoramus," and Boebert calling Greene an "uneducated loudmouth."

- Lara Trump says it's too difficult to decide what she wants more, to become the next Taylor Swift sized pop star singer, or have her father-in-law force Ron DeSantis to appoint her as the next junior US Senator from Florida.

- Trump is reportedly threatening to cancel D.O.G.E. after Vivek Ramaswamy suggested the government can save a lot of money by having administration officials stay at hotels Trump doesn't personally own.

- After announcing she was removing herself from consideration for the Florida Senate Seat Marco Rubio is leaving vacant, Lara Trump just announced she has also removed her cover of Tom Petty's "I Won't Back Down" from consideration for the *Grammys*.

- RFK Jr. accidentally said on a hot mic that Trump smells worse than the head he salvaged from the whale corpse he found on the beach in Massachusetts and tied to the top of his car to drive to New York.

Both Parties In Congress Are Disappointed Ted Cruz Was Reelected

November 8, 2024
Washington D.C.—

Senator Ted Cruz's long career of narcissistically self-aggrandizing political stunts has earned him few friends in politics—actually, no friends.

These are the some of the most charitable remarks his fellow Republicans have said about him:

"I will never not hate Ted Cruz with a fiery passion," said Senator Lindsey Graham. "Nothing he says or does could ever change the fact I've repeated many times before that if someone killed Ted Cruz on the floor of the Senate, no Senators would vote to convict the murderer. I'd even vote to confirm that person onto the Supreme Court because killing Cruz would exemplify such clear and sound judgment."

"I wish Ted Cruz would just stay in Cancun the next time he flies there during a Texan weather emergency," said Senator Shelly Poitter. "I'd love it if the government would deport him to Mexico or Canada, except that releasing the bioweapon of mass annoyance that is Ted Cruz would likely be considered by those governments as an act of war. The United Nations would likely try to prosecute us for human rights violations. But he was born in Canada, not America. The Canadians should have to take him back!"

"In the Senate lunchroom, Ted Cruz always sits alone because, when he tries to join any other table, the people there tell him they're saving the seat for someone, but that someone never comes and sits down," said Senator Wendy Roche. "It almost makes you feel sympathy for him just for a millisecond before you remember he attempted to stop a bipartisan deal by shutting down the federal government all by himself just to promote himself ahead of his presidential campaign in 2016. Anyone who is a perennial presidential candidate like Ted Cruz, who I believe is already drooling over the opportunity to run in 2028, well, it's healthy to just instinctively get the ick from that person."

"The first moment I met Ted Cruz, he looked me in the eyes, and I got my first hot flash of menopause," said Senator Angela Lukeshire. "It's like my body was so disgusted by his creepy, slimy, hair-raising presence that my ovaries did the menstrual equivalent of throwing up and committing fallopian suicide. My ovaries hung themselves!"

"I've heard that Donald Trump has made Ted Cruz do some wildly humiliating things at Mar-a-Lago to be forgiven for the mean things Cruz said about him during the 2016 primary," said GOP Representative John Fludd. "I can't totally confirm for sure because I didn't see it myself, but I heard from a colleague who heard from a Mar-a-Lago cleaning lady that Trump made Cruz do things that made her lose her religion and belief in God because she couldn't believe an all-knowing, all-powerful, loving monodeity would allow such horrifying, blasphemous deeds of self-flagellation and self-penetration as she saw Cruz do."

"Maybe it's because everyone in his life has hated him, but Ted Cruz is so f*cking weird about asking everyone to make an alliance with him," said Senator Paul Whittlinger, "He has asked me like five separate times. Literally, every senator has turned him down. He also asks everyone if we'll sign an oath to vote for him in the next presidential election, but of course, no one has ever signed it. The Senate actually has a suicide pact where roughly 2/3rds of us have all agreed that if Ted ever gets elected as president, we'll all commit Seppuku on election night. Thankfully, I'm positive the American people will never elect Ted Cruz to the White House."

"After everyone was criticizing Ted Cruz for his role in helping instigate the insurrectionist mob on January 6th, Cruz told me that he cared about all the calls for his resignation as much as he cared about Trump's insults aimed at his wife," said Senator Sam Blackwell. "Of all the comparisons he could have made, I just can't get over how weird it was that he chose his wife."

"I once looked at some documents he threw away because he was right next to the recycling bin, but he still chose to throw the paper away in the landfill bin," revealed an anonymity-requesting Congressional janitor, "and on the papers, I could see Ted had doodled a weird number of squirrels all over it. He drew new designs for different denominations of the Dollar all featuring the presidents as squirrels, and he drew some architectural designs for crafting various squirrel houses out of wood, and he had several pages' worth of sketches of new acorn shapes that could theoretically be evolved, and he drew a couple not-safe-for-work sketches of some squirrels getting it on. I confess I don't know much about the anatomy of squirrels, but I believe Mr. Cruz drew their mammaries inaccurately large."

"I don't know what to think about this," said former Cruz staffer Heather North, "but Ted Cruz once got a little drunk after a night of drinking two bottles of rosé wine at a GOP Senate social event, and he whispered in my ear that he was Mothman. Then he flickered his tongue over his lips, and left me to stand next to a light fixture by himself for like fifteen minutes. Later that night he asked me to sign a pledge to vote for him for president in 2028."

BIG IF TRUE XIII

- "Why does this always happen to my best friends?" Donald Trump reportedly asked his staffers this morning after the Gaetz Report revealed that the allegations of his Attorney General nominee, Matt Gaetz, being a sex-trafficking pedophile are "highly credible."

- "Oh, that report, I thought everyone was talking about a different sex-trafficking report," Matt Gaetz just told a reporter who asked why he claimed his ethics report would "fully exonerate" him.

- Trump is reportedly furious with Republicans for refusing to confirm Matt Gaetz, and was overheard shouting into his phone at Mar-a-Lago this morning, "Where am I supposed to find another attorney general with as much blackmail to do what I want as Gaetz?"

- Trump reportedly wants a "do-over" on nominating his cabinet, and says he'll spend more time weeding out the sex offenders this time.

- Elon Musk is reportedly angry that somehow the collapse of the budget deal and the potential government shutdown became his fault when Trump spends eight hours a day when they should be in meetings watching *Fox News* and guessing out loud how big the female hosts' bra sizes are.

- The report on Matt Gaetz's sexual and drug-related misconduct reportedly reveals several sexual fetishes that professional therapists say they have never before encountered or heard of.

- A Cyber Truck transporting a shipment of Elon Musk's semen to a sperm bank so he can "save the planet by procreating more geniuses with his DNA" reportedly caught on fire this morning and exploded.

- Trump is reportedly threatening that, if any tuba players come to his inauguration to play during his speech, the first executive order he'll sign will be a 10,000% tariff on all tubas.

- The feminist mafia "The Cliterati" are reportedly planning to scare away MAGA fans at Trump's inauguration before his speech by handing out tampons to all the men.

- Trump is reportedly furious after the D.O.G.E. committee has recommended presidents only get the funding to golf once a month.

- Mike Johnson's son reportedly just angrily deleted the porn-monitoring app from his phone after his father was revealed to have been helping obstruct the release of the Gaetz Report.

- Trump has reportedly been telling Mar-a-Lago members that his staff has proof Elon Musk abused our immigration laws, and that he therefore has "total control over Musk" because he can have Stephen Miller deport Musk at the moment of his choosing.

- Greenland's governmental social media channels have spent the last several days trolling Trump by posting nothing but pictures of the island's many windmills to dissuade him from annexing them.

- Senator Chuck Grassley is reportedly relieved the Gaetz Report doesn't disclose any embarrassing details about his subterranean f*ck dungeon.

- The parliament of Greenland just introduced legislation that bans Trump and all his descendants for 100 generations.

- A top minister of Greenland said today, "Donald Trump's hands are too small, and his fingers too tiny and covered in fried chicken grease, to ever get a hand on my beloved island."

- A top government official in Greenland says Trump can never come to Greenland because their island strictly bans the importation of foreign mushrooms.

- A top minister of Greenland says his island will agree to become a US territory in exchange for Trump unredacting and releasing all the Epstein files in which Trump's name is blacked out, his tax returns, and transcripts of his nightly calls with Vladimir Putin.

- QAnon said today, "The Gaetz Report is the last straw of Trump betraying the MAGA movement by nominating a cabinet full of sex offenders, traffickers, and harassers, and it's clear Trump was projecting all along when he accused Democrats of being the perverts!"

- A top government official in Greenland says Donald Trump can never come to Greenland because their island bans the importation of foreign mushrooms.

- Elon Musk is reportedly using D.O.G.E. to obtain the unredacted Epstein files so that he has blackmail on Trump to force him to do whatever he wants.

- Evangelical pastors are coming out strongly against Trump's idea to make Greenland a state, with Pastor Randy Mickeldenne remarking, "The European Danish who live there will make the US more gay, or at least more metrosexual, and we believe America is too gay already!"

- A staffer reportedly just showed Trump a picture of the Greenland sharks that can live up to 500 years, and now he says he no longer wants to buy the island.

- A nickname for Trump is reportedly going viral across Greenland and Denmark, and translated into English means "underwear mushroom infestation."

- Matt Gaetz has reportedly been researching the history of the US government all week to find a cabinet appointee who fell deeper and faster into disgrace than him he can punch down at.

- Musk and Trump reportedly just high-fived after they told each other how much money their parents spent supporting them as they were starting out in their careers.

- Trump is reportedly worried his health is not good enough to live another four years and complete his second term as president, and he'll be "one of the embarrassing presidents like Zachary Taylor and William Harrison" who died of natural causes in office. He's also worried JD Vance is too awkward and creepy to continue his legacy.

- The country of Panama just banned the Trump family from entering Panamanian borders for 100 years.

- In his first test of loyalty for Congressional Republicans in his second term, Trump is reportedly demanding the GOP Congress rename the upcoming Martin Luther King Jr. Day as "Donald J. Trump Day."

- A famously homophobic televangelist in Utah says he only filmed the gay sex tape that got publicly leaked today because, "I was so sure Kamala Harris was gonna win and turn America gay anyway."

- After threatening Canada and Greenland, Trump now says he also wants to annex the settlement of "Jonestown" from Guyana because of how loyal the people there were.

- Trump says his vow to end the Ukraine War on his first day as president is "maybe turning into more of a two weeks kind of goal."

"Allegedly!" Screams Trump Nominee For Attorney General Matt Gaetz Anytime Someone Calls Him A Sex-Trafficking Pedophile

November 17, 2024
Washington D.C.—

The Halfway Post reached out to some of Matt Gaetz's friends, and they shared some of the following pickup lines Gaetz uses on women when he's soliciting them for prostitution:

- "I have a *Venmo* transaction for $500 with the emoji of an eggplant in the description with your name on it, girl."
- "You look kind of like Alexandria Ocasio-Cortez, and, despite what I say about her on *Fox News*, I'm obsessed with her."
- "Hey, sweetheart, would you like a twenty dollar bill laundered from Florida by the tax collector of Seminole County to snort this mountain of cocaine?"
- "Hey, Girl, you like guys with rich parents who still call their fathers 'Daddy' when asking for money?"
- "If you send me any nudes, I'll make sure the former and future President of the United States sees it, and I'll let you know what number between 1 and 10 he gives your body."
- "What age would you choose if you could have a fake ID with any age on it? Cause I know a guy."
- "On a scale of 1 to America, how free are you to do coke with me?"
- "Are you a rigged election? Cause you're giving me an insurrection right now."
- "I can't wait to show you off to Nestor."
- "Hey, girl, you're looking at the only guy in Congress who voted against protections for sex-trafficking victims."
- "I have coke. You want coke? I'll give you coke. Here, have some coke. Fine, more coke for me then! You're ugly anyway! F*ck you, b*tch! You're never getting a no-show job for my campaign now!"
- "I may just be really rolling on ecstasy, but your eyes are the most beautiful eyes I've ever seen. They're also really bright. Can you turn them down a little?"
- "Hey, girl, I just crushed a dozen *Viagra*s and snorted them."
- "Are you Joe Biden? Cause I'd love it if you came down into my basement and never came out!"
- "You're looking at the guy who took away Kevin McCarthy's gavel."
- "I get invited to the hottest GOP coke orgies in Washington D.C. at Senator Chuck Grassley's house down in his f*ck dungeon."

Women Are Planning A "Project 2029" That Will Fight Back Against Trump's Toxic Masculinity

December 10, 2024
Washington D.C.—

Democrats are fighting back against Project 2025 by planning a Project 2029 that will include the following policy ideas:

- The *Bible* is very clear that men must not be allowed to waste their seed, so therefore masturbation should be highly criminalized with a minimum punishment of a year in jail.

- Men must start paying child support as soon as conception occurs, and the rate must be no less than 50% of their income in accordance with masculine responsibility as the head of the family, and in accordance with Christian family values.

- *Viagra* and other erectile dysfunction pills are henceforth banned because they go against God's grand, master plan. Maybe men should thank God for blessing them with tiny, flaccid penises, and honor God's intentions for their erectile dysfunction.

- Men must wear jockstraps and protective cups at all times to protect their sperm. Any infertile men will be investigated and prosecuted if gonadal negligence has been suspected.

- Men must start wearing baggy robes over their clothes to school as soon as they reach puberty to cover any visible signs of spontaneous erections they might get. Outlines of erections in their pants will be distracting for the girls in class, and boys will be sent home to change if they do not cover themselves in several layers.

- Men must get a vasectomy at the time of their wife's choosing. Any effort to reverse the vasectomy must be consented to by his wife with written approval presented to doctors. Unmarried men cannot get vasectomies because they might regret someday not having kids. God intended them to be baby makers.

- Unmarried men must have written permission from their mothers to leave the house unaccompanied, or they'll be suspected of prostitution. Without written permission, they must be accompanied by a female relative, either a sister or cousin.

- Courts and judges will no longer consider men's testimony to carry the same evidentiary weight as women's testimony on account of how often men get carried away by their emotional instability.

- Women can legally shoot or abuse their husbands non-fatally for the purpose of correcting their behavior.

- Honor-killing of unfaithful husbands will get a more lenient prison sentence than regular husband murders.

- Women cannot be prosecuted for engaging in pegging of unconscious men if alcohol was involved because those men should have known better than to put themselves in that position. Also, if the victimized men were wearing any type of revealing clothing, they were clearly asked to be pegged.

- Divorcing men is legally permitted and culturally acceptable if they do not return the favor of orgasm.

- No more toplessness rights for men.

- Married men must get a written signature from their wife in order to take out any bank loans.

- Women will get immunity for any violence they perpetrate after men catcalling them on the street in the name of self-defense.

- Woman will be allowed to tell doctors to suture a "wife stitch" during their husbands' anal surgeries to tighten the butthole to enhance sexual pleasure for wives during pegging.

BIG IF TRUE XIV

- A *Fox News* host says that when America annexes Greenland Congressional Republicans should rename the island in his honor as "Orangeland."

- A dozen MAGA fans from northern Florida who snuck into Greenland to start an American colony for Trump just got arrested there, and the leader claimed his only regret is that he has but one life to give for Trump, though the Danish punishment is only deportation.

- A petition of 10,000 MAGA fans in rural Alabama have reportedly pledged to move to Greenland if Donald Trump annexes it, Americanize the island, and "make it feel more like Alabama."

- Mike Johnson has reportedly directed every Republican in the House of Representatives to write a letter to the Nobel Prize Committee to nominate Donald Trump for the Nobel Peace Prize.

- Several MAGA fans who flew to Greenland to try and start an American colony they intend to call "Trumpland" have been detained at the airport for being sex offenders.

- Senator Josh Hawley is reportedly upset with Trump's recent focus on territorial expansion, and said this morning, "Colonizing Greenland and Panama won't address the underlying societal problem in America that people masturbate too much."

- Trump reportedly just appointed *MyPillow* founder Mike Lindell as the National Director of History Education, and says all public school history textbooks will soon be mandated to declare him the winner of the 2020 election over Joe Biden.

- A family of MAGA fans who flew to Greenland this morning to be settlers in a new colony for Trump just flew back this evening already after discovering the people there speak Greenlandic and not English.

- Trump just demanded that Republicans rename the state of New Mexico as "New America."

- The National Security Council just hired a 12-year-old editor to help dumb down the presidential daily briefing to a 6th grade level so Trump will read it.

- A Trump staffer just admitted that Trump always used to take questions from reporters next to his loud helicopter during his 1st term because it helped cover the sound of his incontinence issues and chronic farting, and he'll continue that practice in his 2nd term.

- Trump has reportedly woken up depressed every day this week because soon he has to move back to D.C. and spend the last years of his life doing laborious and ceremonially empathetic work he hates, that gets him daily criticized as an incompetent, sociopathic idiot.

- Trump is reportedly worried the polar vortex this weekend will make his inauguration day in D.C. freezing cold and windy so he'll get sick and die in his first month as president like William Henry Harrison did.

- Trump is furiously marking up maps of this weekend's polar vortex with his *Sharpie* marker to make it stay away from his inauguration in D.C.

- Marjorie Taylor Greene accused the Jewish Space Lasers of somehow pushing the polar vortex south to sabotage Trump's inaugural speech.

- Trump is reportedly terrified the polar vortex winds during his inauguration speech will wave his hair around like a wavy-arm, inflatable tube man.

- Trump is reportedly worried the Polar Vortex will make his inauguration parade down Pennsylvania Avenue so cold that if he incontinently dribbles any pee out it will freeze and he'll make a jangling sound when he walks.

- Trump is reportedly threatening to tariff any news networks that show photos of the National Mall during his inaugural speech if it's largely empty on account of the freezing temperature.

- Trump is worried the polar vortex will make it so cold at his inauguration speech that his stench will be visible steaming off his body during the TV broadcast.

- Pete Hegseth is reportedly furious people online keep mocking him by calling him a "DUI hire."

- Trump reportedly finds it suspicious that JD Vance keeps telling him do his inauguration speech outside to "own the liberals" and "prove he's not afraid of the polar vortex or pneumonia."

- Trump is reportedly no longer planning to walk in his inaugural parade, and will instead drive along in a golf cart.

- Joe Biden says he hid the nuclear codes in a place Trump "will never find: Melania Trump's bedroom.

- The chancellor of Greenland just announced Trump will only be permitted to annex a two square mile landfill in which the island dumps used adult diapers from all its retirement homes.

- After Trump announced he was giving his inauguration speech indoors on account of the cold weather, the chancellor of Greenland taunted him on social media saying, "If Trump can't handle one polar vortex, he can't handle Greenland."

- Trump is reportedly furious that he keeps getting called "Ralph Wiggum all grown up" on social media referencing the dumb, fat character from *The Simpsons*.

- Billionaire Hank Desplessis says his fellow billionaire colleagues humiliating themselves and bring shame upon American capitalism by going along with Trump's "Emperor's New Clothes vibe" by acting like they don't notice his bright, orange makeup, or that he knows anything about the tech industry, artificial intelligence, industrial policy, economics, how the government works, or basic history.

- The brain worm that used RFK Jr. as a host to get close to and sneak into Trump's brain to control him is pissed thinking how unhealthy Trump is, and that its new host might catch pneumonia during the inaugural festivities and die right as the worm obtains total power.

- Trump says he'll unite the country and bring back bipartisan goodwill by deporting Senator Ted Cruz in his first week as president.

- A major costume company is giving away free mushroom costumes to anyone who pledges to wear it to Donald Trump's inauguration.

- Trump is reportedly terrified his MAGA fans will feel betrayed if the media investigates how many immigrant workers he is employing at his properties right now.

- Trump's approval rating among Greenlanders has plummeted to the single digits after Trump canceled his outdoor inauguration speech because it got cold.

- Trump adviser Stephen Miller has reportedly seen the Robert Eggers vampire movie "Nosferatu" five times in the last two weeks, and each time brought a notebook and wrote down various notes.

- The gay dating app "Bear Meets Twink" just announced it's starting an annual political convention for conservatives called "Trump-a-Palooza" because of how profitable other GOP conferences like CPAC and the Republican National Convention always are.

- Joe Biden got through his entire presidency without calling for laborers to arrest their employers, or nationalizing America's iron and steel industries, or ordering all farmers to collectivize their land and crops, or abolishing private property, or turning America communist like Trump said he would.

- Trump is reportedly pissed people are calling him the "Hawk Tuah of presidents."

- Trump forgot to lie about his weight on his records for this presidential term, which means that Trump is officially now recorded in the history books as fatter than Taft.

- The hundreds of Trump protesters who brought tubas, kazoos, and bagpipes to troll his inauguration have reportedly begun playing all across the National Mall, and witnesses say the cacophony can be heard from the Capitol Rotunda where Trump is now set to deliver his speech.

- A surprisingly bipartisan coalition of members of Congress just voted to ban Nancy Mace from the bathrooms of the Capitol today.

- Dozens of the attendees crammed in the Capitol Rotunda for Trump's inaugural speech have described Trump's stench as "nearly unbearable."

- Joe Biden reportedly brought a shotgun to Trump's inauguration saying that he and Trump "have some unfinished presidential immunity business" to take care of.

- BREAKING NEWS: The worm that snuck into Trump's brain from RFK Jr.'s brain just announced it has total control of Trump's body, and it is now the President of the United States and will effective immediately be activating emergency presidential powers to institute martial law, dissolve Congress, and take dictatorial power!

RETRACTIONS

Following fact-checkers' assertions that this political record of the years 2021-2025 is "exhaustively fictional," the entirety of *Satire In The Biden Years: The Worst Of The Halfway Post* has been retracted, with the exception of the fact that Donald Trump's infamous stench has killed several people.

Proof of the olfactory murders has been authenticated by *The Halfway Post*, and will be revealed in two weeks.

Thanks for looking at my book!

If you liked it, please leave a review of it on *Barnes & Noble*, *Amazon*, or anywhere else you find it. Tell your family and friends about it. Loan it to all the liberals and comedy lovers you know. Request your local library get a copy. Gift it to your most MAGA enemies and social media trolls. If you're a Trump fan, bring a copy to your next book burning!

Follow *The Halfway Post* and Dash MacIntyre on your favorite social media platforms, while they last, to interrupt your doomscrolling with graffiti news.

Social Links

Linktr.ee/DashMacIntyre
TheHalfwayCafe.Substack.com
DashMacIntyre.Medium.com
X.com/HalfwayPost
HalfwayPost.Bsky.Social
Threads.net/@TheHalfwayPost
Instagram.com/TheHalfwayPost
HalfwayPost.com

Dash MacIntyre's Books

POLITICAL SATIRE
Satire In The Trump Years: The Best Of The Halfway Post (2021)
Satire In The Biden Years: The Worst Of The Halfway Post (2025)

COMEDY
Apéritifs (2025)

POETRY
Cabaret No Stare (2022)
Moon Goon (2023)
Hotel Golden Hours (2024)

www.ingramcontent.com/pod-product-compliance
Lightning Source LLC
Chambersburg PA
CBHW060554080526
44585CB00013B/565